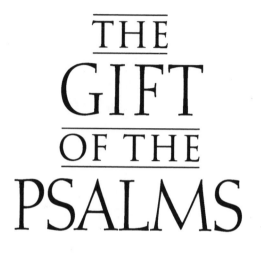

THE
GIFT
OF THE
PSALMS

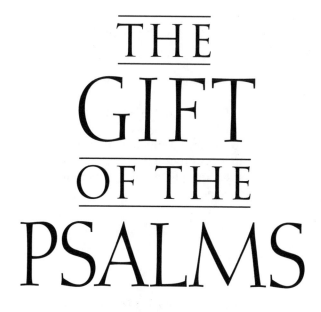

THE GIFT OF THE PSALMS

Roland E. Murphy, O. Carm.

HENDRICKSON
PUBLISHERS

Hendrickson Publishers, Inc.
P.O. Box 3473
Peabody, Massachusetts 01961-3473
U.S.A.

The Gift of the Psalms is a revised version of *The Psalms Are Yours*, published in 1993 by Paulist Press.

The Gift of the Psalms, by Roland E. Murphy, O. Carm.
ISBN 1-56563-474-8
Copyright © 2000 by The Society of Mount Carmel

Printed in the United States of America

First printing—June 2000

Library of Congress Cataloging-in-Publication Data

Murphy, Roland Edmund, 1917–
    The gift of the Psalms   /   Roland E. Murphy.
      p. cm.
    Rev. ed. of: The Psalms are yours. c1993.
    Includes bibliographical references and index.
    ISBN 1-56563-474-8 (pbk.)
    1. Bible. O.T. Psalms—Criticism, interpretation, etc.
I. Murphy, Roland Edmund, 1917– Psalms are yours.   II. Title.

BS1430.2 .M85 2000
223'.206—dc21

                                          00-033476

Dedicated to all the Carmelites
with whom I have recited
the psalms over so many years

R.E. Murphy : The gift of the Ps

Contents

Preface

The goal of this revised edition of *The Psalms Are Yours* remains the same, even if the title has been changed, and I would like to repeat some important observations from the initial preface (1993). The psalms belong to Israel in the first instance. They were written by and for that people of God, and they were born of its beliefs and experiences. Nevertheless, the psalms are Israel's *gift* to you, whoever "you" may be. They are yours if you appropriate them into your way of thinking, in terms of prayer, or aesthetics, or whatever reason that has prompted you to examine them. But before they become yours, you have to recognize how very much they remain also "theirs," the prayerful expressions of an ancient people in an ancient language and with a different worldview. The goal of this book is to help you understand this ancient poetry and make it "yours."

We can be guided by the challenging insights of two gifted theologians. Martin Luther commented on Psalm 12 in the following words:

> None of you can pray a psalm if you have not previously made the words of the psalm your own. But they will then be your own when you have the same feeling and the same spirit in which the words were said. If you pray without this, you resemble those who play a role in a comedy, where the action takes place with proper words, but with a reality that is artificial. What a shipwrecked person really says sounds quite differently coming from the actor who plays the part of the shipwrecked, or a mask, even though the words remain the same. For the former speaks his own words, the latter speaks words that are

foreign, and naturally with a different feeling. For the former, reality and words cohere; for the latter, reality is simulated. (author's translation)

In a similar vein a noted Jesuit theologian, the late Karl Rahner, commented about poetry and Christianity:

> Thus it is true that the ability and practice of perceiving the poetic word is a presupposition for hearing the word of God . . . the poetic word and the poetic ear are so much a part of a person that if this essential power were really lost to the heart, we could no longer hear the word of God in its human expression. In its inmost essence, the poetic is a prerequisite for Christianity. ("Poetry and the Christian," in vol. 4 of *Theological Investigations* [Baltimore: Helicon, 1966], 363; translation revised)

With his typical exaggeration, Rahner touches on a profound truth that holds for readers of any or of no faith. In order to understand the biblical word that is expressed in such highly poetic imagery, we have to be poets ourselves—not that we can write poetry, but we can react intelligently to the images and symbols that crowd the biblical pages. Unless we do this we will not appreciate and fully comprehend the biblical message. Unless we exercise this inborn poetic talent, we will not make contact with the psalms on their own level. The purpose of this book is to give directions and guidance to those who wish to enter into the world of the psalms and to make them their own.

For over half a century the present writer has been occupied with the psalms. This book is the fruit of many lectures and workshops for Protestants and Catholics, clergy and laity. Experience has suggested two basic principles. First, one must read the psalms aggressively, not passively, before having recourse to a commentary or to any notes for help. It is this struggling with the text that enables one to appropriate a psalm. Consulting a commentary to get an "answer" to a question is hardly profitable. The answer is quickly forgotten, even if the explanation may have been accurate. There is no escape from initial reading and rereading of a psalm in and for itself. Not even the comment in the second half of this book, as brief as it necessarily is, should be consulted without an initial confrontation with the actual text of the psalm. Second, there are many preconceptions, many presuppositions, that all of us bring to the reading of the psalms, or any book of the Bible. The first half of this book, a kind of introduction to the psalter, seeks to lay out some of these presuppositions in a manner that is clear and honest. Since there is no escape from presuppositions, we should strive to be aware of them. For example, what is the best choice for approaching the psalms, the best strategy for reading them? According to the literary genres, or according to the history-laden superscriptions, or some other methods that have been developed in the Jewish and Christian traditions? If we truly know the approach we are using, we can be aware of its shortcomings and be careful not to claim too much for it. Particularly important is a knowledge of the ancient world view that is so different from ours. How did the ancients, over a period of some ten centuries, view reality: the world, the makeup of humans, suffering, sinfulness, and so forth? What are the concrete institutions and ideas that played a role in Israel's life: covenant, Temple, Zion, messianism, and so forth? This is a vast area, but certain themes that keep recurring in the psalms call for more explicit treatment. The imagery of the psalms, particularly, has to be understood and absorbed into our way of thinking.

The revision has been serious and extensive, thanks to the insight of Hendrickson Publishers, and especially to the editorial suggestions of Dr. John Kutsko. The two principal parts remain: an introduction and a brief commentary. Both have been entirely rewritten and expanded. Moreover, the commentary is now designed to explain the New Revised Standard Version (NRSV). Hence the many verses and phrases that introduce the comments are drawn from that popular translation. This does not mean that other versions are not brought to bear where the evidence of the Hebrew text or the ancient witnesses demand it. The NRSV itself provides in its footnotes valuable indications of variations from the Hebrew text. But the main purpose of this work is to explain the text of the NRSV as it stands, and that means avoiding unnecessary paraphrase, and explaining what needs to be explained.

This little volume is meant to accompany the actual reading of the biblical text. In that way readers stay fixed on the biblical word, and can weigh their own interpretation against what is offered here. The conciseness of the first edition is still the goal.

In addition, a short and select annotated bibliography on the psalms has been added. Books are cited with an abbreviation or a short title if they appear in the list of abbreviations (pp. xiii–xiv) or in the bibliography (pp. 175–76). Other books will be cited with a full reference in the text.

Easter 2000

Abbreviations

1 Chr	First book of Chronicles
2 Chr	Second book of Chronicles
1 Kgs	First book of Kings
2 Kgs	Second book of Kings
2 Pet	Second letter of Peter
1 Sam	First book of Samuel
2 Sam	Second book of Samuel
ANET	*Ancient Near Eastern Texts* (edited by J. B. Pritchard; 3d ed. with supplement; Princeton: Princeton University Press, 1978)
Bar	book of Baruch
B.C.E.	Before the Common Era (= B.C.)
C.E.	Common Era (= A.D.)
cf.	compare
chap.	chapter
Dan	book of Daniel
Deut	book of Deuteronomy
Eccl	book of Ecclesiastes, or Qoheleth
ed.	editor, edition
e.g.	for example
Exod	book of Exodus
Ezek	book of Ezekiel
FOTL	The Forms of Old Testament Literature
Gen	book of Genesis
Heb	Letter to the Hebrews
Hos	book of Hosea
HTR	*Harvard Theological Review*

i.e.	that is
Isa	book of Isaiah
Jer	book of Jeremiah
Josh	book of Joshua
JSOTSup	Journal for the Study of the Old Testament: Supplement Series
Judg	book of Judges
Lam	book of Lamentations
lit.	literal(ly)
LXX	Septuagint translation (Greek)
ms(s)	manuscript(s)
MT	Masoretic text (Hebrew)
NAB	New American Bible
NEB	New English Bible
NIB	*The New Interpreter's Bible* (Nashville: Abingdon, 1994–)
NIV	New International Version
NJBC	*The New Jerome Biblical Commentary* (edited by R. E. Brown, J. A. Fitzmyer, R. E. Murphy; Englewood Cliffs, N.J.: Prentice-Hall, 1990)
NJPS	*The Holy Scriptures: The New JPS Translation according to the Traditional Hebrew Text (Tanakh)*
NRSV	New Revised Standard Version
NT	New Testament
Num	book of Numbers
OT	Old Testament
passim	at several places
Prov	book of Proverbs
Ps(s)	book of Psalm(s)
Rev	book of Revelation
Sir	book of the Wisdom of Ben Sirach, or Ecclesiasticus
Song	Song of Songs, or Song of Solomon
Tob	book of Tobit
v(v).	verse(s)
Wis	book of the Wisdom of Solomon

Part One: Introduction

❦

CHAPTER ONE

Interpretive Approaches

TRANSLATIONS

Every translation of a work is also an interpretation. The labor of interpreting is inevitable because the translation language (receptor language) can never quite catch the nuance of the original. The Italian saying, "traduttore, traditore," (rendered freely, "translation is betrayal") is perhaps an exaggeration, but anyone who has attempted to translate from another language appreciates its truth.

The fate of any literary composition, especially if it is ancient, is a perilous one in two respects. First, was it copied down correctly in the course of its transmission through the centuries? Second, if it was translated into many languages early on, as the Bible was, what is the quality of these translations? They can be extremely valuable because they bear witness to the state of the text from which they derive (in the case of the psalms, that is Hebrew). The goal of textual criticism—to approximate as closely as possible the original *reading* (not meaning) of a text—is a most difficult task, even if it is unheralded. It is as much an art as a science. The textual notes that accompany the translation of the NRSV are but a faint reflection of the arduous hours of decision making involved in establishing the text to be translated.

There was no special divine providence at work in the preservation of the Hebrew Bible (or Old Testament). The complicated history of the transmission of the biblical text demonstrates the wide variations that are found even before the Christian era. (For example, there are long and short forms of the books of Job and Jeremiah, and the book of Joshua has a complicated textual history.) Traditionally Jews and Christians have fixed on what is called the Masoretic text (= MT), namely, that form of the Hebrew Bible that was handed down in the Jewish community and rendered well-nigh immutable by the notes and marks of the Jewish scholars, or Masoretes, from the seventh to the tenth century C.E. The astounding discovery of Hebrew texts (found near the Dead Sea in 1947) proved that variation among texts existed before the Jewish community agreed on a received text that became the MT. This fact was not really surprising, because differences in the translations of the Bible had been noted long before this discovery. The most famous translation is the old Greek version, called the Septuagint (= LXX), which varied considerably from the Hebrew in some books and dates back to the third century B.C.E. In many cases, this was due not to the whims of a translator (which must always be considered) but to the existence of diverse copies of the text. Only fragments of other Greek translations (Aquila, Symmachus, and Theodotion) have been preserved. Origen's great Hexapla (third century C.E.), which laid out the Hebrew and the Greek translations in six columns (hence the title), was eventually lost to posterity.

Jerome, one of the greatest Christian biblical scholars of antiquity (ca. 340–420 C.E.), devoted his life to the study of the Bible, particularly to the translation of the Hebrew Bible into Latin, which was at that time the language of the common people. His translation became known as the "Vulgate," adopted by the Latin body of Christians throughout the Middle Ages, in contrast to the Greek form used in Orthodox Christianity. (Unfortunately, Hebrew was practically a forgotten language among Christians until the Renaissance period.) Jerome's work on the psalms contributes an interesting point about translations. No less than three translations of the Psalter are associated with him. The "Roman" Psalter was a reworking of the Old Latin translation, which itself had been translated from the Greek version. Jerome revised the Latin in the light of the Greek manuscripts that were then available. The "Gallican" Psalter is an improved edition of the "Roman," because Jerome was able to use the textual material that Origen had made available in the Hexapla. This came to be the accepted Latin translation of the psalms and found its place in the Vulgate Bible. The third Psalter, "according to the Hebrews," was done by Jerome directly from the Hebrew text. It is more exact than the previous Latin Psalters, but it could not dislodge the Gallican Psalter from the Vulgate, so popular had the latter become in the lives and liturgy of the people. These Latin Psalters tell us much more about the popularity and use of the book of Psalms and its influence on the literature of the Western world than they do about the original Hebrew text.

The complicated history of the transmission of the Hebrew text and of the ancient versions or translations is a work that still goes on, and vigorously, thanks to the discovery of the Dead Sea Scrolls. It is a warning to us to be aware of the differences that exist among modern translations, no matter how expert they are. Indeed the general reader can profit by using more than one modern translation of the Psalter. For example, *The New Interpreters' Bible* (Nashville: Abingdon, 1994) uses both the NIV and the NRSV as the basis for its commentary. Even more important than the *fact* of the disparity among the ancient texts of the Bible is this implication: any translation is already an interpretation. The history of the interpretation of the Bible began with the transmission of the original and the ensuing translations. Volume one of the *Cambridge History of the Bible: From the Beginnings to Jerome* (ed. P. Ackroyd and C. Evans, Cambridge: Cambridge University Press, 1970) presents all this interesting background.

Where did the NRSV, the English translation of the Psalter that we are commenting on, come from? Speaking for the translation committee, the well-known biblical scholar, Bruce Metzger, has given the answer in a single sentence: "The New Revised Standard Version of the Bible is an authorized revision of the Revised Standard Version, published in 1952, which was a revision of the American Standard Version, published in 1901, which, in turn, embodied earlier revisions of the King James Version, published in 1611" (Preface to the *New Oxford Annotated Bible* [New York and Oxford: Oxford University Press, 1991], ix). This recent revision, then, ultimately has its roots in the so-called "Authorized Version," or King James Version, almost four hundred years old.

The attention of the reader should be called to the 117 superscriptions added to the psalms, such as "Of David. A Psalm" in Psalm 110. These are comments of ancient Jewish tradition, but are not part of the psalm text. They contain personal names (e.g., David, seventy-three times), liturgical instructions (e.g., "to the leader," fifty-five times), and other designations (e.g., *mizmor* = Hebrew for "psalm," fifty-seven times). These superscriptions have led to different enumerations of the verses. The reader of the NRSV must pay special attention to the verse numbers, because these often differ from the numbers used in the Hebrew text and other translations. Thus, for example, the opening lines of Psalm 51 in the NRSV (vv. 1–2) are numbered 51:3–4 in the Hebrew text because the Jewish tradition counted the superscription concerning David and Bathsheba as the first two verses (51:1–2), which are translated but not numbered in the NRSV. Hence, the reader must be alert to the tradition a translation follows. Generally speaking, the English Protestant tradition deriving from the King James Version, as is the case with the NRSV, does not number the superscriptions (e.g., "To the leader. Of David") that introduce many psalms. Jewish and Roman Catholic versions do follow the Hebrew tradition. Fortunately, not all psalms will be affected, and the margin of difference is usually only one digit. Differentiation between chapter and verse numbers in the Hebrew and Christian versions also occur in other books of the Bible, but not as often. The standard chapter division has been derived from the tradition set by Stephen Langton in the thirteenth century, and the verse division followed a few centuries later. Fortunately, the chapter divisions are usually the same in both Christian and Jewish practice. It is also important for the reader to note the enumeration adopted in commentaries or studies on psalms. This book will adopt the NRSV enumeration.

CHARACTERISTICS

It is well at the outset to consider certain preliminary questions, such as authorship, dating, and psalm collections.

Authorship

Jewish tradition marked David as the author of seventy-three of the hundred and fifty psalms, and the superscriptions for twelve of these even describe the particular event referred to in the psalm. These traditions cannot be verified, and, indeed, substantial arguments against the likelihood of Davidic authorship can be made. We cannot date most of the psalms. Generally speaking, the first chronological divide is the exile, that is, when the Babylonian king Nebuchadnezzar invaded Israel in 587 B.C.E. and removed some of its population to Babylon. Thus, psalms referring to an Israelite king (e.g., 72) would be preexilic. Some psalms seem to reflect the period of exile or afterward (e.g., 126 and 137). It is not all that profitable to speculate about possible authors and dates. Later we will evaluate the "Davidic authorship" from a hermeneutical (or interpretational) point of view.

Collections

The Psalter has been divided into five "books." This is a late and artificial division, indicated by the doxologies (ending "Amen, Amen") that have been inserted in Pss 41:13, 72:18–19 (with the note in v. 20 that the prayers of David have ended), 89:52, and 106:48. Psalm 150 is the fifth book's doxology. These divisions cannot conceal the fact that there are many other collections within these five "books." The superscriptions indicate the psalms of Korah (42–49; 84–85; 87–88), of Asaph (73–83), and of course those of David. Psalms 42–83 show signs of an earlier redaction (or editing) and collection: *Elohim* (the Hebrew word for God) is used two hundred times, in contrast to the divine personal name, *YHWH* (forty-three times), typeset as LORD in many translations, including the NRSV. This is out of all proportion to the occurrence of these terms in the rest of the one hundred fifty psalms. Hence, this group is called the "Elohistic" Psalter. But we know practically nothing about the history of these collections. Nor can we decipher many of the technical terms in the superscriptions, such as "for the leader," etc., which were appended early on, even before the Septuagint (LXX) translation was made for Greek-speaking Jews. We shall see that current scholarship has been attempting to interpret the psalms within the context of surrounding psalms. In other words, the Psalter is in itself a book that calls for unity. Thus, we can ask whether it is possible to interpret a psalm within its present literary context.

Parallelism

The phenomenon of parallelism is generally seen as a characteristic of Hebrew poetry, even if sometimes parallelism seems to appear in what is called "prose" narrative. Parallelism marks two (at times, three or more) lines or cola in relation to each other: the second colon will affirm the first positively (traditionally termed synonymous parallelism, as in Ps 51:2) or negatively (antithetic parallelism, as in Ps 51:17). Let the reader beware; this is not simple repetition. There is continuity between the parallel lines. The thought of the first line is intensified, or specified, or modified somehow as the poetry flows. What is called "synthetic" parallelism expands the first line, as in Psalm 23: "The LORD is my shepherd, I shall not want / He makes me lie down in green pastures." More details could be added, such as word pairs (e.g., "way" and "path") but this can suffice for now. The phenomenon is found throughout the Bible, especially in the prophets and wisdom literature, and it is also present in the other literatures of the ancient Near East.

It would be a mistake to think that the important role of parallelism exhausts the poetic aspects of the psalms. Poetry is not just a literary device. The content or idea of a poem is not communicated simply by a literary analysis, no matter how correct the comment may be. The short commentary that forms half of this book is confined more to the intellectual or noetic level. Commentary can only barely suggest the poetic dimensions of a psalm. It is the reader who must yield to the magic of the poetry and appreciate the quality of the intertwined style and message. Both content and form are joined together in a profound unity that evokes more than the obvious.

LITERARY FORMS

The goal of historical-critical methodology is to ascertain the meaning the written word directly conveys. Recent hermeneutical theories have challenged the dominance of this method, arguing that every interpreter begins with certain inevitable pre-suppositions, and these prevent the method from achieving its intended goal. Still, in spite of these theoretical concerns, the goal can be approached, bringing us at least into contact with the intent of the text. Certainly, the historical-critical method does not exhaust the meaning of a text, which in fact acquires new meanings as it is passed from generation to generation. This is true not just of the Bible but of any literature and foundational texts, as we can see from the meanings that the United States Constitution has acquired over the years.

One of the most important tools of this method is called "form criticism," which attempts to determine the various literary forms or genres that appear in the biblical text. The Psalter provides a fertile field for such investigation, and the scholar most associated with the method is Hermann Gunkel (1862–1932; see the bibliography). He studied the literary types and pointed out their characteristic features, structure, movement, and themes. He was less successful in establishing the *Sitz im Leben,* or setting in life, for the psalms. Later scholars were inclined to identify the original setting in the cultic celebrations of the Temple, and this view still predominates. More recent scholarship has learned to be modest and less specific about the setting. Many, if not most, psalms probably had a setting in the Temple at some stage in their transmission, but some could have originated in a family setting—a household liturgy, as it were (see E. Gerstenberger in the bibliography). The following paragraphs describe the main genres, and these categories also apply to psalms or prayers that occur outside of the Psalter (e.g., Exod 15:1–18 and 1 Sam 2:1–10).

Hymn or Song of Praise

Although in Jewish tradition the entire Psalter has received the name, *tehillim,* or praises, the "hymn" designates a specific literary type of praise. Its basic structure is threefold: (1) a brief but joyous introduction that is a summons to praise the Lord; (2) an enumeration of the reasons to praise God (the two most prominent motifs are creation and the historical deliverance of Israel, which are frequently introduced by such terms as "for" or "because"); and (3) a short conclusion, which may repeat the introduction (Pss 8; 103–104) or express a blessing (Ps 33). Claus Westermann (see his work in the bibliography) prefers to call these hymns "descriptive praise," as distinct from "declarative praise" (categorized by most as "thanksgiving" psalms). Although scholars differ in opinion, the following psalms may be classified as hymns: 8; 19; 29; 33; 46–48; 65; 66; 76; 84; 87; 93; 95–99; 100; 103–104; 111; 113–114; 117; 135–136; and 145–150. On the basis of content, a further division is useful: songs of Zion (e.g., Pss 46 and 48); "enthronement" hymns celebrating the Lord's kingship (e.g., Pss 47 and 97); and the songs of ascents (Pss 120–134, perhaps pilgrimage songs). Sigmund Mowinckel (1884–1965; see his study in the bibliography) proposed a feast of the Lord's enthronement, and he associated some twenty psalms with this celebration. (For a discussion of "Zion" and "kingship," see pp. 54–58). Whether or not such a feast existed, the recognition of the Lord's kingship is clear in such psalms as 47 and 97. With a fertile imagination one can easily recognize a cultic reenactment of the Lord's enthronement, with a procession of the ark of the covenant, the sacred box in the Jerusalem Temple that contained the tablets of the law (see 47:5). Whatever the exact setting, in these psalms the Lord is hailed as king, and his rule is anchored in creation from of old, in his dominion over Israel, and, indeed, in his dominion over the world that he comes to "judge" (96:13; 98:9). The common exclamation "Praise the LORD," or *hallelujah*, occurs in the titles of several psalms (as in 146–150). *Hallelujah* is itself an abbreviated hymn, meaning "praise *Yah!*" short for *YHWH*, "the LORD" (*alleluia* derives from the Latin form).

Psalms of Thanksgiving

These are closely related to the songs of praise, so much so that Westermann classes them as hymns and songs of narrative or declarative praise. He points out that properly speaking there is no word for "thank" in Hebrew. The word so translated as thanksgiving is the same word that means "praise," *todah*. The hymn proper seems spontaneous and not turned toward oneself as "thanksgiving" suggests. Be that as it may, the structure and motifs of the so-called thanksgiving psalms are distinctive enough to deserve separate treatment.

This type of psalm begins with a cry that resembles the opening of the hymn: "extol, praise," etc. The body of the poem consists in the story of deliverance—how a cry for help was answered by the Lord, who is acknowledged as the rescuer. It may be that this prayer was accompanied in the Temple by a "todah" sacrifice, which seems to be the situation in Ps 30:4–5, where the psalmist invites bystanders to join in the prayer and perhaps share in a sacred meal. These psalms tend to draw a lesson from the experience and to proclaim publicly the Lord's faithfulness (Pss 30:5; 116:5–9; 118:5–9). In some cases, thanksgiving is enlivened by a vivid flashback, as the psalmist recalls the distress and even the prayer that was uttered during that trying period (18:4–6; 30:6–10; 41:4–10; 66:16–19; 116:10–12; 118:10–14). It may be that the thanksgiving prayer and sacrifice were vowed by those who suffered, and they are now fulfilling that vow (22:25; 66:13–14) with great joy (30:11). The thanksgiving publicly proclaims the Lord's goodness in saving the psalmist or the people. The prayers bear witness to that fact. Psalm 118 presents such thanksgiving, and it may have been a kind of model in the sense that the cry of v. 1, "O give thanks to the LORD, for he is good; / his steadfast love endures forever!" serves as a response in vv. 2–4 and is repeated in v. 29. This refrain also appears in many other contexts (see 2 Chr 5:13; 7:6; 20:21; Ezra 3:11; Jer 33:11; Pss 100:5; 106:1; 107:1; and throughout Ps 136). A list of typical thanksgiving psalms (of an individual) follows: 18; 22:22–31; 30; 32; 34; 40:1–10 (vv. 11–17 are an appeal for deliverance); 66:13–20 (this psalm is also a mixed type); 116; 118; and 138. While one can distinguish between individual and community psalms, and perhaps consider Psalms 67 and 124 as "collective" thanksgiving, it is important to recognize that thanksgiving is never merely an individual matter. The community is in one way or another involved in the "individual" thanksgiving, since the witness of the individual is directed to the community.

Laments

The term is distinct from lamentation, which is a dirge over a death (e.g., 2 Sam 1:19–27, at the death of Saul and Jonathan) or over a city and people (exemplified in the book of Lamentations).

The lament is really a complaint, a cry to the Lord to be delivered from some distress. It can be either individual or collective, but there are more laments of an individual, about forty, than any other type, and most of them are bunched together in the first half of the Psalter: 3–7; 14 (= 53); 17; 22; 25–28; 31; 35; 36; 38–39; 40:13–17 (= Ps 70); 42–43; 51; 53 (= Ps 14); 54–57; 59; 61; 64; 69–71; 86; 88; 102; 130; and 140–44. Certain subcategories of laments exist, such as prayers of those who have been falsely accused and seek redress (e.g., Pss 7 and 35). In ancient Israel, legal justice was dispensed "at the gates" of the town (see Ruth 4:1–2), where elders would gather to hear a case and give a verdict. There was room for false accusation and miscarriage of justice.

The complaint finds many causes: sickness, enemies, bad luck, and so forth—anything that connotes nonlife; hence, one can be said to be in Sheol (see pp. 34–36). The structure is easily recognized and consists of the following: an appeal to the Lord for deliverance; a description of the complaint; a confession of sin (Pss 32 and 51) or affirmation of innocence (Ps 26), as the case may be; reasons the Lord should intervene (e.g., because of the psalmist's trust); often a vow to offer a sacrifice; and finally, an expressed certainty that the prayer has been heard or an anticipated thanksgiving for when it will be heard (see 31:21–24). The structure of the individual complaint is somewhat flexible. The dry bones of this general description is given life by the frequent cries for help and by the colorful language describing the psalmist's plight—in short, by the ease with which the prayer moves along. The mood varies from being very grim (Pss 39 and 88) to overflowing with trust (22:3–5, 9–10).

The language commands our attention. The laments often portray the psalmist's distress with wild exaggeration. So many images crowd the psalm that the reader is hard put to state just what the psalmist is complaining about (e.g., Pss 22 and 69). Thus some have remarked that the troubles listed in Psalm 22 could not have happened to one person in a whole lifetime, let alone on one occasion: danger from bulls of Bashan, dogs, the mouth of the lion, the horns of wild oxen, etc. (On pp. 46–52, we will discuss biblical imagery, especially that of "enemies.") One could, however, say that our inability to determine the particular reason for a complaint is really an advantage: the images lose their particularity and readers can fit their problems under the broad umbrella provided by such language.

The psalmist's certainty of being heard is an outstanding characteristic of the complaint: "Depart from me, all you workers of evil, / for the LORD has heard the sound of my weeping" (6:8; see also 3:7). This sudden change in mood is hard to explain. Is it a result of the supplicant's strong faith? Or is the psalmist praying *after* having been delivered? Neither of these alternatives adequately explains the sudden transition in so many varied psalms. Some interpreters have suggested that an element found in many other places in the Bible has been omitted here: a divine answer, or oracle, from the Lord. For example, perhaps the many instances of "Do not fear" in Isaiah (41:10, 13; 43:1; 44:2) are examples of a typical oracle that one of the Temple personnel delivered. This is vividly the case in Lam 3:57: "You came near when I called on you; / you said, 'Do not fear!'" This oracle is not repeated in any of the psalms, but it is such an answer the psalmist seeks. (Elsewhere in the Psalter there are several oracles presented, although not as answers: 12:6; 91:14–16; see also 35:3.) So it is reasonable to postulate the kind of divine reply in Lamentations and Isaiah, which in turn begets the certainty that the Lord has heard the psalmist's cry. Claus Westermann has characterized the Psalter as a movement from lament to praise; these are the two poles between which the individual normally moves (*The Praise of God in the Psalms* [Richmond: Knox, 1965]). While there is little movement in such laments as 39 and 88, at the same time, those psalms, like the cries of Job, are not simply cries of despair. They come from faith; the emotional pendulum swings between despair and hope.

Communal Laments

These are individual complaints writ large; they are the lamenting voices of the community. People would have gathered at the Temple on special days marked for fasting or mourning, especially during a drought or some other disaster (see, too, the books of Joel and Lamentations). Among these prayers are the following: 44; 60; 74; 79; 80; 83; 85; 90; 123; and 137. Although the cause of the complaint may vary (e.g., defeat in battle: 44; 60;

74; and 79), the structure agrees more or less with that of the individual lament.

The role and importance of laments deserve greater appreciation than they usually receive. Some may consider complaints and outcries as not "prayerful." But here is an important lesson from the Bible. Israel's historical paradigm, the Exodus experience, was shaped by cry and rescue, as the "little credo" of Deuteronomy 26:5–9 exemplifies. The lament speaks to the finiteness of humans and their needs. Despite this, the lament has almost disappeared from Christian prayer, even though the powerful words of Psalm 22 are recited by Jesus (Mark 15:34). Moreover, these psalms of lament are found throughout the Bible, most notably in the so-called confessions of Jeremiah (Jer 11:18–12:6; 15:10–21; 17:14–18; 18:18–23; 20:7–12; 20:14–18). Anyone who is repelled by the idea of complaining to God should rethink the meaning of faith, which is *not* stoicism.

Psalms of Trust

Scattered through all the psalms are formulas of trust, such as "You are my God" (31:14; see also 22:10; 25:5; 44:4; etc.). This attitude is the basis of any prayer. Without it, why invoke the divinity? Such trust could emerge from Israel's historical experience (22:4, "In you our ancestors trusted; / they trusted, and you delivered them") or personal experience. The theme has created the narrow classification for the psalms of trust (4; 11; 16; 23; 27:1–6; 62; 131), but "trust" permeates the entire Psalter. Be alert to the vocabulary of trust—words like "refuge," "fortress," "shield," "rock," "deliverance," and "shadow."

Other Classifications

The main genres of praise, thanksgiving, and lament have been reclassified in psychological terms as orientation, reorientation, and disorientation (see W. Brueggemann, *The Message of the Psalms* [Minneapolis: Augsburg, 1984]). In other words, praise favors the status quo, the present orientation of one's life with God and people. These songs reflect serenity, well-being, the blessings of God. Disorientation marks the complaint, the setbacks in life about which the disoriented person laments. Reorientation is not so easily distinguished from orientation, except that it signals survival of a crisis and extols God for intervening. It is true that we move into chaos and also out of it, and the psalms in general demonstrate these changes in our life. But the psychological classification does not capture all the structural and motivational details that the traditional classifications reflect.

Several psalms are more easily classified on the basis of content rather than form. We saw above that some hymns have been viewed as "songs of Zion" and also as "hymns of Enthronement" (of the Lord), categories established by content. Some more of these classifications follow.

Royal Psalms is an important and practical classification, based on content. The subject is the king, and this cuts across several classifications. Thus, Psalm 18 is a royal psalm of thanksgiving. Psalms 20 and 21 are intercessions in favor of the king. Psalm 89 has hymnic elements but ends up as a strong complaint. Psalm 144 is a mixed genre, with features of both the hymn and the intercession. Psalm 45 is a wedding song. Three hymns seem to be associated with royal coronation (2; 72; and 110), and these psalms give rise to an interesting question: if they were written before the exile, why were they preserved during the postexilic period when the people had no king? (The discussion of messianism on pp. 54–58 will bring us back to this question.)

Wisdom Psalms is a classification much debated since interpreters do not agree on a list of these psalms. Scholars have not adequately studied the language that is characteristic of the sages, and it is doubtful if we have enough extant literature to do such work. Moreover, the language of the sages was also the language of the common people; it was not the jargon of a small group. Hesitantly, one can propose the following wisdom psalms: 32; 34; 37; 49; 111; and 112. Perhaps the most convincing example is Psalm 37 because it resembles the admonitions in the book of Proverbs, and the opening lines take up a problem that figured prominently in wisdom thought: Why do the wicked prosper? The psalm gives one answer: do not be envious of evildoers! (37:1; see also 73:3); they will get theirs. This problem appears throughout the Bible and receives several answers (see Job and Jer 12:1–4). It might be better to speak of wisdom influence on certain psalms (e.g., Pss 34 and 49), rather than argue for a wisdom classification. Psalms 1 and 119, which have sometimes been classified as wisdom, are better termed "Torah" (or "Law") psalms, based on their contents. While Sirach definitely identified a personified Wisdom with Torah (Sir 24:23), no psalm can be dated with any certainty to his day (about 200 B.C.E).

Acrostic Psalms is also not a true type. It refers to psalms whose structure depends upon alphabetic considerations in one form or another: each unit begins with successive letters of the Hebrew alphabet: 9–10; 25; 34; 37 (also Wisdom?) 111; 112; 119 (also Law?); and 145.

Historical Psalms recount important events in Israel's history: 78; 105; 106; 135; and 136 (Ps 114 is better seen as a hymn). History is used for various purposes, for example, to illustrate God's fidelity to the promises (105) or as a confession of sin (106).

The psalms are often complex in form and content, and we can only briefly mention some of the suggestions this complexity has bred. For example, some psalms may actually be "mixed" forms (e.g., half thanksgiving, half lament; perhaps Ps 40). Another interesting but hypothetical question is that of reinterpretation within a psalm itself (commonly called in French *relecture*), which is perhaps the result of a later addition that re-reads or redirects the psalm. A possible instance of such "conflict" might be in Psalm 51, where the call for the restoration of Temple sacrifice (vv. 18–19) appears to go in a different direction from the call for spiritual sacrifice (vv. 15–17). But is this really a re-reading? It could also have been a tension deliberately created in the psalm from the very start.

While attempts have been made to refine the categories briefly described above (such as Brueggemann's psychological terminology), there is general agreement on the Psalter's literary forms and classifications. Some reconstructions of genre and life setting are exaggerated, but that is a challenge to readers to judge carefully the plausibility of a scholar's approach. And some interpreters oppose the historical-critical method, emphasizing that it is exclusively centered on the past, on what the text meant. To be sure, they correctly point out that we are too rooted in our own modern context to be able to exactly recapture the ancient past, because the very questions we ask the text are conditioned by our present circumstances. Even so, we cannot dismiss the insights into the psalms that this methodology has achieved. The past is not inaccessible to the historian and the interpreter. We can move with a certain continuity of meaning into the present. We do this with other literature (such as Shakespeare and the classics), and we can do it with the Bible. While historical-critical methodology has limits, what it does, it does well.

THE PSALMS IN THE CONTEXT OF A BOOK

The usual approach to the psalms has been to study them separately, with a focus on their presumed liturgical setting. Similarities between psalms are certainly recognized, but usually within a relatively narrow range, such as the enthronement psalms (Pss 96–99). Yet, scholars study chapters of other books of the Bible in their context. A treatment of the psalm in Jonah 2:2–9 would be incomplete if it were not also analyzed *in situ,* as it were. We would ask: what is its function against the background of the narrative?

Instead of the usual custom of treating a given psalm in isolation, a new approach has been urged: interpret a psalm with attention to its position within the Psalter. It certainly is a book in its own right, even if it was formed from many collections that eventually became the Psalter. Not all scholars agree with each other, but the following bibliography can serve to introduce the reader to this approach to the psalms:

> BREVARD CHILDS, *Introduction to the Old Testament as Scripture* (Philadelphia: Fortress, 1979): 304–25; JAMES L. MAYS, "The Place of the Torah-Psalms in the Psalter," *Journal of Biblical Literature* 106 (1987): 1–12; J. CLINTON MCCANN, ed., *The Shape and Shaping of the Psalter* (JSOTSup 159; Sheffield: JSOT, 1993); GERALD SHEPPARD, *The Future of the Bible* (United Church of Canada Publishing House, 1990): 59–98; GERALD WILSON, "The Shape of the Book of Psalms," *Interpretation* 46 (1992): 129–42.

The reader should separate and keep in mind two issues for the discussion that follows. The first is the Psalter's long and complex formation into a book, an investigation that involves many historical reconstructions and hypotheses. Second, the psalms give indications of being meaningfully (not haphazardly) collected and finally combined into one book. If this is so, does the present arrangement offer hints to interpretation? In other words, does the layout of the Psalter help us understand the meaning of individual psalms?

The Formation of the Psalter as a Book

All we know is that many (not just five) collections of psalms preceded the current Psalter. How were these collections arranged in the book? Were the psalms simply placed one after another in a more or less arbitrary manner, or was there a method in their arrangement?

The book of Proverbs presents a comparison. Chapters 1–9 contain relatively long and consecutive wisdom poems, apparently as an introduction to the proverbial sayings in chapters 10–29. With few exceptions (e.g., Prov 26:4–5), these sayings seem quite disparate, with no obvious relationship to each other. It is clear from the headings in the book that it is a collection of collections. But on what basis was an individual collection made? One can point to repetitions of words or catchwords that link sayings together, or there may be a list of sayings that form a clear grouping (e.g., sayings about the sluggard in Prov 26:13–16). On the basis of this kind of evidence one can conclude that the collocation of the disparate sayings is not chaotic or haphazard, though we don't know if this was the work of the final or more intermediate editors or collectors.

The next question one can ask of Proverbs is hermeneutical. Does the arrangement affect the meaning of an individual saying? Yes and no. The proverbs were not formed in bunches but grew out of varied experiences. They are independent of each other, but it is also true that no one saying exhausts reality. A proverb represents a narrow slice of real life, and one proverb can even contradict another. This does not change the meaning of either saying, since they must retain their independence to preserve the meaningful conflict between them and point to the big picture.

The example of the book of Proverbs is helpful in considering the psalms. Within the collections several psalms have been grouped together on the basis of a common topic, catchword, or some other aspect of vocabulary. This is editorial not authorial work. Is it also *interpretive*? I think that more than this is needed for the interpretation of any particular psalm, but editorial arrangement can suggest an overall perspective for the Psalter.

A direct examination of some psalms supports this conclusion. Consider the first two psalms, which have been proposed as examples of contextual interpretation. Psalm 1 is not a prayer; it is a blessing or beatitude that lays down the two ways of living, exemplified by the character of the just and the wicked. The two ways are also neatly described in Prov 1:10–15, 4:18–19, 12:28, and 15:9. Righteousness consists in finding one's joy in the "law of the LORD" and in studying it day and night (Ps 1:2). The wicked will not survive, driven as they are like chaff before the wind. The poem serves as an introduction to the rest of the Psalter, in which the treatment of the righteous and sinners is a central theme. Moreover, the poem simply begins—without superscription—and then paints in a few bold strokes an ideal follower of the Lord. An increasing number of scholars consider the psalm to be a deliberate introduction to the book. The Psalter is being presented as instruction and not merely as prayer, reminding me of the saying, *lex orandi, lex credendi,* "the law of prayer is the law of belief."

Psalm l is not alone in its importance for the structure of the book; it is followed by another one, which is also without a superscription. Psalm 2, a royal psalm, refers to the reigning king in Jerusalem, although the exact setting is difficult to identify. Much depends upon whether the description of the nations' revolt is a real rebellion or only a rhetorical flourish, part of the court style that was more at home in the great empires of the Fertile Crescent than in the tiny kingdom of Israel. In all likelihood, this and other royal psalms came to be interpreted in a messianic, even eschatological, sense. That kind of messianism was rife in the period just before and after the beginning of the Christian era, as is borne out by the fervent national hopes in the so-called *Psalms of Solomon* (60–40 B.C.E.) and reflected in the popular movements described in the NT itself. In 2 Samuel 7 the prophet Nathan delivered the divine assurance that the Davidic dynasty would always reign in Jerusalem, and thus the kingdom of God would be reestablished in and through Israel. When Christians pray and interpret this psalm, especially in the Christmas liturgy, they are looking back at what they consider the fulfillment, whereas Jews are looking forward to its eventual realization.

What then is the relationship between Psalms 1 and 2, and their function within the Psalter? At first sight they appear to deal with two such separate topics—Torah and kingship—that no association seems possible. Some scholars have suggested deliberate editorial positioning. One begins with a "blessing" and the other ends with one (Pss 1:1 and 2:11). Moreover, catchwords imply a relationship: the repetition of the word *hagah* in 1:2 ("to meditate") and in 2:1 ("to plot"), and the reoccurrence of *derek* ("path," "way") in 1:1, 6 and 2:11. The "advice of the wicked" in 1:1 stands in contrast to the command "to be wise, be warned" in 2:10. It has been urged that both psalms are an introduction that gives unity to the rest of the Psalter. The emphasis is not only on the individual and personal morality (Ps 1), but on the preservation of a just order by the Lord's royal agent (Ps 2). Thus a double theme, individual and social, is highlighted from the beginning, and will be reflected in later psalms such as 72 (the just king), and 119 (individual devotion to the Torah).

Conclusion

Brevard Childs has stated well the claim that Psalm 1 is a deliberate indication of how the editorial positioning intended the psalms to be read:

> The present editing of this original Torah psalm has provided the psalm with a new function as the introduction to the whole Psalter. . . . The Torah of God which is the living word of God is mediated through its written form as sacred scripture. With its written word Israel is challenged to meditate day and night in seeking the will of God. Indeed, as a heading to the whole Psalter the blessing now includes the faithful meditation on the sacred writings which follow. The introduction points to these prayers as the medium through which Israel now responds to the divine word. . . . The original cultic role of the psalms has been subsumed under a larger category of the canon. (*Introduction*, 513)

This is an attractive hermeneutical suggestion. It is what has been called the "Scripturalization" of the psalms—when they were collected and made part of the authoritative Hebrew Bible (James Kugel, "Topics in the History of the Spirituality of the Psalms," in *Jewish Spirituality* [ed. Arthur Green; World Spirituality 13; New York: Crossroad, 1986], 113–44, esp. 136). Or, to put it another way, Dietrich Bonhoeffer's question (*Psalms: The Prayer Book of the Bible* [Minneapolis: Augsburg, 1970]) receives an answer. He reflected on how psalms that were the words of humans addressed to God could be viewed as words of God addressed to humans, as part of God's biblical address to his people. The position of Psalm 1 suggests how this is possible. It is a hermeneutical shift given at the very beginning of the book, recommending how the entire book can be read and understood.

I agree that Psalm 1 provides a valuable insight into one level of understanding the Psalter. But it is not the *only* way, nor the only *authoritative* way, of interpreting the Psalter. The canonical approach does not escape the same kind of hypothesizing that characterizes historical-critical methodology. But neither should be seen in an adversarial position; they do not necessarily preclude one another. Both are *levels* of understanding with limited but reasonable credibility. One is not more authoritative than the other; the responsible editor(s) do not replace the author(s). The Bible itself does not lay down rules for authoritative interpretation. This is the work of readers of the Bible, ecclesial or otherwise. And the success of interpretations will depend on factors other than mere authority, such as the carefulness of the reader, the plausibility of the reading, and the relevance of an interpretation. Indeed, different readings may coexist, such as the original one to which the historical-critical method aspires and the canonical one that existed in the context of the entire Psalter.

The second point, the *union* of Psalms 1 and 2, and the hermeneutical perspectives that they open up for the rest of the Psalter, is a much more debatable topic. Two objections can be made against this position. First, the basis for the association of the two psalms (linguistic resonance, etc.) is not convincing; the argument depends mainly on catchwords, and it rests ultimately on the *presumed* view of an unknown editor. Second, the themes of the two psalms are so very different: observance of the torah and subjection to the Davidic ("messianic") king. This double focus weakens the advantage of recognizing the perspective that

Psalm 1 gives to the Psalter and appreciating the range of messages in the Psalter, which go far beyond the promise to David.

Our consideration of the editing of the psalms will end with a comment on the *specific* context that superscriptions sometimes supply. We already saw that superscriptions occur for thirteen of the psalms attributed to David, as well as some others. For example, Psalm 30 is "a song at the dedication of the Temple." It makes no difference whether this is for the second Temple (515 B.C.E.) or the feast of Hanukkah (165 B.C.E.). The superscription removes the psalm from its clear original setting, namely that of an individual thanksgiving, and puts it into the category of what has been called "corporate use." This is not to deny the right of a community to reuse and reinterpret its own traditions. But such a superscription should not negate the psalm's more obvious and undeniable meaning—the thanksgiving of an individual for deliverance. (This is, by the way, the meaning established by historical-critical methodology, as we will see below.) The most appropriate superscription I have found is on Psalm 102: "A prayer of one afflicted, when faint and pleading before the LORD." No frills here; it goes straight to the heart of the matter.

THE PSALMS AND DAVID

I stated above that Davidic authorship was historically improbable and impossible to prove. This ascription of authorship is not an original part of Scripture; it is an editorial (re)classification according to a venerable tradition. However, scholars have asked whether David might provide a new and different lens through which to view the Psalter. Brevard Childs and others have argued that this is so. Childs claims that situating the psalms in the life of a human being, rather than in the liturgy—deculticizing them, as it were—creates a wider hermeneutical context, at least for the Davidic psalms. He writes that "the move toward universalizing the psalm was achieved by relating it to the history of David as a representative man" (*Introduction,* 552). In other words, David is Everyone. The full range of his virtues and vices, hopes and despairs, gratitude and lament, is revealed—the emotional life of a human being with which we can sympathize.

We go through the same kind of experiences and thus can relate to "a psalm of David."

To this one may respond by asking if it is necessary to proceed in such an indirect manner in order to identify with the psalmist, whoever it may have been. Why conjure up a situation in the life of David in order to understand or pray a psalm? It simply seems unnecessary: if we are ultimately to reduce the context to Everyman or universal experience, why start with David? Indeed, the specific situations in David's life to which some thirteen psalms are attributed, *limit* the application to that context. The psalm becomes a "historical" note about a historical character with whom one or another reader may find it difficult to sympathize. The Davidic authorship is an unnecessary constraint.

Gerald Sheppard (in *The Future of the Bible* [United Church of Canada Publishing House, 1990], 84) makes another claim:

> The presentation of David within the book and elsewhere in scripture provides the key sign of the book's coherence, as well as the context of its interpretation as a part of a larger scripture. We begin to realize that the prescriptural hymns can be heard scripturally only when they are heard in just this association with David.

The key terms in this approach are coherence, context, and prescriptural. Although Sheppard's views are more subtle than this brief discussion can portray, each of these terms deserves a comment. As for coherence, is it not obtained at too great a price? Its historical basis is, as Sheppard himself would admit, questionable. The coherence is artificial because the attribution of authorship in fact accounts for less than half of the Psalter. As for context, the giant figure of David provides a context, but neither a necessary nor the only one. As for "prescriptural hymns," if I understand the phrase correctly, this refers to psalms that would have been written and utilized up until the time they were collected and edited in the present book of Psalms, constitutive of "Scripture." This implies that the titles are part of "Scripture," and hence one should not depart from this view if one is going to give a "scriptural" interpretation of a given psalm. In other words, the psalms were "prescriptural" until they were provided with titles. This gives too much power to the superscriptions. For example, Sheppard admits (p. 88),

> Even if, from a modern perspective, the original psalm behind Psalm 3 had little to do with David and nothing to do with this historical event in David's life, it does now in the context of its role as scripture. We cannot make the Bible a better scripture by reconstructing earlier levels of its text and context.

One can agree heartily with his final statement about reconstruction. But it is an exaggeration to say that the superscription situates a text as Scripture and dictates the manner of interpretation. The Davidic interpretation is just as much a reconstruction (by Jewish tradition—and its legitimacy is not to be denied) as the reconstructions of modern scholars (some of which may be valid though all need to be scrutinized). In other words, the superscriptions did not stamp the seal "Scripture" on the final collection of the psalms. Rather, they reflect honorable and respectable tradition that provides one interpretive strategy for approaching the Psalter. The excesses of some modern exponents of the historical-critical method should not force us to adopt the superscription in order to preserve a psalm as being "scriptural."

Alan Cooper makes another strong case for the Davidic interpretation of the Psalter: "The Davidic attribution of the Psalms, in my view, is best understood as a productive interpretive strategy rather than as an historical claim" ("The Life and Times of King David According to the Book of Psalms," in *The Poet and the Historian* [ed. R. E. Friedmann: Chico, Cal.: Scholars Press, 1983], 125). Cooper attempts a *via media* between accepting "a traditional positivistic mode of reading the psalms, rabbinic or Patristic," and simply denying "the veracity of the Bible's own claim about the Psalms" (p. 124). In this connection he quotes an important observation of Hayden White (in *Tropics of Discourse* [Baltimore: Johns Hopkins University Press, 1978], 47)

> to recognize that there is no such thing as a *single* correct view of any object under study but that there are *many* correct views, each requiring its own style of representation. This would allow us to entertain seriously those creative distortions offered by minds capable of looking at the past with the same seriousness as

ourselves but with different affective and intellectual orienta-
tions. ("The Life and Times of King David," 124)

However, I fear that this leads to textual indeterminacy. Cooper
himself concludes that there are "only two sensible and productive ways of reading." One of these is the canonical shape advo-
cated by Brevard Childs (described above). The other is "reading
from an ahistorical aesthetic or literary-critical point of view." He
explains that although the author is beyond our reach, "the imaginary world which is encoded in the text is not. . . . The meaning
of the psalm is nothing more or less than the way we, as readers,
appropriate the text and *make* it meaningful" (pp. 130–31). Both of
these approaches are indeed possible, and they do not necessarily
exclude each other. It seems to me that both depend first on the
use of the historical-critical analysis of the text.

CHRISTIAN APPROACHES TO THE PSALMS

There is no one monolithic "Christian" interpretation of
the psalms or, for that matter, of the Bible. Several approaches
have appeared in the history of Christianity, from the NT through
the patristic and medieval periods into the modern era.

Without pretending to exhaust the variety and value of
these approaches, we will give examples that will highlight the
manner in which the church has interpreted and applied the
psalms. In the NT the appropriation was along two main lines.
First, the messianic interpretation of the royal psalms (e.g., Pss 2
and 72; see the treatment of messianism on pp. 54–58), which
had already begun in Jewish tradition, was thought by the early
church to refer to Jesus. Second, inspired by the image of the "suffering servant" of Isaiah 53, many psalms of lament were viewed
as having a bearing on Jesus' suffering and death (e.g., Pss 22 and
69). The sufferings so graphically portrayed in the Psalter became
a vehicle for understanding and describing Jesus in the passion
narratives. Thus the early Christians "explained" Christ, whom
they saw rooted in the biblical tradition to which they belonged.

The concept of the "fulfillment" of certain psalms and other
OT texts continued beyond the NT and is found in the early apolo-
getic controversies between Jews and Christians. But the NT itself

makes it clear that the affirmation that Christ is the Messiah is a matter of *belief,* not of "proof." The devotional life of the Church went beyond controversies. As the psalms entered the liturgy and the personal lives of the monks, especially, argument yielded to devotion. The interpretation remained christocentric, to be sure, and is perhaps best expressed in the *Enarrationes in Psalmos,* a title Erasmus gave to St. Augustine's commentary and sermons. Augustine makes room for Christ speaking in the Psalter, and also for the presence of his body, the church. The psalms were freely interpreted on an experiential Christian level, with little regard for what we would today consider the historical sense. This approach is now admired from a distance, but hardly practiced. Here is an example of Augustine's comment on Ps 85:1:

> God could not have given a greater gift to humans than to make the Word, through whom he established all things, their head, and to associate them with him as his members. The result is that he is son of God and son of man, one God with the Father, one man with men, so that when we speak to God in prayer we do not separate him from the Son, and when the body of the Son prays, it does not separate its head from itself since he is the one savior of his body—our Lord Jesus Christ, son of God, who both prays for us and prays in us and is prayed to by us. He prays for us, as our priest; he prays in us, as our head; he is prayed to by us, as our God. Let us recognize therefore our words in him and his words in us. . . . Therefore we pray to him, through him, we speak with him and he speaks with us. ("In Psalmum LXXXV," in *Enarrationes in Psalmos* [Turnhout: Brepols, 1956], 1176–77; author's translation)

John Cassian, a contemporary of Augustine, was a member of a monastery in Bethlehem, and he traveled to learn from the desert fathers in Egypt, eventually recording his interviews in his famous *Conferences.* From a certain Abba Nesteros he learned three kinds of spiritual understandings of Scripture—tropology, allegory, and anagogy—as well as the historical interpretation: "One and the same Jerusalem can be understood in a fourfold manner. According to history it is the city of the Jews. According to allegory it is the Church of Christ. According to anagogy it is that heavenly city of God 'which is the mother of us all.' According to tropology it is the soul of the human being, which under this name is frequently either reproached or praised by the Lord" (John Cassian, *The Conferences* [ed. B. Ramsey; New York: Paulist Press, 1997] XIV, 8, 4, p. 510). The seed of this fourfold division already appears in Origen, and it is enshrined in a famous medieval couplet attributed to Augustine of Denmark (thirteenth century): The letter (or literal sense) teaches fact; the allegorical, what you are to believe; the moral (or tropological), what you are to do; the anagogical (or eschatological), what you are to hope for.

Up until the so-called Enlightenment period, this fourfold understanding of the biblical text was standard for most Christians. The allegorical or typological approach had biblical warrant: the recognition of correspondences and analogies between various biblical figures or events, especially between the Testaments. But it was already found within the OT itself. Thus, the exodus deliverance became a type for Deutero-Isaiah (or Second Isaiah, the writer of Isa 40–55), who described the deliverance from the Babylonian exile in terms of the exodus experience. A new exodus was to take place (Is 43:16–19; 51:9–11). Thus, ancient Israelites seem to have practiced typology, and the NT continues to do so, as when it views Adam as a type of Christ (Rom 5:14) and the Passover lamb as a type of the Savior (John 19:36). David, too, reputed as the author of so many psalms, was a type of Christ, the Son of David.

The Reformation and the Renaissance marked a turn in hermeneutics, and they produced a greater sensitivity to history and the historical level of meaning in an ancient text. Is the traditional approach still meaningful today? For those who are already convinced of Christ's identity and role as the goal of OT hope, to read the psalms *only* from the point of view of their typological fulfillment in Christ would prevent them from experiencing the depth and breadth of biblical teaching and history. Typology has been somewhat dismissed because of the exaggerated use made of it by the early writers of the church, where imagination often ran wild. There is also the perception that typology simply does not appeal to the modern mind, and despite all the current emphasis on symbol, the symbolic character of typology has not caught on. Perhaps the best example is the relative neglect of the Epistle to the Hebrews, which sparkles with typology (e.g., Melchizedek and Christ). The indifference may be due to biblical illiteracy, but the line of correspondences between Old and New is not always convincing or congenial.

The fourfold division listed in the medieval couplet (literal, allegorical or typological, moral, and eschatological) conceals a fundamental mistake. It separated out the *littera*, that is, the so-called literal sense or historical fact, from the spiritual meaning, which was placed in the other three categories. What else could one do with the city of Jerusalem? This stripped the OT of spiritual relevance except insofar as it yielded types or moral examples. When "immoral" examples occurred, one was forced into a (non)explanation, as when Augustine characterized Jacob's deception of the blind Isaac in Genesis 27 as not a lie but a mystery (*non est mendacium sed mysterium*). Interpretation of the OT was often rendered jejune by reason of a Christian overlay, reading the NT into the OT. For example, the allegorical approach to the Song of Songs (or Song of Solomon) carried the day over a more literal interpretation. However justified such a "spiritual" meaning may be (i.e., the love between God and the human soul), the tragedy is that the literal meaning of the union between the sexes was bypassed. For Jewish tradition there was a different problem. Their concept of the *Oral* Law, with its written expression in the Talmud and other writings, often came between them and a more historical understanding of their sacred books. For both traditions, historical sensitivity would come later. Perhaps the psalms were somewhat spared. They are so direct in claiming the attention and emotions of the reader that it is difficult, indeed, to escape their immediate impact.

In many Christian circles there is a certain nostalgia for the interpretation of the OT recorded in the ancient liturgies, which reflect typology and Christian aspirations. The validity of such interpretation need not be denied, especially for those who carefully understand and apply it. But such spiritual interpretations, despite their long and glorious history, are not the *only* Christian approach.

Indeed, this traditional Christian interpretation is better called a christocentric approach. This is not necessarily the same as a Christian approach, which can also reach a meaning more in harmony with the literal sense of a passage. For example, a Christian who hears the Jewish *Shema* (which incorporates the cry of Deut 6:4, "Hear, O Israel: The LORD is our God, the LORD alone") can resonate spiritually with that prayer without needing to refer it to Christ. Surely Jesus could read the biblical text and address his Father without allegory or any such maneuver. So also Christians who read the OT as much as possible on its own level are utilizing a Christian approach. They cannot shed their Christian self-understanding, and in many cases their understanding of a given passage derives from a sense of the continuity between the two Testaments. The interpretation remains Christian rather than christocentric. It is important to recognize that the role the OT plays in nourishing the faith of the Christian *after Christ* is different from the one it played in explaining Christ to the first believers. One need not be locked into a patristic or medieval outlook to arrive at a Christian understanding.

Hence, modern readers can interpret the psalms as prayers originally directed to the God and Father of Jesus Christ, *YHWH* of the OT, to whom Jesus prayed: "Our Father, who art in heaven. . . ." This God-centered approach retains continuity with the obvious literal meaning of the words. It also corresponds to a NT ideal: "Through him [Christ], then, let us continually offer a sacrifice of praise to God, that is, the fruit of lips that confess his name" (Heb 13:15). The Christian worships God through Jesus Christ, the mediator, as the venerable ending of liturgical prayers reminds us: "Through Jesus Christ our Lord." Whoever approaches the psalms on that level is worshiping the Father as Jesus himself did. It is one level of understanding and prayer—not the only one, but a basic one. We are free to go beyond it, without neglecting it. People cannot pray what they do not understand. That suggests that we must absorb the worldview of the psalmist and enter into the plea—the substance of the prayer—embracing its forthright stance before God. Can a non-Christian adopt this approach? In part, it would seem so. The mediation of Christ might not be accepted, but the recognition of the God who is reached by these prayers is available to all who are willing to incorporate OT thought and faith. A direct approach to the Psalter matches the basic understanding Jesus had of the Father. He and his followers nourished their spiritual lives with the openness and beauty of the psalms' language.

This may not be satisfactory for Christians who want to worship God from a more distinctive and explicit Christian viewpoint. In that case, the medieval couplet may be more to their liking. This is not something that can be dictated, since movement in prayer is a matter of following the Spirit's lead. For example, Christians need not restrict themselves to OT notions of life, Sheol, and death, and so exclude the belief in eternal life with God. Christians may read many OT texts, quite properly, with a fuller meaning. We can understand such texts as Ps 16:11 in an eschatological sense: "You show me the path of life. / In your presence there is fullness of joy; / in your right hand are pleasures forevermore."

At the same time we should heed Dietrich Bonhoeffer's words about "cheap grace," and not fail to appreciate the level of meaning that is conveyed by the biblical text. It was life in the here and now that is meant, not the next life—and this is surely an important component of religious aspirations. It is not uncommon to hear Christians say with some amazement, "How did they believe in God?" (since "they" had no idea of a blessed future life!). This kind of reaction reveals how much Christians need to integrate the OT understanding of God and of life, if they would appreciate what the NT offers them. Belief means accepting God *on God's terms,* as they are revealed.

In his *Letters and Papers from Prison* (ed. E. Bethge; rev. ed.; New York: Macmillan, 1986), p. 86, Dietrich Bonhoeffer wrote something that all Christians should take to heart:

> My thoughts and feelings seem to be getting more and more like those of the Old Testament, and in recent months I have been reading the Old Testament much more than the New. It is only when one knows the unutterability of the name of God that one can utter the name of Jesus Christ; it is only when one loves life and the earth so much that without them everything seems to be over that one can believe in the resurrection and a new world. . . . In my opinion, it is not Christian to want to take our thoughts and feelings too quickly and too directly from the New Testament.

One may recognize in these words a certain exaggeration, but the exaggeration is in the right direction. The reverence that

Israel and the Jews have had for the sacred name, *YHWH,* became manifest in their substitution of another term, Adonai. This is not due to superstition; it derives from a profound sense of the divine, of awe at who God is. The older Bible translations have kept to this tradition: *Kyrios, Dominus,* LORD. Some moderns insist on Yahweh, the probable vocalization of the consonants of the tetragrammaton, *YHWH,* but this smacks of academic faddishness. The unutterability, the "unsayability," of God's name, the divine transcendence, is the basis of any faith in Christ—and this includes even uttering the name of Christ, who called *YHWH,* "Abba." Similarly the doctrine of the resurrection, which is often glibly accepted by many Christians, is not fully appreciated—not even really comprehended—unless God's creation is first understood.

❦

CHAPTER TWO

Theological Considerations

TERMINOLOGY: SOME KEY WORDS AND CONCEPTS

Modern readers must be aware of the different categories of thought that underlie biblical expressions. In some cases it is practically impossible to separate worldview from theology. Thus, the theological statements about creation in Genesis 1 are inextricably linked to the worldview of the ancient Israelite. We tend to project into the Bible our mentality, our own understanding of self and world. But this is to flatten out the biblical word, its imaginative quality, in favor of our own categories. We fail to savor the imagery and to enter the world of thought in which Israel moved. To that extent we are impoverished and even prone to misinterpreting the biblical message.

God

We may cite as an example the term "God," or "sons of God," or "gods." Most readers of the Bible simply take monotheism for granted as one of the great triumphs of Israelite religion; it bequeathed monotheism to the western world. We accept monotheism as a tidy little package that was a simple matter of reciting the cry of Deut 6:4, "Hear, O Israel: The LORD is our God, the LORD alone."

Instant monotheism! No, this confession of the Lord's uniqueness is at the end of a long historical and theological development. In the early days of Israel there existed a comfortable polytheism that was shared with neighboring states and religions. There were in fact many gods, but it was understood that the Lord was unique among these, the first among equals. Hence we hear the exultant cry of incomparability: "Who is like you . . . among the gods?" (Exod 15:11; see also Ps 77:13). Such statements are not monotheistic. They presuppose, rather than deny, the existence of other gods, and they are better understood as henotheistic: the one, unique, Lord cannot be rivaled by any other.

Moreover, this God is not alone. The Lord is surrounded by heavenly beings (Ps 29:1), or "sons of God," the members of the heavenly court who carry out the divine will. Even the adversary, or satan, is among them (Job 1:6), and there are others like Raphael in Tob 12:12–18 who are sent on missions (hence "angels"). Psalm 29 calls upon this array of heavenly beings to praise the Lord. Only gradually did Israel arrive at a pure monotheism, in which other gods are in fact zeroes. Thus the frequent polemic and ridicule heaped upon them, as in Ps 135:15–18, Jer 10:1–16, and Wis 13:10–19. When one reads that the fool in his heart says there is no God (Ps 14:1 = 53:1), this is not atheism or a denial of the existence of a god. Rather, it states that God is ineffective, inactive—a kind of practical atheism that is born out by the immoral actions of the foolish (14:1).

Soul

This is another word that is often misunderstood, and it occurs frequently in English Bible translations. It is an almost necessary, albeit misleading, translation of the Hebrew term *nefesh* ("vital force"; "soul" in Ps 104:1) and sometimes of *ruah* ("wind," "spirit," etc.; see Ps 104:30). For us the word "soul" carries Greek nuance: the "spiritual" part of the human person, who is made up of body and soul. These are simply *not* biblical categories and should not be imposed upon the text. A human being is breathed-upon matter (Gen 2:7); when God retracts this breath of life (often termed "spirit," or *ruah),* living things die (see Eccl 12:7). Only custom and the constraints of English and other languages lead to the use of this word. There is no handy term for *nefesh;* "person" is not adequate, so translators make do with "soul."

Life, Death, and Sheol

A modern reader has to grasp the essence of certain biblical concepts and understand that Israel refused to raise questions or to philosophize about ideas that we take for granted. Thus, if the soul/body categories are not biblical, how are we to understand life and death? Life means that God breathes on all that live, thus sustaining them (see Gen 2:7; 7:22). At death, the breath returns to God (Eccl 12:7), and the body corrupts. Death means the grave, corruption, the shadowy existence (if it can even be considered as such) of a "shade" in Sheol or the nether world, which was usually imagined in the belly of the earth. However, the rather fanciful descriptions of inhabitants of Sheol that Isaiah 14 or Ezekiel 32 sketch should suggest caution. All descriptions of Sheol are imaginative, since no one ever came back to report information. Even though Samuel could be called up from Sheol (1 Sam 28:14) and David could speak of going to his dead son (2 Sam 12:23), the Israelites did not speculate concerning *what* it was that went to Sheol. They were called "shades," for there was no *real* life after death, only a whisper of existence about which nothing was really known.

Israel's resignation to the fact of death, its acceptance of Sheol, was not unique. It shared this view with most of its neighbors in the Fertile Crescent. Immortality belonged properly to the gods, not to humans. The *Epic of Gilgamesh* is a Mesopotamian story of a human effort to secure immortality, which was ultimately unsuccessful: immortality is for the gods, as Gilgamesh was told (*ANET*, p. 90). Hence, the Bible repeatedly refers to human existence as something very tenuous, as when it is compared to grass that "fades and withers" (Ps 90:6), or when the psalmist laments, "My days are like an evening shadow; / I wither away like grass" (102:11).

> As for mortals, their days are like grass;
> 　they flourish like a flower of the field;
> for the wind passes over it, and it is gone,
> 　and its place knows it no more. (103:15–16 NRSV; see also
> 　39:5–7)

It is no wonder that the psalmist could only have recourse to God:

What, then, can I count on, O Lord?
In You my hope lies. (39:8 NJPS; v. 7 in NRSV)

With such a dim future ahead, all hope was in the present, the here and now, where the Lord might bestow goodness on the people. The same fate awaited both the just and the wicked. But perhaps it can be said that the just suffered more grievously because they perceived that Sheol meant that it was no longer possible to have any *loving* contact with God, whose "steadfast love is better than life" (Ps 63:3). The wicked, who had no genuine relationship with the Lord, were not in a position to realize what life had offered. The psalms frequently refer to Sheol in terms of its effect on praise (Pss 30:9; 88:11; 115:17; see also Is 38:18), as in the following: "For in death there is no remembrance of you; / in Sheol who can give you praise?" (6:5). The point is not that one somehow escapes God or evades the divine power; Ps 139:8 and Amos 9:2 make that clear. Although this idea is used as a motive for the Lord to intervene and preserve the psalmist (6:4–5; 30:9), it presents a deeper reality: the relationship with the Lord that the just had in this life is finished. It is only at the end of the OT era that an undying relationship with the Lord is perceived (see Wis 1:15; 5:15).

Because Sheol means nonlife, it comes to be used metaphorically to describe a distressful situation in this life: sickness, disaster, persecution, and so forth. When the psalmist exclaims (Ps 30:3), "You brought up my soul from Sheol," this means a deliverance from some distress in the here and now; it has nothing to do with physical resuscitation, much less resurrection. Sheol is a powerful image, the term "metaphor" hardly does it justice. Death and Sheol, which are frequently parallel in biblical thought (e.g., Hos 13:14; Isa 38:18), are conceived dynamically (see the comment on Ps 30). They are the great powers that pursue every human being, and, as we all know, they finally get their prey. Hence one can speak of the "power" (lit., "hand") of Sheol (Ps 89:48; see also Hos 13:14), from which no mortal can escape. This concept of the power of Death is not only an important factor in appreciating the biblical mentality, it is the key to our understanding many biblical texts. Thus in the Song of Songs 8:6, love and passion are compared to Death and Sheol: "Love is as strong as death." What is the essence of the comparison? Strength. Death/Sheol is the most powerful force that humans face; no one can shake loose from that grip. Hence Song 8:6 is a tremendous tribute to true human love, which can be compared to Death/Sheol for its otherwise matchless strength.

Heart

The psalms use the term "heart" with some of the same ambiguities it has in modern English. Hans W. Wolff calls it "the most important word in the vocabulary of Old Testament anthropology" (*Anthropology of the Old Testament* [Philadelphia: Fortress, 1974], 40). Two forms occur (*leb* and *lebab*) 858 times in the OT, and almost always of human beings, although twenty-eight times it is used of God (perhaps Hos 11:8 is the most famous instance). Naturally, the physical organ is meant, especially in the descriptions of sickness (Ps 38:10, "my heart throbs"). Because it is an internal organ, it comes to stand for something hidden, inaccessible; only God knows the secrets of the heart (Ps 44:21). Sheol and Abaddon (a term for the realm of the dead, meaning "[place of] Destruction," often used synonymously with Sheol) are open before the Lord, so how much more the human heart (Prov 15:11)! The Lord can look at the heart and not be deceived by exterior signs, as the choice of David over his oldest brother, Eliab, reveals (1 Sam 16:7). The heart is the seat of desire (Ps 21:2) and other emotions. Yet it is very frequently a synonym for intellectual activity: in Deut 29:4 the eye is for seeing, the ear for hearing, and the heart for understanding. The psalmist prays, "Teach us to count our days / that we may gain a wise heart" (Ps 90:12). The key to Solomon's wisdom is the "listening heart" for which he asks, and which the Lord gives him (1 Kgs 3:9–12). Of course, in biblical thought sheer mental activity is hardly ever separated from action. Hence "heart" also indicates the will and decision of a person. Sensitivity to God's grace is indicated by the "natural heart" in Ezek 36:26: "A new heart I will give you, and a new spirit I will put within you; and I will remove from your body the heart of stone and give you a heart of flesh."

As mentioned above, God too has a heart, and it is the source of divine plans (Ps 33:11, "the thoughts of his heart"). In

Gen 6:6 God is grieved "to the heart" for having created human beings that have turned out to be so evil. Hence it can be said that God repents (Hebrew *naham*) about something that has been done or planned (see Gen 6:6; Jer 18:8; Jonah 3:10). Obviously this has nothing to do with repentance over sin. The meaning is "to regret something" or "to change one's mind." Here again care should be taken not to simply impose Greek categories of thought (God is "pure act," so how can God "change?") into a biblical framework. The Hebrew mind had no difficulty in conceiving a God who *reacts*, even a God who suffers (e.g., Hos 11:1–9; 13:4–14).

Other Physical Expressions

Another part of the human body that the Psalter frequently mentions is "kidneys," which most English translations gloss with more "suitable" English words like heart, mind, or soul. It is often paired with heart and designates the deepest feelings (see Pss 7:10; 16:7; 73:21). Even the word "liver" occurs and is translated as "soul" in Ps 16:9 or "heart" in Ps 108:1.

"Flesh" frequently connotes the sexual sphere in English, but in the Bible it means simply what is human and mortal, as opposed to the divine. We read in Isa 31:3, "The Egyptians are human, and not God; / their horses are flesh, and not spirit." What at first might appear banal is a cutting comment about the vaunted Egyptian power—it belongs only to the human sphere. In a benign usage, God remembers that the people are flesh (Ps 78:39) and withdraws the divine anger. The realm of the flesh is frailty, just as the realm of the spirit is strength and life (Job 34:14–15).

Name

It might be thought that "name" should not cause difficulties, but not so. We have already discussed the mystery and awe contained in the sacred Name (see pp. 30–31). First revealed dramatically to Moses in Exodus 3, God's name never lost that aura expressed in Exod 34:5–6, when the Lord descended in the cloud and stood with his servant and proclaimed: "'The LORD, the LORD,' a God merciful and gracious, slow to anger, and abounding in steadfast love and faithfulness." The very mention of "the *name*" (*shem* in Hebrew) was one way for Israel to understand the divine presence. Deuteronomy states that while the Lord dwelt in heaven, "the name" was present in the Temple of the holy city (e.g., Deut 12:5), and this becomes a theme of the so-called Deuteronomistic theology (e.g., 1 Kgs 8:29); that is, the somewhat unified theology found in the books of Deuteronomy through 2 Kings. Without this sense of the power of the name, we will have difficulty understanding the significance of the Lord acting for the sake of the divine name, as Ezek 20:44 vows: "You shall know that I am the LORD, when I deal with you for my name's sake." Hence it may not be easy for us to resonate meaningfully with the refrain of Psalm 8 (vv. 1 and 9): "O LORD, our Sovereign, / How majestic is your name in all the earth!" Or with the spirited ending of Ps 7:17: "I will give to the LORD the thanks due to his righteousness, / and sing praise to the name of the LORD, the Most High." Even the powerful biblical expressions "blessed be the name of the Lord" and "in the name of the Lord" become bland if we fail to appreciate this background.

The psalmist asks the Lord to protect the faithful who are in need (5:12) and knows that the Lord will be the joy and exultation of all "who love your name" (v. 11). One can say that the name is shorthand for the person, but this explanation does not catch the flavor and full meaning of the concept. Human names are also significant. Individuals receive meaningful names, as when the "man" (Hebrew *adam*) is formed from the dust of "the ground" (Hebrew *adamah;* Gen 2:7). Leah names her son Asher (meaning "happy") because his birth has made her happy (Gen 30:13). The name can even indicate a person's nature: "Nabal [lit. 'folly'] is his name, and folly is with him" (1 Sam 25:25). A name change pointed to the superiority and power of the one who made the change (Abram to Abraham in Gen 17:5; see also Jacob/ Israel in Gen 35:9–11).

Presence/Face

The concept of the presence of God is not unlike that of the name. There is no question that the true dwelling place of the Lord is in "heaven," where the members of his court praise him

(Ps 29). But even so, Israel had a deep sense of the mystery of the divine presence, as Solomon's prayer in 1 Kgs 8:27 shows: nothing could really contain God, whether the heavens or the Jerusalem Temple. And, moreover, the Lord was present among his people, as the psalms' lively language makes clear. The supplicants were not talking to themselves, nor did they speak only "as if" the Lord was present.

Psalm 139 testifies to this awareness of the divine presence. The intimacy is intense: "You have searched me and known me." God knows what the psalmist will say; around and about, the divine "hand" rests (vv. 4–5), and there is sheer astonishment at such a relationship. Anywhere in the universe, even in the heart of darkness, God holds fast the psalmist (vv. 7–12). Almost playfully the thought is entertained: "Where can I go from your spirit? / Or where can I flee from your presence?" Of course, it is not a question of trying to escape; there is simply an overpowering admiration—neither height nor depth! No matter what the poet might imagine, in view of the divine knowledge, guidance, and pursuit, there is no escape—the divine concern extends even to "my mother's womb" (v. 13). This is the active divine presence that the poet experienced and described.

Another aspect to divine presence is the "face" of God. The danger of "seeing God" is a well-known theme, beginning with the warning to Moses that to see God's "face" (*panim*) would mean death (Exod 33:20–23). There is a startling reversal of this in the language of the psalms. One does not die; rather, one seeks and even sees the face of God (translations of the psalms frequently render "face" with "presence"), as in the following: 11:7 ("the upright shall behold his face"); 16:11 ("in your presence" = with your face); 17:15 ("I shall behold your face in righteousness"); 21:6 ("the joy of your presence" = your face); 27:4, 13 ("behold/see the beauty/goodness of the LORD"); 36:9 ("in your light we see light"); 42:2 ("behold the face of God"); 61:7 ("forever before God" = in God's presence forever); 63:2 ("I have looked upon you in the sanctuary, beholding your power and glory"); 84:7 ("the God of gods will be seen in Zion" [uncertain text]); 140:13 ("the upright shall live in your presence"). Psalm 42:2 vividly expresses this desire: "My soul thirsts for God, for the living God. / When shall I come and behold the face of God?"

What was once considered dangerous is now a source of blessing. It is not clear how this reversal came about. Perhaps the beginning of the change is present in the priestly blessing of Aaron (Num 6:25–26): "The LORD make his face to shine upon you, and be gracious to you; / the LORD lift up his face upon you and give you peace." In any case, the emphasis is not upon a naked encounter or anything approximating the meeting of Moses with the Lord. Even Moses' experience is described with some ambiguity (see Exod 24:9–11; 33:11).

Furthermore, it seems that these encounters are mediated by the experience of God in the Jerusalem Temple. That intimate phrase, "seeing the face," with all its echoes in Israel's history, could now be understood safely. For in the Most Holy Place the Lord was present, yet invisible—enthroned on the ark of the covenant, his footstool, and guarded by the two cherubim. We may call this a spiritual or liturgical presence. The metaphor of the "face' is also important in other experiences of the Israelites. It was only natural that in a period of adversity one referred to God "hiding" the face (Ps 30:7; 104:29). There is an unmistakable boldness in biblical language concerning a God who has eyes, mouth, and ears—who sees but cannot be seen, who hears Sarah's laugh when she is eavesdropping (Gen 18:12–13), and who speaks to prophets.

CREATION

We cannot adequately discuss such a large topic here, but the remarkable images with which creation is portrayed in Hebrew poetry call for attention. Most people are aware of the rather controlled and trouble-free process of creation in six days by the word of the Lord (Gen 1). Even here, however, there is a hint of chaos in the expressive Hebrew phrase, *tohu wavohu* (Gen 1:2, "formless void"). But any sign of a real struggle has been muted; the creative acts are effortless, a mere word. The Genesis creation narrative (as well as other portions of the "pre-history" in Gen 1–11) has been compared with the Mesopotamian epics *Enuma Elish* and *Atrahasis*. For the psalms, however, the more pertinent background is the Canaanite worldview expressed in the poetry of ancient Ugarit, dating from around the fourteenth century B.C.E. The biblical poets, inspired by these myths, enlarged on the theme of creation as the overcoming of chaos. (The thinking behind the chaos theme has been described as mythological, suprahistorical, simply imaginative, or a combination of these, but we need not resolve this question here). For our discussion, the German word, *Chaoskampf,* battle with chaos, sums up this whole world of creation thinking.

The passages in the psalms that reflect this viewpoint are easily identified. The obvious creation psalms, such as 8, 19, 104, and others, require little comment. But the following psalms need some explanation: 74:12–17; 77:11–20; 89:8–14. This will serve the reader well, too, since the ideas expressed in these poems are also scattered throughout the Bible (see Job 38–41 and Isa 27:1; 43:16; 51:9–10).

Psalm 74:12–17 describes the actions, which are called saving deeds or "salvation" (and this association of creation with salvation should be kept in mind), that the Lord, the King, performs. These divine deeds include breaking the heads of the dragons, crushing the heads of Leviathan, and then performing the well-known creative acts involving day and night, moon and stars, etc. Three terms have a striking Ugaritic background: sea (or *Yam*), Leviathan (or *Lotan,* a twisting seven-headed sea monster; see Isa 27:1), and dragons (*tanninim*). In the Ugaritic texts these are the opponents whom Baal, the Canaanite storm-god, overcomes. The details of his battles (also with *Mot,* or Death) are controverted. But it is clear that the Israelites drew from a *Chaoskampf* story that had some of the details we see in the Ugaritic texts in order to portray their God's creative activity. The allusions in Psalm 74 are convincing in this regard.

Psalm 77 has none of the striking references that mark Psalm 74, but the waters from the deep and also the storm phenomena are signs of the Lord's wonders and might, as he redeemed his people: "Your way was through the sea, / your path, through the mighty waters; / yet your footprints were unseen" (77:19). However, the reference is to the exodus, not to creation, to the Lord who has won victory over Sea by leading out his people "through the sea." The use of the myths was flexible—they could be applied to various activities of the Lord, the creator and redeemer of Israel.

Psalm 89:8–14 recalls the creative activity of the Lord and introduces another name for the sea monster that personifies chaos, Rahab (see also Isa 51:9). The text moves from creation to the covenant that God has established with the people. This is a lament that contains a kind of rhetorical trap for God. The psalmist repeatedly praises the Lord's steadfast love and faithfulness throughout the psalm until he arrives at his real grief: the Lord has gone back on his word by allowing king and people to be defeated (the precise occasion is difficult to determine).

Jon Levenson has argued (in *Creation and the Persistence of Evil* [San Francisco: Harper & Row, 1988]) that biblical creation is not intrinsically irreversible. These mythological allusions in the Bible indicate that chaos survives and hence can return. For example, when the Lord plies Job with satirical questions as to how Job would handle Leviathan (Job 41:1–8), it is implied that the divine victory is not total. Leviathan could conceivably break loose from the divine control. Hence creation is not intrinsically irreversible. This would yield a biblical explanation for the persistence of evil in the world created by God. The Lord is not quite in charge. In reply, one may ask if these mythological allusions can bear all that theological weight. Leviathan may still "exist," at least in the world of myth. But the casual dismissal of this monster of chaos in several texts (Job 41:1–8; Ps 104:26) is rather an indication of impotence. Even the "final" (eschatological?) slaying of Leviathan (Isa 27:1) seems to be symbolic; it cannot evade the divine constraint.

The argument turns on the ontological validity of mythological allusions, a philosophical question. I would claim that the mythopoeic approach of the ancients in this instance was the only way available for them to conceive of reality. To transfer that level to the ontological level of Greek and western thinking is another move, and it is not a simple carry-over. Evil and suffering remained a mystery to the ancient Israelite, as also to modern western "theodicy." On the mythological level, it does not appear that these biblical texts tried to explain evil by implying that the Lord had a loose rein on Leviathan/Chaos. Instead, we find in the biblical imagery an effort to glorify the Lord, who is never portrayed as defeated; the conflict is apparently one that he cannot lose. The *Chaoskampf* mentality is our way of summarizing the Hebrew appropriation of the mythology, but there appears to be an underlying belief in divine omnipotence, even if that term is never used. In the Lord's speeches in Job, conflict seems to be downplayed, if not denied, when chaos is portrayed as a babe in swaddling clothes:

> Who shut in the sea with doors
> > when it burst out from the womb? —
> when I made the clouds its garment,
> > and thick darkness its swaddling band,
> and prescribed bounds for it,
> > and set bars and doors,
> and said, "Thus far shall you come, and no farther,
> > and here shall your proud waves be stopped"? (Job 38:8–11)

Does such a passage leave any hope for Sea to burst its bonds? Or to come through the doors? This imagery may be interpreted as even contradictory: swaddling clothes and barred doors. Is this more than a lively imagination (or "poetic license") reflecting on the ambivalence of water in any age, both beneficial and also threatening? The very manner in which these contradictory ideas are joined together suggests caution in transferring them to the ontological plane that characterizes western thought.

Understanding creation in terms of the *Chaoskampf* is necessary because it is somewhat foreign to modern thought. While this is far from an adequate treatment of creation in the Bible, we can briefly indicate some descriptions of the creation process, which are found especially in Genesis 1, Job 37, 38–40, and Prov 8:22–31. These texts may interest the scientist who is concerned with ancient as well as modern views of beginnings. However, that is not the point of the poets who employ the creation themes. They are not interested in creation for creation's sake. These texts have unmistakable theological purposes: in Genesis 1 it is the ease of creation and also the theological emphasis on the Sabbath; in Job it is the power, variety, but also the puzzling aspects of creation; and in Proverbs it is the association of Woman Wisdom (the personification of wisdom as a woman) with the created world. The psalms never speak of creation in a detached manner.

There is an accompanying sense of wonder, of confidence, even of admiration. Psalm 104 highlights continuing creation, the providential blessings with which the Lord has graced the world, and it explodes in wonder at the Lord's wisdom (v. 24). In a display of personal pride in his composition that is rare in the OT, the psalmist hopes that this joyful praise will be found acceptable to the Lord (v. 34), and he ends with an unusual panache: the only drawback to creation is sinners—let them be eliminated. In Psalm 33 the Lord is clearly praised for creation by word (vv. 6–9; see also Ps 147). Psalm 8 indicates the awesome marvels of the sky, only to contrast them with the even more astonishing creation of humanity—creatures that are just a little less than the members of the immediate divine family, the members of the heavenly court. With such a rank, it is perhaps not surprising that they have been given a share in the divine rule over the rest of created beings. Vivid imagination also colors Ps 19:1–6, which celebrates the mysterious language of "the music of the spheres," and in it the sun (not Shamash, the Mesopotamian sun-god) makes its rounds as hero and bridegroom. All in all, a creative, endearing, and admiring presentation!

SALVATION

An important word in the Psalter is "salvation." What does it mean? In religious language it is commonly understood as "salvation from sin," due to the NT influence. But the biblical notion includes much more. It refers, par excellence, to the actions of the Lord on Israel's behalf. In the songs of praise, whether individual or communal, salvation is understood in many different ways: the deliverance of Israel in the exodus, in the return from Babylon, or in an individual's personal experience (sickness, persecution, etc.). In a most general sense it means being delivered out of some distress and into a condition that to some extent connotes *shalom* or well-being. Moreover, it has many synonyms that designate the effects of salvation, such as "peace," "life," and other positive notions. Deliverance can also be indicated in spatial terms, as to move out of a tight spot (Ps 4:1, "You gave me room when I was in distress").

Several hymns celebrate the "salvation" or saving intervention of God in Israel's history: from the patriarchs, to the beginning of the monarchy under Saul, to the reigns of David and
Solomon, to the divided kingdoms and their eventual destruction, and to the return of the exiles from Babylon. The so-called
"historical" psalms, in particular, allude to events in Israel's history for various purposes. For example, Psalm 78 draws lessons
from the record of its rebellious history, from Egypt to David.
The mood of Psalm 105, in contrast, is hymnlike, commemorating the Lord's fidelity to the promises to the patriarchs, the divine
aid during the Egyptian plagues, and the rescue from Egypt because of the "word" (i.e., promise) to Abraham. Psalm 106, despite its hymnlike beginning, confesses the manifold infidelities
from the time of Moses to the monarchy, invites Israel to repent
of its sinful past, and offers a plea to God that the people be gathered together "from among the nations" (v. 47).

Perhaps the most electrifying summons is the opening
verses of Psalms 107, 118, and 136: "O give thanks to [= praise]
the LORD, for he is good, / for his steadfast love endures forever."
The effect is particularly clear in Psalm 136, because the second
line is repeated in a refrain that occurs through all the verses. The
psalm itself unites the themes of creation and salvation history,
from Egypt down to the grant of the land "as a heritage" (v. 21).
The repetition expresses the heart of the psalm because it celebrates one of the prime characteristics of the Lord, namely, his
steadfast love (*hesed*, a rich word variously translated as love,
kindness, etc.). The term stands for the total relationship of the
Lord and Israel: all his saving interventions, all his goodness, the
promises and the covenants. Psalm 77 dares to ask: "Has his
steadfast love ceased forever?" (v. 8), a question brought on by a
"change" in the right hand of God (v. 10, i.e., God's mighty help).
We can assume that the writer is speaking for the community,
when some national catastrophe has driven them all to the brink.
But hope reasserts itself in the recital of the wonders of the exodus (vv. 11–20); there is no giving up. The Lord's "steadfast love"
will return; it is the rock bottom of Israel's faith. Psalm 63:3 tells
why: "Your steadfast love is better than life." That is an astonishing
statement, because "life" is the prime value in the perspective of
the OT. It is life in the here and now, which means the beneficent

presence of the Lord as opposed to the emptiness, the nonlife, of Sheol. Life is not worth living without the divine *hesed.*

ENEMIES, VIOLENCE, AND VENGEANCE

Salvation has meaning for the individual, as well as the community. The appeal, "Save me!" occurs frequently (e.g., Pss 7:1; 54:1; the Hebrew *hoshi'eni* lies behind the familiar cry, Hosanna). This is a natural beginning for a lament, along with "Hear my voice," and other urgent appeals. From what is the psalmist (or the people) to be saved? The foremost danger is enemies, but there are also the various troubles of life, such as threat of death, old age, wild animals, physical sickness, sinful behavior (Ps 51), and the innumerable evils that afflict humankind.

To interpret these dangers it is important to understand the *language* with which they are described. In one sense, the language is so formulaic that it is difficult to take it seriously. One can readily empathize with a given psalmist, but when the laments repeat the same old tired complaints, there is an understandable urge to skip over their problem. How is one to deal with the broad class of enemies: liars, mockers, hypocrites, men of blood, and people who are false, bold, tyrannical, and above all, innumerable? Within even one psalm these predicates tumble one after another. Various theories have been proposed in an effort to be more specific. The enemies are calumniators who are judging the psalmist of criminal action, or they are magicians who weave a spell (Ps 10:7) against the psalmist, or they are the rich who are exploiting the poor. None of these hypotheses can be verified. One may ask a different question: are they really human beings? The descriptions are so extreme and exaggerated that they seem to portray superhuman hostile and evil powers that the psalmist cannot handle. Hence the symbols of death and destruction associated with the enemies—they lay traps, shoot arrows, and lie in ambush like lions ready to pounce on the innocent.

Perhaps the reader of the psalms should understand the enemies as personifications of evil. This is not to deny that enemies can refer in some cases to actual human beings. But the characterizations are driven by a greater reality: evil is at work, and the suffering psalmist is beleaguered and driven to the broad and bold representations found in the laments. These are types that gradually became stylized in the language of the lament. The ancient world was much more opaque to the individual than our world is to us. We can name our problems: various types of illness, real and identifiable persons, or social or political systems. We have cancer, AIDS, and you name it, but the ancient world could not give a malady a name, without the same knowledge of sickness, let alone identify its cause. Was the problem an evil spirit? Then how much more trouble could such spirits be? The ancients were quite conscious of an unknown, hostile world that they described symbolically. Psalm 91, a beautiful prayer of trust, warns of an unspecified "terror of the night," "the pestilence that stalks in darkness," and "the destruction that wastes at midday." The perennial issue, the conflict of good and evil, finds concrete expression in the characterization of the just and unjust. Moreover, the psalmist's use of this language to describe his or his community's condition is deliberately intended to motivate the Lord to intervene. The lament considers the situation a matter of life and death (the serenity expressed in Ps 90 is unusual). Thus, understanding this aspect of the language of the psalms will help us deal with prayers that seem offputting.

The imagery is not always so extreme. No effort is required to identify with the following lines:

Save me, O God,
    for the waters have come up to my neck.
I sink in deep mire,
    where there is no foothold;
I have come into deep waters,
    and the flood sweeps over me. (Ps 69:1–2)

At the same time, this imagery points to a paradox. We don't know the precise situation of the psalmist, but this turns out to our advantage. The language is so broadly pitched that we can fit our problems into the complaint. If the psalmist were precise and specific, we might find it hard to apply those details to our own situation, and being unable to identify with them, we might lose enthusiasm for the prayer. How many times have we heard of the physical complaints of acquaintances—a boring experience! It is not easy to enter into and identify with the particular sufferings of another. We find it difficult to shed our own concerns, and the troubles of others become remote. We may sympathize, but we hardly identify.

Another issue is the tone of vengeance in some psalms, a problem that is exacerbated by the Psalter's role in the liturgy. One reaction to the violence and vengeance has been to eliminate the so-called "offensive" passages. Thus a Roman Catholic liturgical directive of 1970 has permitted the omission from prayer books and from the Divine Office (a daily liturgy centered on the Psalter) of three psalms (58; 83; 109) and parts of nineteen others (e.g., Ps 137:7–9). Such a "solution" is self-defeating and an irrational censorship of the Bible. What is the purpose? To shield the reader from disturbing, even ugly, thoughts? This negative approach is oblivious to the harsh reality of modern life, which can be well characterized by the old Latin saying, *homo homini lupus* (humans are wolves to each other). The implication is that only "pious thoughts," not reality, are to be considered as prayer material. No, such violence should be confronted by a violent generation that has inherited World Wars and witnessed ethnic cleansing. Identification with the mood and will of the psalmist is not always the best way to approach a psalm; confrontation can be accompanied by meditation. That means that the reader sees the futility of being "shocked" by the past, and looks at the present, the violent generation to which he or she belongs. One can allow the vengeance expressed in a psalm to point an accusing finger to the spirit of revenge that lurks in the human heart. We are not strangers to the craving for revenge. We see it in the media interviews in which aggrieved people stoutly affirm the statute of capital punishment.

These psalms challenge us to think and to meditate; they cannot "scandalize." The early fathers of the church never evaded such confrontation; many of them could recite the 150 psalms from memory. They tended to view the enemies as the devil Satan, the powers of evil, or as personal wicked tendencies. At times this might appear naive, but it is honest, not evasive. This approach does not allow prayer to be dominated by our own choice and mood. It takes us out of ourselves and into both the suffering and the sinful human family to which we also belong. The psalms bring a much-needed corporate dimension to our prayer. James L. Mays (*The Lord Reigns: A Theological Handbook to the Psalms* [Louisville: Westminster/John Knox, 1994], 46–54) explores the corporate nature of the Psalter. Even psalms written in the first person can be the voice of the community and of the individuals in it. The "I" of the psalms has been expanded to "We" already in the OT (e.g., Ps 66:1–12 and 13–20), where corporate identity was a much stronger feeling than it is in our culture. It has been said that over the course of time we read tenfold of what is really printed, because our thoughts and memories, our very selves, are contained in what we read. Not only our selves, but also the great spirits of the past, such as Augustine, Luther, Calvin, and many more. The corporate self should also include those of other cultures and climes who are oppressed or violated. Or, to put it another way, the Christian should have a sense of the body of Christ.

We mentioned above one of the most tender prayers, Psalm 139, whose opening lines are familiar to every Bible reader: "O LORD, you have searched me and known me." The first eighteen verses describe the intimate relationship between God and the psalmist. But verses 19–22 (notice, not vv. 23–24) are excised by some censors, presumably because of the hatred:

> O that you would kill the wicked, O God,
> and that the bloodthirsty would depart from me—
>
> . . . .
>
> Do I not hate those who hate you, O LORD?
> And do I not loathe those who rise up against you?
> I hate them with a perfect hatred;
> I count them my enemies. (Ps 139:19, 21–22)

We can react in various ways to these verses. The least desirable is to criticize the psalmist in the name of an allegedly higher ethical standard. What good does this accomplish? If it gives one a feeling of superiority, that attitude is wrong, harmful, and unprofitable. Finding "fault" is beside the point, unless it is followed by an assessment of the violence and hatred that the reader has some share in. Indeed, these statements directly imply fidelity to God:

your enemies are my enemies. This is in effect a statement of loyalty, but it is lost on anyone who merely passes moral judgment. Admittedly, the identification of enemies can become a dangerous justification: *my enemies are also yours.* This is a rationalization not uncommon among human beings. But if readers honestly face and ponder these emotional expressions, they will profit from the experience. In fact, the last two verses (vv. 23–24) reveal the heart and honesty of the psalmist, who is not self-satisfied or complacent, but fully aware of personal doubt: "Search me, O God, and know my heart. . . . See if there is any wicked way in me, and lead me in the way everlasting" (i.e., in the ways of old).

Some may not be convinced by the previous considerations, arguing that feelings of hatred and revenge are simply out of place in their prayers. Their uneasiness may stem from the way in which they "pray" them. The usual way of using the Psalter in prayer is to identify with the words of the psalmist. Those words and sentiments, especially when expressing praise and hope, become the vehicle of personal aspirations. The difficulty arises in cases where readers cannot bring themselves to identify with hatred for others. Is another approach possible? Yes, *hear* the word! Hear the agony and even the sinful violence of human beings—in the context of prayer. These expressions of rage exemplify the demonic in every human heart. No one is exempt from feelings of revenge. When they are heard in prayer, they serve first to illumine and then perhaps even convict our own feelings.

We have already mentioned the practice of eliminating certain parts of the psalms for purposes of "piety." This is not only an artificial and dishonest procedure, it is theologically questionable. Why do we read our Bible? Merely to confirm our own views? Consider a serious principle at stake here: we cannot afford to be selective about our biblical canon. In recent scholarly discussion the issue of a canon within the canon has emerged. That is to say, a given book or books become the key to interpreting the whole canon and are allowed to snuff out others less "spiritual" or less "popular." This is an unsatisfactory theological procedure, because it fails to attend to the whole spectrum of the biblical word. In a similar way, men and women who live in a world marked by violence and revenge should not fail to confront these same realities in the Bible.

The laments are not an inferior type of psalm, although they seem to be the least imitated and perhaps among the least recited by personal choice. The reason may be that they are understood merely as complaint, as "whining," or more seriously, as contravening the will of God. True, Christ urged us to "turn the other cheek," "to forgive our enemies," and so on. And the image and example of Christ should govern our freedom in praying to the Father. But Jesus shuddered before his own suffering, reciting the opening of Psalm 22 on the cross ("why have you forsaken me?"). Or consider the striking verse of Hebrews 5:7, "In the days of his flesh, Jesus offered up prayers and supplications, with loud cries and tears, to the one who was able to save him from death." While the gospels do not give us an inner psychological portrait of Jesus, and hence it is difficult to draw specific conclusions, those words, "loud cries and tears," from the Letter to the Hebrews are suggestive. The Gospel of John has chosen to portray Jesus meeting his fate without a hint of interior distress (e.g., John 18:1–11), but there was a struggle: "Not my will, but yours be done" (Luke 22:42). Jesus was not a Stoic; he voiced his feelings and was nourished by the laments of the Psalter. The genre of intimate lament has virtually disappeared from Christian prayer (except when it appears in the Psalter), but Christians still have much to learn from it.

It has often been said that the Psalter is a school of prayer—not in the sense that it provides 150 more prayers to add to one's list. Rather, it teaches us about the various ways of approaching God. Personal notes of praise, love, and trust are sounded, even in the midst of all the self-centeredness that characterizes a lament. "Taking refuge," either as a noun or verb, occurs in the psalms thirty-seven times (out of fifty-eight in the entire Bible); two-fifths of all the occurrences of *batah* ("trust," as verb or noun) are in the Psalter (about fifty times). The implication is not simply that the psalmist has nowhere to turn (which may be true), but that it is only on the Lord that one can rely with certainty. Notes of complaint and lament do not have the last word; motifs of intimacy with God sweep the reader into a complete relationship. As already noted, the movement of most psalms is from lament to praise. Psalms 39 and 88 seem to be the most forlorn, with little hope expressed. Still, these are prayers brought before God, even if in a given instance the psalmist is without enough spirit to voice the confidence that moved him to compose the prayer.

SIN AND SUFFERING

The ancient world clearly connected sin and suffering. Distress was a sign of divine displeasure, and one "explained" suffering as some kind of punishment. Prosperity, on the other hand, was a sign of divine blessing. Human attitudes were thus applied to God. In a sense this view is hard to fault. It shows a sense of responsibility, of awareness of the results of wrongdoing. In the end, the wicked will have to pay for their wickedness. A typical example of this even-handed retribution is Ps 11:5–7:

> The LORD tests the righteous and the wicked,
>   and his soul hates the lover of violence.
> On the wicked he will rain coals of fire and sulfur;
>   a scorching wind shall be the portion of their cup.
> For the LORD is righteous,
>   he loves righteous deeds;
>   the upright shall behold his face.

In all that occurred, the Lord was directly involved, the primary agent of weal and woe (Isa 45:7; Amos 3:6).

Some might envision the moral universe of the OT as a veritable machine, as if there is an *intrinsic* connection between act and consequence: a good deed produces a good result (reward); a bad deed produces a bad result (punishment). God does not intervene, does not need to, but is like a "midwife" who supervises this moral order. This view is exemplified in Ps 7:15–16, which describes the mechanical effect of evildoing:

> They make a pit, digging it out,
>   and fall into the hole that they have made.
> Their mischief returns upon their own heads,
>   and on their own heads their violence descends.

Several other passages indicate such a connection between deed and consequence (see Ps 57:6; Prov 26:27; Eccl 10:8; and Sir 27:26).

But in practical terms, one must ask if they ever understood reality to be so automatic. While there is a certain thrill, an appropriateness in what Shakespeare called "hoist with his own petard" (*Hamlet,* III, iv, 208), who is so simple-minded as to take this as an "order" of things, a kind of "boomerang" effect in human activity? How long did one have to wait before discovering that the wicked did not fall into the pit that they dug for the righteous? In the name of poetic justice, they should fall, but reality was another thing. Besides, one could never control the Lord. Even the casting of lots does not escape divine control (Prov 16:33).

If retribution failed to occur, was it because the system that God set up malfunctioned? Psalms 58 and 82 appear to try to shift the responsibility for a just rule from the Lord to the members of the heavenly court. They are, as we have seen, "gods" (see Ps 29:1), and we can infer from these psalms that they have some responsibility for the administration of justice in the world. Because they fail in their duties, they shall die, just as mortals do:

> "How long will you judge unjustly
>   and show partiality to the wicked?"
>
> . . . .
>
> I say, "You are gods,
>   children of the Most High, all of you;
> nevertheless, you shall die like mortals,
>   and fall like any prince." (Ps 82:2, 6–7)

Even so, whether God was directly or indirectly involved, what message did this convey to one who was suffering? Was distress a sign of sin and well-being a sign of virtue, as Job's friends thought? The very existence of complaints in the Psalter shows that retribution could not be viewed so neatly. And some psalms complain how unfair it is that the arrogant and evil prosper. Psalm 37 attempts to solve this problem: Do not be envious of evildoers, for they will be punished—somewhere, somehow! Most of the laments in the Psalter freely admit some guilt, but there are many impassioned pleas for deliverance from unmerited troubles (e.g., Ps 26; and the so-called "confessions" of Jeremiah, Jer 12:1–4). Ultimately, the Lord is not viewed as a mechanical dealer of justice. God can be moved; hence the psalmists ply him with expressions of trust and loyalty and with requests for *hesed*. In a sense the supplicants in the OT were in a bind. The demand for justice had to be manifested in this world, otherwise divine justice was a sham. The Lord "must" intervene.

Moreover, is there not a mystery about suffering that goes beyond the obvious and external standards of justice and injustice? To a certain extent, the recognition of the *test* allows Israel to face this mystery (see Pss 17:3; 26:2; 139:23). The wisdom of the Proverbs tells us that God is the tester of the human heart. Mortals may consider themselves "right," but it is the Lord who probes hearts and thereby reveals truth and reality (Prov 21:2; 16:2). And let us not forget the profound mystery of undeserved suffering on behalf of others to which Isa 53:3–9 and Matt 20:22–23 refer.

ZION, MESSIAH, AND KINGSHIP

The conquest of Zion (that is, Jerusalem) was a strategic coup from every point of view. While it was not a very large (Jebusite) city, it was neutral, belonging to none of the Israelite tribes. David gave the city its biblical status: "the stronghold of Zion, now which is the city of David" (2 Sam 5:7). Its distinctive religious importance came when David brought the ark of the covenant there (2 Sam 6; Ps 132). When the Temple was built, Zion was understood to be God's "holy hill" (Ps 2:6), "the city of our God," (see Ps 48:1 and Isa 60–62). The heart of its importance rested in the belief that the Lord's name was present there (see 1 Kgs 8:29). Several psalms, essentially hymnic in form, have come to be called "Songs of Zion" (Pss 46, 48, 84, 87, and 122). Two of these can also be characterized as pilgrim psalms (Pss 84 and 122). The true home of Israelites, wherever they may be, is Zion, according to Psalm 87. Divine protection makes Zion inviolable, as Psalms 46, 48, and 76 claim. This theme of inviolability, particularly associated with the prophet Isaiah (Isa 10:32–33; 33:6; 37:22–32), later becomes a problem for the inhabitants of Jerusalem. (Any religious truth, no matter how proper in itself, can be abused.) One hundred years later, when they assume that

God must protect them because of the Temple, Jeremiah warns that the Lord requires them to act morally if they wish to be saved from their enemies (Jer 7:1–7).

Nonetheless, the presence of God that suffuses the psalms is intimately connected with Zion and the Temple—this is holy space, a phenomenon that may seem strange to the modern person. The presence was not static; it was achieved through liturgical celebration or *re-presentation*. And oracles, delivered probably in the Temple, were also a form of theophany, the manifested presence of the LORD: "Hear, O my people, and I will speak, / O Israel, I will testify against you. / I am God, your God" (Ps 50:7).

Intimately connected with the divine presence is the king: "I have set my king on Zion, my holy hill" (Ps 2:6). The Lord adopted the king as a son (Ps 2:7). At one time this kind of language was regarded merely as court style. It is that, but it shouldn't be disregarded as simple hyperbole, since it stems from the divine commitment to the Davidic dynasty (see the oracle of Nathan in 2 Sam 7). Instead of David building a "house" (i.e., temple) for the Lord, it is God who will build a "house" (i.e., dynasty) for David: "Your house and your kingdom shall be made sure forever before me; your throne shall be established forever" (2 Sam 7:16). The functions and powers of a king in the ancient Near East were very extensive. He was a sacral as well as a political figure and played a central role in the liturgy. Thus David acted as priest (2 Sam 6:17–19), and "David's sons were priests" (2 Sam 8:18). Solomon also offered sacrifices (1 Kgs 3:3–4), although among the court officials Zadok and Abiathar are mentioned as "priests." Royalty were anointed, and priests only later ("anointed" is the literal meaning of messiah). The incident in 1 Samuel 24, when David has Saul at his mercy and is urged by his followers to kill him, conveys the status of the king. David stealthily cuts off a corner of Saul's cloak, but is immediately troubled: "The LORD forbid that I should do this thing to my lord, the LORD's anointed, to raise my hand against him, for he is the LORD's anointed" (v. 6).

Thus the number of royal psalms in the Psalter is not surprising (Pss 2; 18; 20–21; 45; 72; 89; 101; 110; 132; 144:1–11). Sigmund Mowinckel (*The Psalms in Israel's Worship* [Nashville: Abingdon, 1962], 78–80) introduced the notion of "democratization" of royal psalms: that is, certain psalms were originally royal, but came to be applied to the average Israelite in the liturgical usage. Be that as it may, the royal psalms deal with concrete situations, such as a wedding (Ps 45), a battle (Pss 18, 20, 21, 144); and a defeat in battle (Ps 89). It is likely that Psalms 2, 72, and 110 are associated with some royal celebration (coronation or anniversary). These prayers illustrate the importance of kingship for Israel, but what do they say to the modern reader? Are they of just antiquarian interest? And most importantly, why were they ever preserved? For all intents and purposes, Israel lost the kingship with the fall of Jerusalem in 587 B.C.E. It was the high priesthood that presided over the restored community in the postexilic era. Nonetheless, these psalms were preserved. The most reasonable explanation is that they were reinterpreted to refer to the future. Was this merely wishful thinking? No, because the Davidic *covenant* promised that a descendant of David would always sit upon the throne in Jerusalem (see Pss 89:39 and 132:12). Royal messianism never faded out in Israel's difficult history; many references in the prophetic writings nourished the hope (e.g., Amos 9:11; Hos 3:5; Jer 23:5–6; and especially the so-called "book of Immanuel," Isa 7–11). The assurance of a dynasty crystallized in the expectation of a future individual messiah, and the Gospels use it in the personal way to refer to the Christ (see Raymond E. Brown in *NJBC*, 1310–13 [§ 77:152–63]).

In fact, the messianic hopes in the NT era are very complex. The Qumran documents speak of "anointed ones of Aaron and Israel," a rather enigmatic phrase that indicates a union of priesthood and kingship, a priestly messiah and a Davidic messiah. A "prophet" is also mentioned, probably the expectation of a prophet like Moses (see Deut 18:15, 18; John 1:21). In the NT the title "Son of Man" is favored by Jesus over messiah. It seems that he plays down his role as messiah (what scholars call the "messianic secret," which is especially present in Mark), because the messiah he intended to be was contrary to the popular notion, namely, that of a victorious leader who would throw off the yoke of the Romans (see the disciples' question, "Is this the time when you will restore the kingdom to Israel?" in Acts 1:6). The foregoing considerations lead to the conclusion that messianism, understood strictly as *royal* messianism, is not as important in the Gospels as it was once thought to be. It appears principally in the infancy narratives (e.g., Matt 1:1; 2:4; Luke 1:32). The followers of Jesus believed that he was *the* Messiah, the promised one, and they looked to many other OT passages to confirm this belief. The acceptance of Jesus was based on more than a genealogical relationship to David. What effect does this have on our understanding of the royal or "messianic" psalms? It means that they are not *predictions.* The postexilic community that preserved them reinterpreted them as bearing on the future and thus kept that hope alive. Christians should realize that in the literal sense these psalms are not prophecies of a future messiah. They refer to the currently reigning king *in the light of the covenant with David.* The Christian liturgy reinterprets these psalms just as the postexilic Jews did, only it understands them as having come to a completion in the past, in the appearance of Jesus the Christ. Christians consider these prayers preeminently fulfilled in Jesus. Hence they are used in the Christmas liturgy in the spirit of the infancy narratives of Matthew and Luke, that is, to celebrate the birth of the Messiah. Relative to the literal historical meaning of these psalms, this is an accommodation to the liturgical significance of the feast of the Incarnation.

This discussion of the messianic king is incomplete without considering the kingship of the Lord. James Mays in *The Lord Reigns* (p. x) states that this liturgical proclamation, "the Lord reigns," is "the nuclear and organizing metaphor for the theology of the psalms." It is a thematic sentence, an "organizing center" for the Psalter. The phrase, "the Lord reigns" (or "the Lord is king"), occurs in Psalms 93, 96, 97, and 99 (similar in content are Pss 95 and 98; see also 47:7). We saw above how Mowinckel ingeniously anchored them in Israelite liturgy. He postulated that these and other psalms were associated with a feast of the Lord's kingship. The celebration is analogous to the celebrations for earthly kings, and the proclamation "the Lord reigns," is like the cry, "so and so has become king!" (e.g., for King Jehu in 2 Kgs 9:13). The cry in the psalms is not announcing something new, of course. Yahweh has been king from of old, but now the kingship is celebrated liturgically. Of course the Lord is greater than all gods (Ps 97:7, 9), and divine sovereignty is rooted in creative power. Hence God rules over *all* peoples, for their gods are mere idols. To Israel he has given a choice heritage (Pss 47:2–4; 95:3–7).

The royal image of divinity permeates the psalms. The basis of this kingship is that the Lord is creator of all and, in particular, the creator of Israel—a foundation that evokes God's power and providence. In his supreme power, the actions of reigning and judging are unified (Pss 96:13 and 98:9). The Lord is portrayed as "coming" to judge, which has led to the eschatological interpretation of a final judgment. But judgment does not necessarily contain the threatening note that we often associate with royalty. In the laments, the psalmist appeals to God's judgment as a means of safety, that justice may be served. Thus Ps 43:1 seeks the divine judgment, even demands it.

In the Bible it seems that every divine attribute is modified in some way: divine wrath by divine mercy, and so also royal power by divine condescension.

CHAPTER THREE

Praying the Psalms

FROM UNDERSTANDING TO PRAYER

The previous considerations of this introduction have had a particular purpose; they are oriented toward an enjoyable and productive praying of the psalms. They provide background and, I hope, some insights into prayers that seem to be so different from our modern style. The discussion of interpretive approaches and literary genres is meaningful only if it has contributed to the understanding of these psalms. For we cannot pray what we do not understand. If we do not have a basic grasp of the worldview of the psalms, we are at a disadvantage. The context of the Psalter is a context of prayer; its Hebrew title is *tehillim* (= praises). However, prayer does not depend simply upon study; one must leave room for the free, unaccountable movement of the Spirit. So the following reflections on the psalms and prayer are offered with a certain tentativeness: they are suggestions, challenges, not a blueprint.

What do we mean by "praying" the psalms? A traditional definition of prayer is "conversation with God." The psalms easily qualify on that score. Most of the time the psalmist is addressing the Lord directly in the second person, "thou" or "you." In other instances the psalmist may be speaking for the community, identifying with them or urging them to praise God. The reader's relationship to the psalmist is of paramount importance. Normally one who uses or "prays" the psalms identifies with what the psalmist says. In chapters one and two we have indicated the possibility of bypassing the identity approach when encountering passages that are disturbing (vengeance, etc.). But bypassing does not mean dismissing. Rather, we address the violence, meditate on it, and weigh realistically the surges of violence and vengeance that permeate our daily existence. We confront human sinfulness and take a stand. Indeed several psalms retain a meditative quality (e.g., Ps 90) that provokes a thoughtful pondering, a kind of lingering. This can issue into direct dialogue with God; the prayer is spurred by the reflection on the psalm. In the case of other types of psalms, such as hymns and songs of thanksgiving, the situation is clearly different: straightforward identification with the words of the psalmist is a natural attitude.

It follows that attention to the various types of psalms described earlier in the introduction will be helpful. The mood communicated by these types is perhaps more important for sincere prayer than are the details of structure. It is not necessary that the mood be uniform throughout; indeed, it might be advantageous to move through a psalm according to the changes in mood. How is one to react to such mood swings? Can a person experiencing joy enter into the spirit of a lament, or can a sad and depressed person exult? No general answer suffices; each case is different. It would seem easier for a joyful person to absorb a lament for obvious reasons; the lament would not be upsetting, and identification with all who are in need can be quite salutary. However, a joyful hymn could more easily turn to ashes in the mouth of a depressed person. Of course, individuals can select psalms that are appropriate to their personal conditions. But this should not lead to merely subjective choices. Exposure to the full range of the Psalter is the ideal. Moreover, a certain personal discipline is called for; prayer is not a selfish exercise to relieve or confirm one's subjective feelings. It is outgoing, in praise of God. By definition it is God-centered, not self-centered. Consider also that the Psalter has been described as a movement from lament to praise. In other words, we are not left to wallow in self-pity or personal anguish. We are lifted up beyond ourselves into the greatness and mystery of God.

LITURGICAL PRAYER

The Psalter has always been used in the liturgy. In many Eucharistic celebrations, the recitation of a psalm, usually selected parts, serves as a "response" to the first reading from the Bible, generally agreeing with the tenor of that reading. It may come as no surprise that in the current lectionaries the lament is not as popular a choice as hymns of praise.

The manner of reciting the psalms has varied in the history of Christianity. Today the normal practice is to have a leader (or cantor if the psalms are sung) read a short refrain followed by a verse or more of the psalm, after which the worshipers repeat the refrain. The centuries-old Divine Office (also the Anglican "Evensong"), cultivated especially by monastic Orders, is another type of oral performance. In this devotional practice, which incorporates most of the 150 psalms, the two sides of a choir alternate reciting the verses of a psalm. Such a reading of the psalms in a congregrational setting is easy and simple, since the worshipers, even if they are numerous, can easily follow along. But there are some caveats to such a recital. For one, the mechanical alternation of verses can lead to monotony. Moreover, the alternation does not consider the structure of a given psalm. Thus, what should be (or can be) effectively delivered by a solo voice is simply taken up by the group on the other side of the choir, because it is their "turn." For example, if one attends to the structure of Psalm 46, the recitation would take a different form than a plain alternation of verses. The refrain, "The LORD of hosts is with us..." in vv. 7 and 11 (and probably to be inserted also after v. 3) should not be treated as simply another verse, or the effect of the prayer is weakened. Similarly, the affirmation of v. 10, "Be still and know that I am God!" calls for a solo voice, as the structure suggests, or it is lost in the routine alternation. It is ironic that the (liturgical) voice of God is obscured in this and other instances, and this chokes the power in several psalms The breaking in of God's voice should be dramatic and distinct in a case such as Ps 95:8–9: "Do not harden your hearts, as at Meribah, as on the day at Massah in the wilderness, when your ancestors tested me, and put me to the proof, though they had seen my work" (and continuing through vv. 10–11). In some instances a solo voice is appropriate even when it does not represent the divinity, especially where a leader appears to be giving instructions to a group: "Rejoice in the LORD, O you righteous. . . . Sing to him a new song" (Ps 33:1–3). Psalm 15 illustrates the effect of an intelligent analysis on the recital of a psalm: it opens (v. 1) with a question, "O LORD, who may abide in your tent?" and the remainder of the psalm is a reply, describing the type of person whom the Lord welcomes to the liturgical service (perhaps the last sentence in v. 5 is a separate, or third, part). Distorting structure and meaning is a high price to pay for neat ceremony. But the careful study of a psalm can lead to powerful and meaningful liturgical performance.

PERSONAL PRAYER

An old monastic form of personal prayer is the *lectio divina,* or sacred reading, which has become popular in our times, especially in the communities of Latin America. It is applicable to any text of the Bible, not exclusively to the Psalter. Usually four steps are prescribed: *reading, meditation, prayer,* and *contemplation.* These more or less flow into each other and need not be rigidly separated.

The purpose of the *reading* (*lectio*) of the biblical text, repeated as often as helpful, is to hear what the text is saying. This is not oriented toward historical exegesis but simply to understand the text in the spirit of Deut 30:14, which sees the word as present; it is not up in the sky or across the sea, "The word is very near to you; it is in your mouth and in your heart for you to observe." The reading is active, marked by obvious questions: Who? What? Where? Why?

Meditation is designed to take the past text into the present moment. This is actualization: what does the text say to me today? How is the present like and unlike that of this ancient text? This is neither a speculative nor a neutral insight. What force does the text have in one's heart? If we keep repeating it, ruminating on it, the power of the word will be revealed, especially when the text is drawn from the Psalter. The parallelism of the lines helps us to meditate on the affections and desires within a psalm.

We can linger over certain phrases that are intensified by their artful repetition, which is really more a deepening and extension of meaning than simple repetition. Here the words of John Cassian, whom we have quoted before, are particularly insightful. He is summarizing the doctrine of Abbot Isaac on prayer:

> For then the sacred scriptures are revealed more clearly to us—in a certain way, their flesh and blood are exposed when our experience not only understands, but anticipates this understanding, and the meaning of the text is arrived at, not by explanation but by reality. We share the same heartfelt affection with which the psalm was written or sung; we become the authors, as it were. We anticipate the thought, rather than follow it; we capture the meaning without knowing the letter. (*Conferences* X, 11; author's translation)

This doctrine values experience and treasures life above understanding, since understanding is only the first step. While "meditation" is described from the point of view of the individual, it also has a corporate effect when it is voiced and shared in a (small) community. Each individual, by sharing the "meditation" with others, spurs them to seek and apply the manifold meanings of Holy Scripture.

Prayer is not like the third rung in a ladder. One cannot really say when meditation passes into prayer, and it is not governed by any mechanical regulation. Prayer is not to be delayed until the "proper" time. If an individual has arrived at a fairly clear picture of what the biblical text is saying to him or her, the question is now: What does the individual want to say to God? In any case, one should at least begin with a prayer for help. But the expansion in prayer has no limits; it can burst forth in lament or in praise, in keeping with the movement of the text and the action of the spirit. The prayer can even consist in reading aloud again the psalm or biblical text with which one began.

Contemplation is the last step, but at the same time it is a beginning. It is not static, but the ever recurring encounter with God. At this point one should be ready for a deeper sense of the presence of God and the need to take one's rest in him.

Prayer should be real, the outflow of one's experience of God. If that experience is meager, almost nonexistent, the psalms can offer an appropriate shock. For they illumine many corners of human experience, even areas that seem beyond divine reach. The psalms, particularly the laments, recognize separation from God. But separation becomes the occasion of reaching out. We are reminded of the dogged earnestness of Moses in Exod 34:9: "If now I have found favor in your sight, O Lord, I pray, let the Lord go with us. Although this is a stiff-necked people, pardon our iniquity and our sin, and take us for your inheritance." These words share an attitude that permeates the Psalter: trust in God. It matters not if God is the final recourse, or if in one's view God is the cause of the vigorous, even condemnatory, "why?" that is addressed to him. The "why?" is itself a prayer, an utterance that calls for the basic measure of trust. Even Job, despite everything, never gave up.

The psalmist may use the motif of trust to move the Lord to action, as in many of the individual and communal complaints. Psalm 22:4–5 provides a striking example:

> In you our ancestors trusted;
>> they trusted, and you delivered them.
> To you they cried, and were saved;
>> in you they trusted, and were not put to shame.

The threefold repetition is particularly effective. Psalm 27 is a lament, but the complaint is lost in the affirmation of trust: "The LORD is my light and my salvation, / whom shall I fear?" (v. 1). The metaphors used for the Godhead reflect this attitude—the Lord is rock, fortress, and refuge (Ps 62:2, 6–7); hence the psalmist can urge the community: "Trust in him at all times, O people; / pour out your heart before him; / God is a refuge for us" (62:8). Psalm 130, the famous "de profundis," takes away, almost surreptitiously, any basis for God to be other than merciful: "If you, O LORD, should mark iniquities, / LORD, who could stand?" (130:3).

In recent times certain forms of meditation have developed the "mantra" style of prayer, which consists in the repetition of significant words or phrases. Although the term historically belongs to Eastern religions, Christian spirituality has adopted it. There were equivalents in Christian practice, like the traditional Rosary, or the Jesus Prayer. The rosary consists of NT passages:

the Lord's Prayer and selections from the Annunciation and Visitation scenes in the gospel of Luke (1:28, 42). The Jesus Prayer is profoundly biblical in sentiment and based on passages from the Gospels (Luke 18:13, 38): "Lord Jesus Christ, Son of God, have mercy on me, a sinner." Many colorful and programmatic lines from the psalms are apt for this kind of meditation: "Into your hand I commit my spirit" (Ps 31:5). Personal consideration will doubtless determine the choice.

Finally, here is an honest and practical question: What about distractions? The reality of distractions cannot be denied, and avoiding them depends on an individual's determination, attention span, and discipline. There is no reason to be anxious or disturbed over what is a normal human failing. Rather, one can adopt the calm attitude of St. Thérèse of Lisieux:

> I should be desolate for having slept (for seven years) during my hours of prayer. . . ; well, I am not desolate. I remember that *little children* are as pleasing to their parents when they are asleep as well as when they are wide awake. . . . Finally I remember that: "*The Lord knows our weakness, that he is mindful that we are but dust and ashes.*" (*Story of a Soul* [Washington, D.C.: ICS Publications, 1976], 165)

FROM PRAYER TO UNDERSTANDING

It is well to attempt a summary of the remarks in this introduction that are most pertinent to prayer. We must begin where we are, that is, Christian, Jew, Muslim or whatever. Inevitably, my suggestions are Christian, but perhaps they may help non-Christians as well.

Modern readers cannot deny that they bring a perspective to the psalms that differs from that of the ancient Israelites, despite a sincere attempt to capture the nuances of the Hebrew text. Here attention should be called to the distinction already drawn between christocentric and Christian reading. A christocentric interpretation, as we have seen, means that one reads the psalms with direct reference to Jesus Christ. While such an approach has many illustrious proponents, there is often an artificiality in the way the text is stretched. Christ can be said to be a personal center, the *telos* or goal of biblical focus, but he is not the literary center. On the one hand, a Christian recognizes the goal of the divine plan of redemption in the paschal mystery accomplished in the person of Jesus Christ. On the other hand, God's design is recorded in the literature of his chosen people. The mystery has to do with person; the literature of the Old Testament reflects the path that was seen to lead to that person. The Old Testament or Hebrew Bible, *as literature,* cannot be flattened out and reduced to only a Christian dimension. Jesus Christ is the focus of the New Testament, not the Old. In Christian terms, it is the Father of Jesus Christ who is the focus of the Old Testament. Hence a merely christocentric reading is incomplete; it does not grasp the psalms at the level on which they were written. Why not pray from Thomas à Kempis's *Imitation of Christ* or from the *Confessions* of St. Augustine, if one is going to insist on a direct reference to Christ? The Christian liturgy itself speaks of an approach to the Father *through* Jesus Christ.

Still, a Christian can insist that he or she is not an Israelite and is really unable to pray these psalms on any kind of literal historical level. That situation is true of everyone—all stand in traditions that have developed beyond that of the psalms. Therefore, the important step is to establish the nature of the continuity (and discontinuity as well) between the Testaments. Ideally, this approach would honor the meaning inherent in the biblical text, and then go on to expand it in a fuller meaning without arbitrariness. Thus, when a psalmist speaks of sin, of distress, of salvation, of the puzzle that God is, one can fit this in a continuous way into one's own experiences. While the perspective goes beyond, it continues what is in the text. A different nuance is added, but the meaning of the psalm is taken seriously.

In this way the Old Testament enriches a Christian reading of the Bible. Even the discontinuities between the Testaments can have great theological and practical value. Some Christians live too easily with the truths of Christian eschatology, resurrection, and eternal life. Thus, the Hebrew concept of Death/Sheol is not to be dismissed; it offers us a more complete perspective on the meaning of life and death. A failure to appreciate the OT often lies behind one-sided and even shallow doctrines we mistakenly call Christian. The Israelite welcomed life in this world as the gift of *YHWH*. That faith was not focused on half of reality, the next world, but on this world, in which a Christian must also live.

The psalms kindle that joy of life, regardless of the mixture of life's triumphs and troubles. May your understanding of the psalms lead to prayer, as your prayer leads to understanding.

Part Two: Commentary

❧

CHAPTER FOUR

A Brief Commentary
on the Psalms

The reader should pay attention to the valuable footnotes provided to the NRSV translation. They usually indicate verses of doubtful translation and meaning, and provide some evidence from the ancient versions for the doubtful readings. "Cn" indicates "correction," that is, a reconstructed reading of the original text, in the judgment of the translators. Since the meanings of most of the technical terms in the superscriptions (e.g., Ps 22, "The Deer of the Dawn") are simply unknown to us, there is no point in commenting on what we do not know. The same is true of the mysterious *Selah* that occurs seventy-one times in thirty-nine psalms (e.g., Ps 3:2, 4, 8). Italic print will be used to introduce a lemma, or heading, that calls for comment; for example, Ps 76:2: *Salem:* an older name of Jerusalem (Gen 14:18). Sometimes the words of the psalm are also printed in italics, and thus call attention to the biblical text. Within the context of a psalm, bold numbers indicate verses.

Psalm 1. See the treatment of this psalm above in the "Psalms in Context" section in the Introduction. This is not a prayer, but a blessing. It has been prefixed probably in the postexilic period as an introduction to the psalms that follow. The theme of the two ways (v. 6), righteous and wicked, is reflected throughout biblical teaching (e.g., Prov 4:18–19; Deut 30:15–19), and especially in the Psalter. Structure: vv. 1–3, the way of the righteous; vv. 4–5, the way of the wicked; v. 6, the role of the Lord. **1.** *Happy:* a typical congratulatory formula, frequent in the psalms and wisdom literature (Prov 3:13 and Ps 2:11). Literally, a "man" is blessed, but the word is not gender specific and is hence translated as "those." That is standard practice in the NRSV translation. **2.** *Law:* lit., "teaching," and by extension, the Pentateuch (cf. Sir 24:23 and Ps 119). Constant preoccupation with, even *delight,* in the Law is the positive trait of the righteous, balancing the description of their virtue in v. 1. **3–4.** The comparisons to *trees* and *chaff,* frequent in the OT (Jer 17:8; Ps 35:5), continue the contrast between the just and unjust. **5.** The *judgment* is probably that pronounced by the community, but it is susceptible of being interpreted as eschatological and rendered by God. **6.** *Way:* frequently refers to one's manner of life; similarly, Acts 9:2 describes the first Christians as those who belonged to the "Way." See the Introduction (pp. 19–22) for a discussion of the editorial positioning of Psalms 1 and 2.

Psalm 2. A royal psalm, perhaps composed on the occasion (or anniversary) of the king's accession to the throne in Jerusalem. The exaggerated court style (universal reign, divine backing, the *anointed* as *son*) is characteristic of the ancient Near East, but here it is rooted in the promise made to David in 2 Sam 7; cf. Ps 89:19–37). Structure: vv. 1–3, revolt of the nations; vv. 4–6, the divine reaction; vv. 7–9, the divine decree; vv. 10–11, a warning to rebel kings. **1–2.** The revolt of vassal nations was frequent enough in antiquity, but here it may be just a motif befitting the hyperbole of court style. In the postexilic period the royal psalms came to be interpreted as referring to an eschatological future David. The relationship between the *anointed* (Messiah or Christ) and *YHWH* is clear from v. 6 (also 2 Sam 7:14); hence the derisive laughter of God, as in Ps 59:8. **7–9.** It is not clear whether the king or a court official pronounces this decree of the Lord concerning the king's adoptive sonship and worldwide reign. (For a discussion of the issue of adoption, see J. J. M. Roberts, "Whose Child Is This: Reflections on the Speaking Voice in Isaiah 9:5," *HTR* 90 [1990]: 115–29). **10–11.** Despite the uncertain text (see NRSV footnote), the warning to the *rulers of the earth* is unmistakable. See the treatment of Zion and Messiah in the Introduction (pp. 54–58).

Psalm 3. An individual lament, though dominated by the affirmation of trust. Tradition attributed it to David, as are Psalms 3–41; on Absalom, see 2 Samuel 15–16. Structure as in NRSV paragraphing: vv. 1–2, the complaint; vv. 3–4, affirmation of trust and confidence; vv. 5–6, despite myriads of enemies, no fear; v. 7, the appeal, with confidence that the prayer has been heard; v. 8, a blessing invoked on the people of God. The verbs here are practically timeless, describing the appeal to God and a steady answer. The issue is "salvation" (translated as *help, deliverance,* vv. 2, 8). Although *many* claim God will not *help,* the psalmist affirms confidently that God will do so (v. 8a). It is impossible to determine the setting. If the poem was originally uttered by the king, who may have invoked the blessing on the people (v. 8b), it came to be "democratized" and used by the ordinary Israelite.

Psalm 4. A complaint permeated by trust. Structure: v. 1, an appeal, based on past deliverance; vv. 2–5, a confident challenge and warning to opponents; vv. 6–8, affirmation of joy and confidence. **1.** *God of my right:* a saving God who defends the right of the suppliant by delivering him. **2.** *You people:* these cannot be identified, except by the description of their conduct, which merits the warning by the psalmist. **6.** *Many:* they are not specified; v. 6a may be their yearning for a change. For their prayer in v. 6b, see Num 6:25–26. **7.** The psalmist compares his own happiness to the proverbial joy on the occasion of harvesting.

Psalm 5. An individual lament. Structure: vv. 1–3, a confident cry for help; vv. 4–6, reasons for confidence: the Lord will not tolerate evildoers in the Temple; vv. 7–8, but the psalmist can worship there; vv. 9–10, an imprecation upon the wicked; vv. 11–12, an appeal for the righteous: joy and blessing. **3.** *Plead my case:* perhaps means to prepare a sacrifice. Prayer *in the morning* is mentioned several times (Pss 46:5; 59:16; 90:14; and 143:8). **4–7.** For the exclusion of the sinful, see the "examination of conscience" in gate liturgies in Psalms 15 and 24; only the faithful such as the psalmist should dare to approach God in the Temple (vv. 8–9). **9.** *Open graves:* because words of calumny and corruption are spewed forth from their *throats.*

Psalm 6. An individual lament, one of the traditional "penitential" psalms: Psalms 6, 32, 38, 51, 102, 130, and 143. Structure: vv. 1–3, a complaint and cry for help; vv. 4–5, reasons for the Lord to intervene; vv. 6–7, description of suffering; vv. 8–10, certainty of having been heard. **1.** Apparently a stereotyped formula (cf. Ps 38:1 and Jer 10:24). Human suffering is a sign of divine displeasure; sickness or any distress came to be interpreted as an indication of sinfulness—hence the reactions of the three friends to Job's sufferings. **4–5.** God should intervene because of *hesed,* or covenant loyalty, and because after death there is no loving contact with the Lord in Sheol. The psalmist must survive in order to praise God. This is a frequent motif (Pss 30:9; 88:10–12; 115:17; and Isa 38:18). **8.** *All you workers of evil:* not easily identified; are they evil spirits that cause his suffering? **9.** The repetition of *the LORD has heard* is striking. What is the reason for this certainty? The words could have been recited after the recovery, but more likely they are a reaction to the deliverance (the so-called "oracle of salvation") promised by one of the Temple personnel.

Psalm 7. An individual lament, perhaps a prayer of one who has been unjustly accused. Structure: vv. 1–2, a plea for deliverance; vv. 3–5, a protestation of innocence in the form of an oath; vv. 6–8, an appeal to God to show justice to the one who deserves it; vv. 9–11, further appeal to God, the righteous judge; vv. 12–16, a description of God's punishment of the wicked, whose own evildoing brings them down; v. 17, a vow to offer thanksgiving sacrifice for deliverance. **1.** *My pursuers:* these seem to be those whom the oath of v. 5 invited to "pursue" him; they accuse him of some wrongdoing, and he appeals to the Lord for deliverance. **3–5.** The casuistic style (if, then) is typical of an oath of innocence (cf. Job 31). **6–11.** A vigorous appeal to the Lord as universal judge; the psalmist boldly asserts a personal innocence that will stand up to divine scrutiny. The Lord's *indignation* always focuses upon evildoers. **12–16.** A description of the punishments that God will inflict. The metaphors in vv. 14–16 are familiar in the OT (Job 15:35; Isa 59:4; Prov 26:27; and Pss 9:15–16; 28:4). They include: conception that fails to result in birth; falling into the hole one has dug for another; and evil recoiling on one's own head. But the psalm also asserts that God produces such effects, so retribution is not merely a mechanical correspondence between deed and consequence. See the discussion under "sin and suffering" in the Introduction (pp. 52–54).

Psalm 8. A unique hymn of praise of God as creator. Normally a hymn calls upon people to praise God, but not here. A communal refrain (vv. 1a, 9) forms an inclusio for an individual hymn of admiration (vv. 3–8). **1a.** *Name:* God's own being, whose majesty is reflected on earth; the name is the person. **1b–2.** The text is difficult, probably corrupt; it may mean that the divine *glory* is the more evident because of the modest means, *infants*, that God has chosen to silence his *foes* (perhaps the powers of chaos or sinners?). **3–4.** An individual addresses God directly in awed tones describing the contrast between the divine and the human in God's creation. **5–8.** Yet what God has done with mere mortals is even more astonishing: they are just a little less than the *elohim*-beings (see NRSV footnote) of the heavenly court. Moreover, God has deigned to have them share in his dominion over all creation. Contrast this tone with the matter-of-fact style of Genesis 1. Heb 2:5–9 transposes vv. 4–6 to the new creation in Christ.

Psalms 9–10. Originally these two psalms were one, combining thanksgiving and lament, in an imperfect acrostic pattern (here every second line in the MT should start with successive letters of the alphabet). There is no real structure to the poem; the physical layout of the NRSV indicates the several themes that succeed one another: thanksgiving (vv. 1–2), deliverance (vv. 3–4), and divine judgment and kingship over all peoples (vv. 5–12; 17–20; and 10:15–16). But there remains the scandal of the arrogant wicked (Ps 10:1–11, in the style of an individual lament), followed by a confident appeal to God to save the oppressed (Ps 10:12–18). **14.** *Daughter Zion:* cities were often personified as women. The *gates* in Zion are the center of activity in the town. **15–16.** Cf. the comment on Ps 7:14–16. **10:1.** The metaphor of God's distance appears again. In v. 11 the wicked think that God has not seen what they have been doing, but God does see (v. 14)! **4.** The criterion for the existence of God is a practical

one: is God active? **11.** *Hidden his face:* a frequent motif expressing divine indifference, displeasure, and any negative reaction
(Pss 13:1; 30:7; 44:24; 69:17; 88:14; 104:29; etc.). **12–15.** This
strenuous urging is motivated by the belief expressed in vv. 16–18.

Psalm 11. The overall affirmative mood of the psalm indicates that it is a psalm of trust (vv. 1a, 4, 7). Structure: vv. 1–3, advice to flee; vv. 4–7, the reply to this advice. **1–3.** Differing
interpretations are given to these verses. NRSV understands vv.
1b–3 as part of a dialogue in which the psalmist receives (friendly
or hostile?) advice to flee because the wicked have the upper
hand. *The righteous:* some interpret this as referring to a helpless
God (see v. 7). **4–7.** The confident reply to the danger is that the
all-powerful God sees everything from his holy temple in the
heavens, and thus is testing everyone, distinguishing between the
wicked (vv. 5b–6) and the righteous (v. 7). *Cup:* here a metaphor
for divine punishment, from which the wicked must drink (see Ps
75:8). *Behold his face:* as in the blessing of Num 6:25–26; contrast
the "hiding" in Ps 10:11.

Psalm 12. A lament of the community (v. 8). Structure:
vv. 1–2, description of distress; vv. 3–4, imprecation on the evil
tongues; vv. 5–6, a statement of the Lord, and reaction; vv. 7–8,
confidence in divine protection, despite the continuing situation. The moral debacle is reminiscent of Psalm 11, except that
Psalm 12 describes the action of the ungodly only in terms
of their wicked, lying words. **2.** *Double heart:* lit., heart and
heart. **3–4.** The imprecation strikes at the organs of speech.
5. An example of an "oracle of salvation," probably spoken in the
name of the Lord by one of the Temple personnel. The assurance
does not refer explicitly to the evil tongues of vv. 3–4, but in contrast v. 6 praises the *promises* (lit., "words") of God.

Psalm 13. A lament of an individual. Structure: vv. 1–2, the
complaint; vv. 3–4, the request with motivation; vv. 5–6, certainty of being heard, followed by a vow to acknowledge the
Lord's goodness. **1–2.** *How long:* thrice as emphatic as Ps 6:3. It is
not possible to specify the distress, except for the vague reference
to *enemy. Hide your face:* see comment on 10:11. **3.** *Light to my*

eyes: strength and will to live; the eyes are the organs of the body that express life (Ps 19:8) or its opposite (Ps 38:10). **5.** *Trusted:* better, "trust," with an indication of the thanksgiving song in v. 6.

Psalm 14. A lament that has a duplicate in Psalm 53 in the so-called Elohistic Psalter. Structure: vv. 1–3, the complaint about the fools; vv. 5–6, God's deliverance of the righteous; v. 7, a wish for the Lord to help the people. **1–3.** The atheism of the "fool" is practical, not theoretical; see comment on Ps 10:4. But the fool cannot escape the divine gaze (cf. Ps 11:4–6). *Not one:* this is an exaggeration, since the existence of the righteous is indicated in v. 5. **6.** *You:* addressed to the evildoers described in v. 4. **7.** The hope expressed in this verse possibly refers to a return from exile.

Psalm 15. This is commonly described as a liturgical entrance psalm, or "gate" liturgy pronounced antiphonally on the occasion of entering the Temple (cf. Ps 24:3–6 and Isa 33:13–16). Structure: v. 1, question; vv. 2–5, answer. **1.** The question is addressed to the Lord, presumably by someone at the *tent,* an archaizing term for the Temple; the mood is "who dares?" **2–5.** The reply centers on practical social morality: truth, no slander or hurt of neighbor, honoring the difference between the *wicked* and those who *fear the LORD,* fulfillment of oaths, interest-free lending (see the condemnation of usury in Exod 22:25), and avoidance of bribery.

Psalm 16. A psalm of trust. Structure: vv. 1–6, a description of the psalmist's loyal relationship to the Lord alone; vv. 7–11, words of trust in the Lord for the gift of life. **2b–4.** The text is probably corrupt; perhaps the psalmist indicates a rejection of all gods, except the Lord. **5–6.** The metaphors are reminiscent of the partitioning of the land (cf. Josh 13–19 and Ps 142:5). *Cup:* this is in contrast to the cup in Ps 11:6 (see also Ps 23:5). **7–8.** A remarkable statement of awareness of God's guidance and intimate presence. *I shall not be moved* expresses exactly the idea in Ps 15:5. **9–10.** The happiness (cf. Ps 14:7c) of the psalmist is secured by the Lord's delivering from *Sheol = Pit,* a symbol for any distress (cf. Ps 30:3). **11.** A view of a happy life, the enjoyment of intimacy of God because of intense devotion. Ps 73:23–28 is an extended commentary on *the path of life.* The perspective of these verses is limited to this life, but the text is open-ended, and it was later applied to Christ's resurrection in an extended meaning (cf. Acts 2:25–31 and 13:34–37, where the LXX translation is used).

Psalm 17. An individual lament. Structure: vv. 1–5, a confident cry, with affirmation of innocence; vv. 6–12, a request to be delivered from beastly enemies; vv. 13–15, renewal of request, with the certainty of being heard. **1–5.** The psalms often advance the motif of personal righteousness as a reason for the Lord to intervene: Pss 7:8; 18:20–24; 26:1–7, 11, etc. This is not the same as self-righteousness; it can be a declaration of loyalty, and also often an indication of puzzlement or questioning in the face of personal distress (cf. Job's affirmation of his integrity in Job 6:1–10, 24; 7:20). **3.** The challenge for a testing is bold, and it occurs also in Ps 26:2. However, in Ps 139:23–24, there is a different nuance; the psalmist asks the Lord to test and see if there might be some fault, and then to lead him or her back. **6–8.** The appeal turns from integrity to the Lord's *steadfast love* and protection under the divine *wings* (Deut 32:10–12). **13–14.** Again, the appeal is renewed to punish the *wicked,* who are portrayed as lions (vv. 10–12). The meaning of verse 14 is uncertain; NRSV seems to understand it as an imprecation against the unjust and their descendants. **15.** The psalmist hearkens back to the righteousness theme of vv. 1–5. *When I awake:* it may be inferred that he has spent the night in the Temple. *Behold your face:* the phrase is paradoxical because such a view is dangerous (Exod 33:20), but the phrase comes to be used for an experience of God in the Temple (see also Ps 11:7).

Psalm 18. A royal thanksgiving hymn for victory over enemies; a parallel recension appears in 2 Sam 22:2–51. Structure: vv. 1–3, hymnic introduction; vv. 4–30, the first description, in terms of a theophany, of the king's desperate plight and the Lord's storming intervention to save him on account of his loyalty; vv. 31–48, a second description, more concrete, of the marvelous deliverance in battle by the God who trained the king; vv. 49–50, concluding praise. **1–3.** See Ps 144:1–2. **4–5.** The metaphors derive from the ancient myths concerning Sheol/ Death; these were conceived as dynamic powers that hunt out human beings, so that even the living can be ensnared by them (Pss 30:3 and 89:48). *Perdition:* lit., Belial, a synonym for Sheol. **7–19.** In a stormy (vv. 11–14) theophany, God the Warrior rides down (Ps 68:4) on a *cherub* from the heavenly *temple* to reach out and snatch the king from the *mighty waters* (vv. 15–16, symbolic of the original chaos), that are identified with the royal enemies (vv. 17–19). **20–24.** *Righteousness* was the reason the Lord *delighted* (v. 19) in the psalmist; see comment on Ps 17:1–5. **25–30.** A somewhat didactic conclusion concerning God, whose way is *perfect* (*tamim,* v. 30), and who rewards those who are *blameless* (*tamim,* vv. 23, 25). God is *loyal* to the *loyal,* but he matches the wickedness of the *crooked* (vv. 25–26). **31–48.** This thanksgiving hymn details minutely the action of God on behalf of the king; the battle and victory (cf. vv. 41, 43) are unknown. **34.** *A bow of bronze:* an exaggerated metaphor for a powerful bow. **49–50.** The conclusion to the hymn underscores the Lord's *steadfast love* to the *anointed* (the reigning king) and the Davidic line (Ps 89:19–37).

Psalm 19. A hymn of praise that unites two themes, creation and torah. Structure: vv. 1–6, God's glory revealed in the world; vv. 7–10, the wonders of the Law (although some argue for the presence of two independent psalms, the whole is connected, in that the Law reveals the divine will, while the divine glory becomes clear through nature); vv. 11–14, the final portion is a personal reaction: loyalty to the Law, even if there are "unknown faults" (e.g., Lev 5:2–4; Ps 90:8). **1–4.** The *voice* proclaiming the divine *glory* is soundless, yet it is heard everywhere on *earth*— quite a revelation! **5–6.** Preeminent in the divine handiwork is the sun (Shamash, the sun [god], was a divinity in the ancient world), boldly compared to both a bridegroom coming forth from the bridal chamber where it rests for the night, and a soldier-giant. **7–10.** Praise of the Law: each verse relates a characteristic, followed by a good effect. An association with wisdom literature appears in *fear of the LORD* and the comparison to *gold* and *honey* (Prov 1:7; 8:10; 24:13–14). **12–14.** The hymn ends with a prayer in which the psalmist hopes (cf. Ps 104:34) that the poem is pleasing to the Lord, who is called *redeemer* (*go'el*, lit., one's next of kin on whom one can rely for aid; cf. God's activity in Exod 6:6 and Isa 43:1).

Psalm 20. A royal psalm, requesting God's aid in making the king victorious. The structure is guided by the pronouns *you* (vv. 1–5, 9), *we* (v. 5), and *I* (v. 6). The change in person may indicate a solo prayer (vv. 1–4; 6–8) with choral responses (vv. 5, 9). **1–5.** The good wishes for the king derive from his special relationship to the *God of Jacob* who reigns from *Zion.* **6–7.** Victory is certain because it comes from the Lord, not by human means (Pss 33:16–17; 147:10–11; and Prov 21:31).

Psalm 21. A royal psalm, expressing thanksgiving for the many blessings bestowed upon the king. Structure: vv. 1–7, a description of the Lord's goodness to the king; vv. 8–12, an address to the king, assuring him of victory over his enemies; v. 13, conclusion: an echo of v. 1, in which the community praises God directly.

Psalm 22. Lament of an individual, ending with a powerful prayer of thanksgiving. The opening words are on the lips of the crucified Jesus (Matt 27:46; Mark 15:34; other verses are alluded to, e.g., John 19:34). Structure: vv. 1–21, the complaint, with repeated requests (cf. *far* in vv. 1, 11, 19), description of suffering, and expressions of trust (vv. 4–5; 9–10); vv. 22–31, a thanksgiving, in which the psalmist invites the community (vv. 23–26) to share, and the proclamation of worldwide worship of the Lord. **3.** *Enthroned on the praises of Israel:* a mysterious and unparalleled phrase, emended in some translations. **3–5.** The basis of trust is the Lord's deliverance of the people in the past. Here it serves as a reminder of why the Lord should not remain far off. **7–8.** The sneer and words of the enemies reflect the belief that one who suffers must be a sinner. **12.** A wide range of animals (lions, oxen, etc.) symbolize the enemies (see also vv. 20–21). *Bashan:* the Transjordan area east of the sea of Galilee, noted for its lush growth and its cattle (cf. Amos 4:1 and Ezek 39:18). **14–15.** Symptoms of physical sickness alternate with the attacks from wild animals; the imagery is extravagant and deliberately exaggerated. **16b.** The final line is corrupt; the MT reads, "like a lion my hands and my feet." Any translation is a guess. Note that the NT does not quote this line. **18.** Such actions indicate that the enemies regard death as certain. **20–21.** Again the imagery is extreme. The MT reads "you have answered me" (see the footnote in the NRSV). **22–26.** These verses mark a sharp transition to a thanksgiving ceremony with a *congregation,* presumably in the Temple where the psalmist fulfills the *vows* (v. 25) he had made in gratitude for deliverance (v. 24). **25.** *From you:* perhaps "because of you." **26.** Bystanders (to whom the last line is spoken directly) presumably share in the thanksgiving sacrifice (as in Ps 30:4). **27–28.** The universalism is not unusual in the OT, but it is striking in this context. **29–31.** The text is uncertain and translations differ considerably, as one can gather from the textual notes. The NRSV seems to say that all mortals, living and dead, will honor the Lord, just as the psalmist does. Future generations will remember this deliverance, to the praise of the Lord.

Along with other texts, such as Isaiah 53 with its description of the suffering servant, this psalm provided the primitive Church an insight into the meaning of Christ's sufferings. In itself, this is one of the most powerful laments in the Psalter, but its sudden shift to thanksgiving and praise is surprising. It has been called an anticipatory thanksgiving that reinforces the lament itself. Many interpreters regard the ending, and also other portions, as a later addition, the result of a *relecture,* or re-reading, of the psalm, but this remains speculative, and little is to be gained by picking apart the "original" pieces.

Psalm 23. A psalm of trust, structured in two parts: vv. 1–4, God as shepherd; vv. 5–6, God as host. **1.** The ancient Orient generally conceived of the king as shepherd, and the metaphor is frequently applied to the Lord who pastures his people (Ps 79:13; Isa 40:11; and Ezek 34:15). **2–4.** The vivid terms deriving from shepherding cover the contingencies of life as well: the *rod* to ward off enemies, the *staff* for sure guidance. The metaphors of caring for sheep in vv. 2–3 blend into personal care of the psalmist. *The darkest valley* may be a more exact translation for the traditional "valley of the shadow of death" signaled in the NRSV footnote. **5.** The picture of God as table host, perhaps at a sacrificial meal in the Temple, is all the more impressive because of the *enemies* that are watching. **6.** Now the psalmist is "pursued" by divine *goodness and kindness. Dwell in the house of the* LORD: not meant literally, but as a metaphor for divine shelter (Pss 27:4–5; 61:4; and 63:2–4).

Psalm 24. A processional hymn, with an entrance torah and liturgical entrance. Structure: vv. 1–2, praise of the creator; vv. 3–6, the entrance torah, question and answer; vv. 7–10, procession of the king of glory into the Temple. **2.** Sea and River are in frequent parallelism in Hebrew poetry, and seem to reflect an Israelite version of the Canaanite motif of Baal's victory over *yam* (= Sea) that appears in biblical descriptions of creation (see Pss 74:13–15; 89:9–11; and the discussion of "creation" on pp. 40–44 in the Introduction). **3–5.** The question asks for the qualifications of worshipers, as in Psalm 15. Four prerequisites are demanded: freedom from bribery, purity of heart (i.e., a clean conscience especially as regards neighbors), avoidance of idols (lit., what is vain or false), and, finally, a commitment not to harm others by lying oaths. The reward of the worshipers is the Lord's *blessing,* a full and prosperous life. **7–10.** The questions and answers continue in antiphonal style, perhaps as worshipers carry the Ark (on which the Lord is invisibly enthroned) in procession. The *gates* are personified as bowing and rising up at the approach of the *King of glory.* LORD of hosts is the title, Lord Sabaoth, associated with Shiloh (1 Sam 1:3; cf. Ps 48:8), and perhaps here the "hosts" stand for his army.

Psalm 25. A gentle lament of an individual, in acrostic style (see comment on v. 22). The psalmist is aware of sinfulness and hated by enemies, and he prays for deliverance and guidance. Structure: vv. 1–7, a confident appeal; vv. 8–15, a teaching about the "way" (vv. 8–10, 12; see vv. 4–5) that is central to the prayer; vv. 16–22, a series of requests. A wisdom influence pervades the psalm. **2–3.** *Shame:* a frequent reference in the Psalter, and three times here, dealing with status before both God and humans. **6–7.** *Mindful:* lit., "remember" and requested three times. The *steadfast love* recalls Exod 34:6, and is taken up again in v. 10. **12.** Typical wisdom exerts itself in the portrayal of the Lord as one who teaches the *way*. **22.** This verse, a prayer for Israel, falls outside the alphabetical sequence that structures the poem. It is introduced by the letter *pe*, and this seems to be a didactic device to arrive at a twenty-two-line poem (the *waw* verse has been omitted), which spells out the root *'lp* (= "to teach") in the opening letters of vv. 1, 11, and 22 (see also the comment on Ps 34:22).

Psalm 26. A lament of an individual, perhaps one who has been unjustly accused. Structure: vv. 1–3, request for justice; vv. 4–8, affirmation of innocence; vv. 9–12, request renewed, with affirmation of innocence. **1–3.** "Walking in integrity" forms an inclusio with v. 11. This is a legitimate denial of guilt (cf. the bribery in v. 10), and not an arrogant claim of self-justification **2.** *Test:* see the comment on Ps 17:3. **4–7.** This negative confession (Job 31) precedes a ritual of cleansing by water (cf. Exod 30:17–21). **9–10.** A petition to be saved from the death that is the lot of a sinner; v. 10b seems to refer to the venality of the judges. **11–12.** See v. 1. *Level ground:* a frequent metaphor for ease of walking along the "way" (also Ps 27:11).

Psalm 27. A lament of an individual. Structure: vv. 1–6, a poem of trust in God for protection, with particular emphasis on the Temple; vv. 7–14, the complaint, ending with certainty of being heard (v. 13), and an oracle of encouragement (v. 14). Although some scholars have claimed that two poems have been combined, poems emphasizing trust and complaint, these are normal parts of a lament. **1–3.** For the Lord as *light*, see Isa 10:17. *Devour my flesh:* the *evildoers* are implicitly compared to wild animals (cf. Ps 22), and metaphors of war appear in v. 3. **4–6.** The *Temple* is the center of life and worship (v. 6); the psalmist may not really *live* there (cf. Pss 23:6 and 26:8). **7–13.** The *face* of the Lord has two aspects: one must *seek* it by worshiping in the Temple (Ps 42:4), but it may also be hidden, signifying a rejection (Deut 31:17). For v. 11, see Ps 25:4 and 26:11. Verse 12 indicates false accusation as a reason for the lament. **13–14.** The expression of the certainty of being heard precedes encouragement to hope in the Lord, which is addressed in the singular (to the psalmist or to the community?). *In the land of the living:* while I live, or perhaps for living in the presence of God in the Temple (see Pss 52:5 and 116:9).

Psalm 28. Lament of an individual. Structure: vv. 1–2, invocation and plea; vv. 3–5, punishment requested for the wicked; vv. 6–9, certainty of having been heard, with a prayer for king and people. **1.** *Pit:* A frequent synonym for Sheol, or the netherworld; see comment on Ps 16:10. It could be a metaphor for sickness, but the mention of the *wicked* in vv. 3–6 suggests that the psalmist faces some sort of persecution. **4–5.** The handiwork of the evildoers is in contrast to the handiwork of God who will tear them down, never to be rebuilt; they are enemies of God, hence the imprecation. **6–7.** A sudden change to an expression of certainty of being heard, and thanksgiving, as in many other laments (see comment on Ps 6:9). **8–9.** Another sudden move, an appeal on behalf of the king *(anointed)* and people (for *shepherd* see Ps 23:1).

Psalm 29. A hymn calling upon the members of the heavenly court to praise the Lord. Structure: vv. 1–2, the call to worship; vv. 3–9, description of the Lord's power; vv. 9c–10, the acclamation of the heavenly court; v. 11, a prayer for the people. An unusual hymn, in that it calls for worship in heaven above, followed by the reason: the Lord's thunderous power on earth. It has been claimed that the psalm is an adaptation of an ancient Canaanite hymn (similar to Ugaritic examples) to Baal, the storm-god. It describes the course of a storm-god advancing from the Mediterranean across the Lebanon range to the wilderness of Kadesh to the east. The "voice of the LORD" is the thunder that sounds seven times in this journey. **1.** *Heavenly beings:* originally "the sons of El," the high god of the Canaanite pantheon. These were eventually domesticated as the heavenly court that advises, and does the bidding of, the Lord (cf. Gen 1:26; 6:2; Job 1:6; Ps 89:6; and the treatment of monotheism on pp. 32–33 in the Introduction above). Notice the "staircase" parallelism: abc/ a'b'd, a feature of both Hebrew and Ugaritic verse. **3.** As often in the Bible, *voice* can mean thunder. The *mighty waters* are the waters above that were separated at creation (Gen 1:7) and upon which (cf. v. 10) the Lord is enthroned. **5–9.** Even the majestic cedars (Ps 104:16) are broken, and the Lebanon (= *Sirion,* a Phoenician name) mountain range trembles as the Lord progresses inland. **10.** *Flood:* see v. 3; the king receives the adulation of the court (vv. 9c, 10b). **11.** This prayer for Israel has the appearance of an addition to the poem.

Psalm 30. A thanksgiving psalm. Structure: vv. 1–3, praise of the Lord for deliverance from death; vv. 4–5, an address, presumably to bystanders, encouraging them to share and to learn from this event; vv. 6–10, a flashback to the days of distress; vv. 11–12, an address to God praising him for the restoration. **2–3.** *Healed:* perhaps from sickness, but *Sheol* could serve here as a metaphor for a deathlike distress. Of course, he was not literally resuscitated. **4–5.** If the action is in the Temple, the psalmist addresses *faithful ones,* the bystanders. They are to share in the rejoicing and learn from this experience that all will turn out well (v. 5). **6–10.** In this flashback, characteristic of a thanksgiving psalm, the psalmist relives the days of overconfidence and the hiding of God's *face* (see comment on Ps 10:11). The prayer that was uttered at that time uses Sheol as a motive for God's intervention: there is no praise of God in the netherworld. **11–12.** A graphic picture of restoration, leading to the thanksgiving; sacred dancing was known in Israel (cf. 2 Sam 6:16).

Psalm 31. The psalm has been compared to a collage, since it contains many echoes of other biblical sources. It has been variously classified as both a lament and a thanksgiving; elements of both genres appear, but the ending may be only anticipatory. Structure: vv. 1–8, a mixture of complaint and strong expressions of trust (vv. 3, 5; cf. 14–15); vv. 9–18, description of troubles and appeal for deliverance; vv. 19–24, a thanksgiving song. **5a.** These words are on the lips of Jesus in Luke 23:46. For the *hand* (= power) of God, see v. 15; the hand of the enemy appears in vv. 8 and 15. The *spirit* is the "life breath" (Gen 2:7). The tone is serene confidence in the Lord's care; in v. 5b read "you (will) redeem me," a Hebrew perfect tense expressing certainty. **8.** *Broad place:* a symbol for freedom of movement away from the *enemy.* **9–13.** In a second phase, the poet describes his distress in terms suggesting mortal sickness and human hostility. **13.** This bears a close re-semblance to Jer 20:10a (see also Jer 6:25 and 20:3). **15.** *Times:* the actions and events that fill up the space of time; an expression of confidence. **17–18.** Cf. Ps 25:2–3. **19–24.** In giving testimony to deliverance, the psalmist recalls the past in a flashback (v. 22), and encourages the Lord's *saints* (i.e., faithful ones). For echoes of other works: compare vv. 1–3a with Ps 71:1–3; v. 12b is similar to Jer 22:28; and the ending in v. 24 is similar to Ps 27:14.

Psalm 32. A prayer of thanksgiving, with overtones of wisdom teaching; one of the seven "penitential" psalms; see comment on Psalm 6. Structure: vv. 1–2, introductory beatitudes; vv. 3–7, exhortatory teaching on the benefit of confessing one's sin; v. 8, a divine oracle; vv. 9–11, admonition, assurance, and exhortation to the just. **1–2.** This is the conclusion to which the psalmist has come, the lesson that he or she seeks to inculcate. Sin is *covered,* i.e., removed (v. 5). **3–5.** Suffering finally led the psalmist to a realization of wrongdoing, and the need to "confess" or acknowledge it before God. **6.** *Mighty waters:* as in Pss 18:16 and 29:3, the phrase reverberates with echoes of chaos, which are here symbolic of the deathlike situation of suffering and distress. **7.** *Glad cries of deliverance:* probably refers to the neighbors' sharing in the joy of the psalmist's safety. **8.** This appears to be an oracle from the Lord whose *eye* is on the psalmist, which one of the temple personnel probably pronounced at the thanksgiving celebration. **9.** The plural verb (in Hebrew) indicates that this admonition is for a group; a "teaching" follows it in v. 10. **11.** A concluding call to the *righteous* who are present, to celebrate the Lord's intervention (cf. the ending of Ps 31:23–24).

Psalm 33. A song of praise because of the Lord's creative word and control of history. This is an "alphabetizing" poem of twenty-two lines, the number of letters in the Hebrew alphabet, but it exhibits no acrostic sequence (see Ps 38). Structure: vv. 1–3, typical hymnic introduction, a call to sing praises to *YHWH;* vv. 4–19, reasons for the praise: the Lord's word and work as they appear in creation and in history; vv. 20–22, concluding acclamation. **3.** *New song:* this phrase occurs frequently (e.g., Pss 40:3; 96:1; Isa 42:10), and may have various nuances, among them the

Lord's ever-renewing action. **4.** *Word* and *work* anticipate the development in the hymn: vv. 6–12 and 13–19. **6–12.** The word is manifest in creation (vv. 6–9) and in the *counsel* (vv. 10–12) by which God controls all *peoples,* with predilection for the *people whom he has chosen.* **13–18.** God's vision of all creatures, with an *eye* (v. 18) especially upon those who *fear* him. For another picture of God's vision of the human race, see Isa 40:22. **16–17.** A frequent proclamation (see comment on Ps 20:6–7). It functions here in view of vv. 18–19, which assure the deliverance of worshipers from *death.* **20–22.** The Lord's activities described in the body of the hymn warrant these varied reactions.

Psalm 34. A thanksgiving psalm, with clear wisdom influence. The acrostic sequence is the same as for Psalm 25 (see the comment on Ps 25:22). The superscription is not a likely historical reference; it should read Achish, not Abimelech (cf. 1 Sam 21:10–15). Structure: vv. 1–3, hymnic introduction, which anticipates the message of the psalm, the Lord's care for the *humble* (Hebrew *'anawim); vv.* 4–10, the acknowledgement of the deliverance develops into a didactic exhortation to trust and fear the Lord, a basic wisdom theme; vv. 11–22, an instruction, typical of wisdom teaching. **7.** *Angel of the LORD:* one of the heavenly court, executing the Lord's orders (Ps 35:5 and 91:11). **9.** *Holy ones:* the adjective *qadosh* rarely refers to humans; normally it denotes the superhuman world. **11.** A sapiential call (Prov 4:1; 5:7, etc.) introduces a series of admonitions and maxims favoring the just over the wicked. **12.** The sense of the question is that all desire a long prosperous life. **15.** For the *eyes of the LORD,* see Ps 33:18. The doctrine of retribution follows the optimistic teaching of Proverbs, but there was a strong tide of doubt as to the validity of this doctrine in the wisdom tradition, as the books of Job and Ecclesiastes prove. In general, the viewpoint in the Psalter is similar to that of Proverbs, as the programmatic Psalm 1 also indicates (the two ways).

Psalm 35. A lament of an individual. Structure: vv. 1–3, invocation of divine help with legal and military metaphors; vv. 4–8, imprecation against unjust enemies; vv. 9–10, an anticipatory thanksgiving; vv. 11–16, renewed complaint; vv. 17–26, a renewed appeal, with imprecations; vv. 27–28, an invitation to friends to rejoice as the psalmist praises the Lord for deliverance. The structure illustrates the complexity of the poem. **3b.** This has the ring of an oracle of the salvation for which the psalmist hopes. **5.** For *chaff,* see Ps 1:4; for the *angel of the LORD,* see Ps 34:7. **7–8.** For this kind of imagery and imprecation, see the comment on Ps 7:12–16. **12–14.** Practically an affirmation of innocence; perhaps there is an unjust accusation (see vv. 19–21). **21–22.** Note the contrast between what the enemies and the Lord have seen. Similarly, there is a contrast between the hostile words of v. 25 and the words of the friends in v. 27.

Psalm 36. The lament of an individual who trusts in the Lord's covenant loyalty ("steadfast love," *hesed,* in vv. 5, 7, and 10). Structure: vv. 1–4, a description of evildoers; vv. 5–9, a hymnic statement of confidence in the Lord's protection; vv. 10–12, a request for continued help against evildoers. So understood, the poem can be taken as a unit rather than as a composite. **6.** *Mighty mountains:* lit., "mountains of God," a superlative. The psalm compares the divine decisions about all creatures to the great Deep (*tehom,* as in Gen 1:2). Thus they are beyond human comprehension. **7.** The metaphor of *wings* is frequent (e.g., Ps 17:8). **8–9.** The sustenance given by the Temple resembles that of a rich banquet. The highly expansive metaphors continue: The Lord is the source of *life. In your light:* the light of God's face that shines on the faithful (cf. the priestly blessing in Num 6:25). The light of the Lord's face is the reason *we see light.* To "see the light" is to live (Ps 49:19 and often). Of course, this is the good life, filled with God's blessings, that the text envisions here, but this is also an open-ended vision. **10–12.** The request is for a continuance of *steadfast love,* demonstrated by deliverance from the *wicked.*

Psalm 37. If ever a psalm could be classified as wisdom, it is this one. This is so because the psalm consists of couplets that would be at home in the Book of Proverbs, and because of its structure in the acrostic pattern. Each Hebrew letter opens two full lines, a stanza, as printed in the NRSV. Otherwise, the structure is loose, since it is governed by imperatives (vv. 1–9, 27, 34, and 37), proverbial sayings (vv. 2, 8–9, 16, and 21), and by a steady contrast between the just and the wicked. (vv. 16–40). The writer champions the traditional doctrine of retribution: the just will *inherit the land* (vv. 3, 9, 11, 22, 29, and 34), but the wicked will be *cut off* (vv. 9, 22, 28, and 38). God rewards and punishes in this life; judgment may be slow, but it will surely come, so one should not be upset over delay (vv. 1, 7, and 8; cf. Ps 73:3). **1.** The implication is that retribution has its downside; there is no automatic mechanism at work; one must wait for justice. **2.** *Grass:* a symbol of short duration; this common metaphor (e.g., Isa 40:7) comes from the rapid desiccation in Palestine caused by the sirocco or the sun; here it refers to the short-lived prosperity that the evildoer is to experience. **3–4.** These exhortations are obviously felt to be necessary in view of harsh reality. **11.** Inheriting the *land* has the overtones of the divine promise (Gen 12:1), fulfilled for Israel, for the land belongs to the Lord (Lev 25:23). It is promised to the *meek ('anawim),* the needy who have only the Lord to rely upon. **16.** This "better"-saying is typical of wisdom teaching; see Prov 14:16; 16:18; Eccl 5:9. **18.** *Forever:* as elsewhere in the OT, this has the meaning of indefinite duration, not eternity; however, the idea is capable of expansion into a life that is undying (Wis 1:15) or eternal (John 17:3). **30–31.** *Wisdom* and *law* ("teaching," or torah) are identified in Sir 24:23 and Bar 4:1. **35–36.** An example of how insubstantial and transitory is the prosperity of the wicked; it *has* to be so. For the lot of the righteous, see vv. 25–26. But the argument from experience is selective and ultimately unproductive. Like the Book of Proverbs, a psalm like this must be held in tension with Psalm 73 and other portions of the Bible (Job). It does not affirm that a just order exists. As v. 1 correctly implies, injustice already exists, but the psalm is a call for (blind?) trust in the Lord.

Psalm 38. A lament of an individual; the third "penitential" psalm. Structure: v. 1, opening plea; vv. 2–8, complaint and confession of sinfulness; vv. 9–20, expressions of confidence (vv. 9, 15, and 16) and renewed complaint (vv. 10–14; 17–20); vv. 21–22, final petition. **1.** See Ps 6:1. **2.** *Arrows . . . hand:* common metaphors for the sufferings portrayed in the stereotypical descriptions that follow. **3–4.** The association of sin and suffering is clear, and the prayer aims at warding off more suffering. **5–12.** The description of drastic sufferings and ostracism reminds one of Job's predicament: sores, mourning, abandonment, and enemies. It is not possible to pinpoint the exact situation; as in Psalm 22, suffering is presented broadly so as to include the troubles of everyone. **13–14.** The silence of the psalmist is unusual; he refuses to engage with spiteful neighbors; instead he speaks to God in whom he hopes (v. 15). These lines offer a motive for the Lord to intervene. **18.** For the third time sinfulness is admitted (cf. vv. 3–4). **21–22.** This final appeal creates a poem of twenty-two lines, an "alphabetizing" psalm (Ps 33).

Psalm 39. A gentle lament of an individual (vv. 2–3) in a meditative mood. Structure: vv. 2–3, a description of the psalmist's silence; vv. 4–11, outburst of complaint, with renewed appeals for deliverance; vv. 12–13, final appeal. **1–3.** Without the customary introduction, this lament describes a struggle to be peaceful and silent before the *wicked.* Finally the complaint cannot be held back. The reason for the silence is not clear: temptation to apostasy? or fear lest the suffering (v. 10) be misinterpreted by the wicked? **4–6.** Reflection on the brevity of life is a common topic in the Bible (e.g., Ps 90; Job 7:7–10; 9:25–26; and Isa 40:6–8). Resignation to human mortality was an accepted fact in the OT. This meditation can hardly be the reason for the silence; perhaps it serves to move the Lord to intervene. **8–10.** The *fool* is often shorthand for the wicked in the wisdom books; perhaps they used the suffering psalmist as an example of divine indifference. The silence in v. 9, in contrast to v. 2, is a sign of submission to God and the *blows* (v. 10) that were the punishment for sin. **11.** *Like a moth:* a moth-eaten garment is a symbol for human transience, as in Job 13:28 and Isa 50:9. **12.** The metaphors convey the tenuous grasp that humans have on life. The *ger,* or alien, describes the patriarchs, who were merely resident aliens in the land; that is what life is like in this world. **13.** Like Job (7:19), the psalmist asks God to look away. In contrast to Ps 33:18–19, the present text realizes that the divine gaze can be harmful and punishing. It is no small virtue of this poem that it ends on a dark note, nonlife in Sheol (cf. also Job 7:21; 10:20–22), despite the hope (v. 7) in God.

Psalm 40. Many consider this a "mixed" psalm, a thanksgiving (vv. 1–10) joined to a lament (vv. 11–17), especially because of the reappearance of vv. 13–17 as Psalm 70. Yet, praise and thanksgiving precede lament elsewhere, as in Psalms 9/10, 17, 44, and 89. Structure: vv. 1–3, a description of deliverance and its effect; vv. 4–5, a beatitude and a short hymn of praise; vv. 6–8, a teaching about radical obedience; vv. 9–10, fulfillment of a vow to give thanks publicly; vv. 11–15, petitions (vv. 11, 13) and complaints (vv. 12, 14–15); vv. 16–17, confident petition. **1–3.** The customary direct address (cf. Ps 30) is here muted to the third person, but the metaphors are similar *(pit). New song:* see Ps 33:3; in the present case, a "new" song is fitting because of the deliverance. **4.** The beatitude is a kind of teaching intended for bystanders. **5.** This sudden praise goes beyond the immediate situation to the Lord's actions for the people. **6–8.** The teaching that obedience is better than sacrifice is familiar (cf. 1 Sam 15:22; Isa 1:11–17; and Hos 6:6, etc.). This is not a choice between material and spiritual sacrifice, nor a condemnation of sacrifice in itself. Rather, it is a rejection of the insincere manipulation of ritual. The emphasis is on interiority, as *open ear* and *heart* indicate. *Scroll of the book:* the torah or law, which itself does prescribe sacrifice. **9–10.** An extraordinary emphasis on the public acknowledgment of the saving intervention of the Lord. **11–12.** These verses are a turning point in the structure of the prayer; v. 11 can be related to the previous verses as a confident conclusion, while v. 12 initiates a complaint that the following verses fully develop. *For:* the Hebrew particle is better understood as "indeed." **13.** This verse is familiar to those who pray the liturgy of the hours, or divine office. **15.** *Aha:* a vivid expression roughly equivalent to, "you have it coming to you" (cf. Ps 35:25). **17.** The psalmist describes himself in the frequent phrase *poor and needy ('ani we'ebyon),* who are almost automatically the objects of the Lord's concern.

Psalm 41. A lament of an individual. Structure: vv. 1–3, introductory beatitude; vv. 4–10, plea and complaint; vv. 11–12, a statement of confidence. **1–3.** This is an unusual beginning for a lament, and it constitutes an argument for those who construe the poem as thanksgiving. Perhaps it calls attention to those who would care for such as the psalmist; pity for the "poor" (v. 1) will be rewarded. **4.** Those who interpret the psalm as thanks-giving regard "I said" as a flashback to an earlier complaint. How-ever, it can also be a prayer that is recited in the present situation. **8.** *Deadly thing:* lit., a thing of "Belial" which is a syn-onym of Death/Sheol in Ps 18:4–5. **9.** *Bosom friend:* lit., "the man of my peace." The usual "enemies" is sharpened here to traitor-ous treatment from an intimate. **12.** Despite the admission of sin in v. 4, there is a recognition of a deeper integrity that moved the Lord to save the psalmist and entitle him to remain in the divine presence (perhaps the Temple). *Forever:* see the comment on Ps 37:18. **13.** This doxology is a later editorial addition that closes the Davidic collection (Pss 3–41), the first "book" of the five in the Psalter.

Psalms 42–43. There is general consensus that the two psalms constitute a single poem, since there is no title for Psalm 43 and the refrains in 42:5, 42:11, and 43:5 bind the two parts to-gether. The separation into two psalms perhaps arises from the fact that the first is a complaint, while the second is a confident request. Structure: The refrains suggest three stanzas in which complaint is loosely mixed with longing, reminiscence, petition, and confidence. The usual interpretation is "biographical" in the sense that the psalmist is in the north (v. 6), suffering somehow (42:7–9 and 43:2), and yearning to be back in Jerusalem where he has participated in the liturgy (42:4 and 43:4). **42:1.** *Korah-ites:* according to 2 Chr 20:19, a group of temple singers; the superscriptions attribute Psalms 42, 44–49, 84–85, and 87–88 to them. **2.** Recall the paradox here—to "see the face of God," once a sure death (Exod 33:20), is now used for spiritual experience in the Temple (e.g., Ps 11:7 and see comment on 17:15). **3.** *Where is your God?:* a stereotyped question, often addressed by a hos-tile group (Pss 79:10; 115:2; and Mic 7:10). **4.** This happy re-membrance serves to emphasize the desolation caused by separa-tion from the Temple. **5.** A personal soliloquy is unusual in the Psalter. **7.** The roar of the waters suggests chaos and suffer-ing. **43:3.** *Light . . . truth:* are personified here as guardian spirits to protect the psalmist. Usually it is "steadfast love" and "faithful-ness" that guard the faithful, as in Pss 25:10; 36:5; 40:10–11; and

57:3, 10. Here light is needed to find the path to the *holy hill* and the Temple.

Psalm 44. A lament of the community. Structure: vv. 1–8, a hymnic recall of God's deliverance of the people in the past; vv. 9–16, a complaint about the present distress; vv. 17–22, a protestation of innocence; vv. 23–26, a demand for deliverance. The precise historical situation cannot be determined. The psalm contains a curious mixture of first person singular (vv. 4, 6, and 15) and plural (vv. 1, 5, 7, and 9–14), however that switching is to be explained (solo voices? the role of the king?). **1.** *God: 'Elohim* is substituted for *YHWH*, a revision of the so-called Elohistic Psalter. **2.** The past salvation history, in which the sole deliverer was God, is recalled to serve as a contrast with the present distress, just as Ps 22:4–5 contrasts the trust of the fathers with the sufferings of the psalmist. **3.** *Light of your countenance:* always a sign of divine favor (e.g., Ps 4:6), to be contrasted with v. 24, where God is charged with hiding his face. **4–8.** The attribution of victory to the Lord alone is a common motif (Deut 8:17–18 and Josh 24:12). **9–16.** The complaint is that the Lord has deserted the warriors (v. 9, practically repeated in Ps 60:10 and 108:11). The language is bold, pointing out the poor bargain that the Lord has made (v. 12). **17–22.** As in the individual laments, the motif of innocence appears: v. 20 poses a hypothetical guilt, but vv. 21–22 deny it. Indeed, it is on the Lord's account that they are being slaughtered! **24–27.** An ultimatum is delivered. The sleeping God (see Pss 7:6 and 35:23) must wake up! The divine "forgetfulness" (v. 24) cannot stand, since Israel did not forget (v. 20).

Psalm 45. A wedding song for an Israelite king. It is not to be interpreted allegorically, nor can a specific king be identified. Structure: v. 1, self-presentation by the psalmist; vv. 2–9, praise for the king for his comeliness, virtue, and warlike ability; vv. 10–15, admonition to the bride, urging her to wifely devotion, and describing the wedding (apparel and procession); vv. 16–17, a concluding address to the king. **1.** The tone and style of the writer suggest that he is a court poet, who presents himself here and at the end (v. 17). **3–5.** The military prowess of the king is singled out for praise. **6.** *O God:* the NRSV understands this to be a vocative, addressed to the king. He can be called an *elohim*-being because of the idealized superhuman qualities with which he was invested, as a son of God (see Ps 2:7). The use of the term *elohim* was fairly broad, to judge from the application of this word to the ghost of Samuel coming up from Sheol (1 Sam 28:13). However, the appellation is applied to the king only here, and other translations of this verse are possible, such as "your divine throne" or "your throne is divine" (see the NRSV footnote). **7.** *Righteousness:* the ideal of justice was particularly associated with royalty, at least in theory (cf. Ps 72). *God, your God:* before the Elohistic recension of Psalms 42–83, the phrase would have been "*YHWH,* your God." *Oil of gladness:* probably a symbol of the joyful gifts of riches and blessings (v. 8) that his *companions,* the other princes, do not have. **8–9.** An elaborate description of the wedding; Ophir is located either in south Arabia or east Africa, and was famous for its gold (1 Kgs 10:11, 22). **10–12.** The address to the Queen may indicate that she is from Tyre. The description of the procession resumes in vv. 13b–15. **16–17.** The poet assures the king of a dynasty, and again (cf. v. 1) the poet refers to himself, and in a somewhat boastful way (cf. Ps 104:34).

Psalm 46. A hymn of praise, one of the Songs of Zion (Pss 48, 76, 84, 87, and 122), which focus on Zion and on the Temple as the dwelling place of the Lord. The Songs have characteristic motifs such as conquest of the Sea (chaos), holiness, and divine presence. The precise setting in the liturgy cannot be specified, despite Mowinckel's "enthronement" feast (see p. 10 in the Introduction above). The psalm has a clear structure of three stanzas, partially indicated by the refrain (presumably uttered by the community) in vv. 7 and 11. **1–3.** The presence of God, hailed in the refrain, is the reason for the confidence that chaos (earthquake and *sea)* never prevail. Many restore the refrain of vv. 7 and 11 after v. 3. **4.** *River:* no such body of water exists. This language reflects the mythological background of the dwelling of the gods from which life-giving waters come. The verse so describes the Lord's residence, and the "river" stands in contrast to the threatening waters of chaos; it symbolizes the divine presence, like the "waters of Shiloah" in Isa 8:6. In this stanza the emphasis has shifted from chaos to *nations. Most High:* lit., *'elyon,* the Canaanite designation of the chief god, El, in the pantheon, applied here to the Lord (cf. Ps 47:2). **5.** *Morning dawns:* perhaps a reference to the answer given to prayer after a night in the Temple (Pss 5:3; 17:3, 15, and often). **8–9.** This invitation is difficult to understand; is it to be a vision of words, or some kind of mime? Moreover, who is addressed—the community or the nations (v. 10)? What is announced is the end of war, a reign of peace. **10.** *Be still:* thus begins an oracle delivered in the name of the Lord by one of the Temple personnel; its audience is the whole world. **11.** Note that the refrain reflects partially the name of Isaiah's famous "sign," Immanuel, "with us is God."

Psalm 47. A hymn of praise, celebrating the enthronement of the Lord as king, whether or not this was celebrated at a specific feast; see also Psalms 93 and 96–99. The interpretation of these psalms varies, with different scholars referring it to: (1) a specific historical event; (2) the eschatological or end time; and (3) a liturgical rehearsal of the Lord's kingship (most likely). Structure: vv. 1–4, a call to worship Elyon because of the favor done to Israel; vv. 5–7, a description of a procession with summons to praise; vv. 8–9, a proclamation of kingship, with description of the assembly. **1–2.** The directive is universal (cf. v. 9), because Elyon (cf. comment on 46:4) is a *great king,* an expression also used by Assyrian monarchs, over the world, and specifically (vv. 3–4) because of his choice of Israel. **5.** *Gone up:* the verb strongly suggests a cultic rite of mounting a throne (perhaps the Ark of the covenant carried in procession?). The *trumpet* blasts are characteristics of the celebration (2 Sam 15:10; 2 Kgs 9:13) when a new king would be proclaimed (2 Kgs 11:12, 14). A feast of enthronement of the Lord need not imply that he was not considered king before; rather, eternal kingship is actualized in the liturgy. **6–7.** Cf. vv. 1–2. **9.** The universal note is sounded again (vv. 2, 8), but now the *peoples* are intimately united (v. 9b) with Israel in the celebration. *Shields:* foreign rulers who protect their subjects (cf. the parallelism in Pss 84:11 and 89:18).

Psalm 48. A song of Zion (cf. Ps 46). Structure: vv. 1–3, praise of the great King defending his holy mount; vv. 4–8, the panic that the sight of the city of God causes its foes; vv. 9–11, proclamation of praise by the community; vv. 12–14, a summons to procession. **1–3.** *The city of our God:* cf. the great work of St. Augustine, *De Civitate Dei (The City of God). Great King:* see the comments on Pss 46:4 and 47:2. *In the far north:* lit., the heights of Zaphon (= north). Jerusalem is not in the far north. The psalm may be associating Zion with Mount Zaphon, which is the Mount Olympus of the Canaanite deities (in the Ugaritic texts), where Baal dwelt also. Cf. Isa 14:13 and Ezek 28:14. Seven epithets, all extravagant (e.g., *joy of all the earth*), are used to describe Zion, which is inviolable and impregnable because God defends it (Pss 46:4–7 and 76:2–3). **4–8.** As in Pss 2:4–9 and 76:2–3, Zion brings panic to the enemy but victory and joyful pride to its residents. This is an imaginary description; hostile enemies flee at the mere sight of God's city. *Tarshish:* site unknown, perhaps in or near Spain; the reference is to seagoing ships. **10.** *Victory:* lit., "justice," *sedeq,* which often has the nuance of a justice that saves. **11.** *Towns:* lit., "daughters," as surrounding towns were often described. **12–14.** The summons to examine Zion may be literal or figurative, but the purpose is to communicate to succeeding generations the sense of divine leadership. *Forever:* this final phrase of the MT, *'al mut,* is thus rendered by NRSV without any note; it is virtually untranslatable.

Psalm 49. It is difficult to specify the genre of this psalm. It is often termed "wisdom" (v. 3) because of its meditative style, and its topic, the frailty of life and human possessions. Moreover, it takes up the troubling situation of those who are rich because they have placed their trust in riches (vv. 5–6, 16; cf. Pss 37 and 73). The reply to this problem takes the form of high confidence (vv. 1–4) that a solution is to be announced. Structure: vv. 1–4, a ponderous introduction asking for attention to what follows; vv. 5–12, a consideration of death—it cannot be paid off, for it rules over the wealthy as well as the poor. The ending is a kind of refrain (v. 12; cf. 20); vv. 13–15, a contrast between the fate of fools and that of the psalmist; vv. 16–20, an admonition concerning those who trust in their riches. The text is uncertain in places, as the several textual notes in the NRSV indicate, but the main ideas are fairly clear; ultimately God "redeems" (v. 15). **1–4.** This solemn introduction is striking; it emphasizes the importance of what is to come: *wisdom.* There is no other biblical reference to a connection between music and wisdom utterance. **5.** *Persecutors:* lit., "supplanters," like Jacob the "heel-grabber" (Gen 25:26; 27:36). **6–9.** The emptiness of riches; no one can buy off the Pit, i.e., death. *Ransom:* literally it is a material payment, but it also can be a metaphor for God's deliverance from Egyptian slavery (Ps 78:42 and Deut 7:8). **10–12.** Since life is a gift of God, death reigns supreme, even over the wise and the powerful. In this respect humans resemble animals (v. 12), as Qoheleth also claimed (Eccl 3:19–20 and 9:3). **13–14.** Death befalls particularly the *foolhardy,* probably those who trusted in riches while alive. The NRSV footnote indicates that the MT reading favors the upright in Sheol. Since this is contrary to the OT view, a corrected reading is presented. **15.** This is perhaps the most important verse. It stands in contrast to v. 8, which asserted that no one could give a ransom against death. Here it is God who ransoms the psalmist. Is this merely a claim that the Lord delivers him or her from "persecutors" (v. 5)? Or does the context indicate that God's ransom is more—literally and completely delivering *from the power of Sheol?* Commentators differ on this question. In favor of God redeeming from death is the contrast with v. 8, and also the use of the verb *receive,* which, by its use in the "taking" of Enoch (Gen 5:24) and of Elijah (2 Kgs 2:11), and the taking to glory in Ps 73:24, suggests a fuller meaning. Be that as it may, the verse is at the least a strong reaffirmation of the trust in God that v. 5 also expresses. **16–19.** This admonition also reflects back on the uselessness of "fear" (v. 5). The fate of those who find their happiness in riches is inevitable: Sheol, where one never sees the *light.* **20.** The Hebrew of this verse is not identical with v. 12. *Abide* should be replaced by "understand." The difference is slight, but it gives a sapiential twist at the end of the psalm, which proclaimed *wisdom* and *understanding* in v. 3.

Psalm 50. This is obviously not a prayer, but the genre is difficult to describe. Is it a lawsuit or a prophetic judgment liturgy? The structure is clear, however: vv. 1–6, the Lord appears in a theophany in Zion and issues a summons to judgment; vv. 7–15, the first speech of the Lord concerning animal sacrifices;

vv. 16–21, the second speech, now addressing the wicked, indicting them for disobedience to the divine commands; vv. 22–23, an admonition to choose appropriate sacrifices. **1–2.** The entire *earth*, as well as *Zion*, feels the effect of the Lord's speaking. **3–4.** The description of the theophany is reminiscent of other texts (e.g., Ps 18:7–15; Deut 33:2, etc.). The witness of *heavens* and *earth* forms part of the typical lawsuit language (see Deut 31:28 and Isa 1:2). **5.** This is an ideal description of those who are summoned, namely those who covenanted in sacrifice at Sinai (Exod 24:4–8). **6.** The *heavens* of v. 4 are now to give witness to the justice of the coming judgment. **7.** The opening is typical of prophetic proclamations, as in, e.g., Isa 1:10. *God, your God:* i.e., *YHWH,* your God (cf. the comment on Ps 44:1). **8.** It is curious that the tirade against animal sacrifices begins in this negative style, since the acceptance of sacrifice in v. 5 makes it clear that the criticism is not a condemnation of ritual in itself. **9–13.** Whoever relies on mere sacrificial victims misunderstands who the Lord is; all things belong to God, and hypocritical conduct will be rejected in the sarcastic question of v. 13. **14–15.** God will respond to *a sacrifice of thanksgiving,* which is usually vowed by a person in *trouble.* Psalm 30 would be a typical example of thank-offering that accompanied a meal in which the bystanders shared. **16–21.** Not only formalism in worship, but evildoing receives condemnation in concrete fashion. Worship is genuine only if the covenant stipulations concerning theft, adultery, etc., are observed. **21.** The silence of God—a failure to punish the wicked for their wrongdoing—has been misinterpreted, so now comes the threat. **22–23.** The choice is theirs: destruction or *salvation.* The superscription attributes this psalm, as is also the case for Psalms 73–83, to Asaph, who receives liturgical notice in 2 Chr 29:30 (see Ezra 2:41).

Psalm 51. The fame of this "penitential" psalm is only partially explained by the superscription that needlessly puts it in the context of David's sin with Bathsheba. In the MT this counts for two verses; MT 51:3 = NRSV 51:1. The prayer also exhibits remarkable depth and character. Structure: vv. 1–2, an appeal for mercy; vv. 3–5, confession of sinfulness; vv. 6–12, requests for absolution and renewal; vv. 13–15, a vow to praise God; vv. 16–17, the sacrifice that God desires; vv. 18–19, a plea that Zion be restored for sacrificial worship. **1–2.** Four imperatives, all dealing with the removal of the sinfulness (not sickness or enemies) that weighs down the psalmist; the emphasis is extraordinary. **4.** One should understand between lines *ab* and *cd* a phrase like "I say this." The admission of sin is explicit so as to exonerate God of any accusation of unjust treatment of the psalmist. *You alone:* there is the heart of sin, even if it involves harm to the neighbor. **5.** The sense is that the psalmist is totally sinful, wrong from the start. This has nothing to do with maternal conception or intercourse, much less with original sin (which is not a biblical phrase). See Gen 8:21; Ps 58:3. **6–11.** The images become those of interiority (*truth, heart,* and *spirit*). **7.** *Hyssop:* a plant used to sprinkle water or blood; cf. the ritual cleansings in Leviticus 14. **8.** *Joy and gladness:* perhaps the festivities that accompany a thanksgiving sacrifice after one receives forgiveness (cf. the acknowledgment indicated in v. 13). **9.** God's "hiding the face" is here a sign of forgiveness, in contrast to its usual meaning of rejection, as in Pss 69:17 and 88:14. **10–12.** The inner renewal is reminiscent of Jer 31:33–34 and Ezek 36:26–27; read the NRSV footnotes. *Holy spirit:* used only here and in Isa 63:10–11, designating the enlivening effect of God's work in the psalmist. *Joy of your salvation:* the happiness that God's forgiveness brings; see "God of my salvation" in v. 14. **14.** *Bloodshed:* lit., "bloods," i.e., from death, or deliverance from the consequences of violent wrongs, or possibly "bloodguilt" (when sinners die in their sin, Ezek 3:18–21). **15–17.** A startling statement. The psalmist offers as *praise,* not a *burnt offering,* but himself, his *broken spirit* and *heart;* he becomes the victim of sacrifice. See also Pss 40:6; 50:14. **18–19.** Whether or not these verses are a later addition, they stand in deliberate tension with vv. 16–17. They request a restoration of Zion and a resumption of the usual Temple worship.

Psalm 52. The genre of the psalm is difficult to define. It begins with an indictment of a wicked person, and ends with the deliverance of the righteous and with expressions of trust. The mention of Doeg in the superscription refers to 1 Sam 21:7 and 22:6–19. Structure: vv. 1–5, indictment and condemnation of a wicked person; vv. 6–7, the reaction of the righteous at the downfall of the wicked; vv. 8–9, the psalmist's trust. **1.** *Mighty one: gibbor* has the general meaning of champion or hero. No one in particular is meant; this is rather a type of a domineering and unscrupulous liar (vv. 2–4). **6–7.** The ridicule of the *righteous* at the downfall of the wicked adds another trait: trusting in *riches*. **8–9.** The speaker of these lines stands in contrast to the wicked of v. 7; his *trust* is in the Lord's *steadfast love.* The *olive tree* is a hardy, all-purpose growth, important in the life of the ancient Palestinian; here it highlights personal vigor. The comparison to trees is common (Pss 1:3; 92:12; and 128:3).

Psalm 53. See Psalm 14, of which this is a variant form. Also, the sacred name has been replaced by "God" in this Elohistic Psalter; see the comment on Ps 45:7. The text of v. 5 is uncertain, as the NRSV footnotes indicate, and it differs from the parallel in Ps 14:5–6. In the NRSV, the verse is a threat to the *ungodly.*

Psalm 54. A lament of an individual. The reference in the superscription is to 1 Sam 23:19–24 and 26:1–25. Ziph is a desert town south of Hebron. Structure: vv. 1–3, a cry for help against godless enemies; vv. 4–5, an affirmation of confidence, followed by imprecation; vv. 6–7, a vow to offer a thanksgiving sacrifice for the deliverance. **1.** *Name:* as usual, this signifies the person of the deity, and the verse forms an inclusio with the mention of thanksgiving in v. 6 to the *name.* The psalms frequently invoke the "name," and its protective aspect is illustrated in Ps 20:1, 7. **5b.** This is an imperative directed to God. **7a.** *He:* possibly "it," referring to the sacred name in v. 6 (cf. v. 1).

Psalm 55. A lament of an individual. The structure is loose; there is a mixture of complaints and imprecations. Structure: vv. 1–2, appeal; vv. 3–8, complaint; vv. 9–11, imprecation and complaint; vv. 12–15, complaint about an intimate friend and imprecation; vv. 16–19, confidence in deliverance by God; vv. 20–21, denunciation of a smooth-talking friend; vv. 22–23, exhortation to rely on the Lord, and a final imprecation. **4.** *Terrors of death:* an apt expression for all the troubles that assail the psalmist. **6–8.** This desire is unrealistic; the psalmist cannot escape so easily. The wish is all the more surprising in view of the fact that it does not include a flight to the Lord's protection; but the metaphors are appealing. **12–14.** The complaint is sharpened by the treachery of a particularly close friend. **15.** As often in the Psalter, the text personifies Death/Sheol as powers that will take the enemy to themselves (cf. Num 16:33 and Prov 1:12). **16–19.** Despite the *battle* (note the profusion of metaphors), the psalmist is convinced that he will be saved. **20–21.** *My companion:* this is not in the Hebrew, but the reference seems to be to the false so-called *friend* of v. 13. **22.** It is not clear who is speaking to whom; it is perhaps an oracle of a Temple official urging trust in the Lord, or perhaps the words of the psalmist. **23.** *The lowest pit:* lit., "the well of the pit." Whatever the precise meaning, there were levels in the imaginative descriptions of Sheol (see, e.g., Ezek 32:18).

Psalm 56. A lament of an individual. The characterization of the "dove" in the superscription is really not translatable. For David at Gath, see 1 Sam 21:11–16 (NRSV, 10–15). Structure: vv. 1–4, appeal and complaint, ending with trust (v. 4, refrain, with v. 11); vv. 5–7, renewed complaint with imprecation; vv. 8–11, a statement of confidence (refrain in 11; cf. v. 4); vv. 12–13, statement of a vow to give thanks. **1.** *Gracious:* better, "merciful," as in Ps 57:1. **2.** The identity of the *enemies* remains vague throughout; it is not clear if the reference is to evil people or foreign nations (cf. vv. 5–7). **4.** *Flesh:* this designates the sphere of the human and finite (cf. Isa 40:6 and also the echo below in v. 11). **7.** *Repay:* as the footnote indicates, this is a conjecture; the MT has "save them" (for trouble), perhaps meant sarcastically. **8.** The sense is that God collects and preserves the tears of the psalmist; they are not wasted, but are precious to the deity. God also keeps a book on his valued subjects (see Mal 3:16 and Exod 32:32–33). **9.** This verse appears again with slight variation in Ps 116:8–9. **13.** *Light of life:* or possibly "light of the living." The light is opposed to the darkness of the dead in Sheol (Job 10:22); God has delivered the psalmist from Sheol.

Psalm 57. A lament of an individual. The superscription contains an allusion to 1 Sam 22:1, or to 24:4 (NRSV, 3). Structure:

vv. 1–3, a confident petition to the Lord for saving intervention; vv. 4–6, the complaint, interrupted in v. 5 by the refrain (v. 11); vv. 7–10, anticipatory thanksgiving; v. 11, refrain. **1.** *Shadow of your wings:* as in Pss 17:8 and 36:7, the image derives from the picture of a bird protecting its nest, and here it perhaps refers to the safety of the Temple. **2.** *Fulfills his purpose:* better, "does good" or "provides." **3.** *Steadfast love* and *faithfulness* are guardians sent to protect the psalmist (see v. 10 and comment on Ps 43:3). **4, 6.** These metaphors are common in the Psalter, especially falling into the *pit,* a trap set for others (e.g., Pss 7:15–16 and 9:15–16). **5.** This exclamation is a surprising interruption; it refers to the heavenly residence from which God's works and actions manifest the divine *glory* (see v. 11). **7–10.** This thanksgiving recurs in Ps 108:1–5, where it introduces a complaint that is a repetition of Ps 60:5–12. **8.** *Awake the dawn:* the psalmist anticipates the dawn by his rising early to sing praise. Parallels to this idea occur, from Ovid to Shakespeare and beyond. **11.** The refrain also in v. 5; cf. also Ps 36:5.

Psalm 58. The genre of this psalm is not clear. The problem is twofold. Who has authority to speak thus? Who is being addressed? The enigmatic *'elem* of v. 1 is usually changed to *'elim,* gods or divine beings, the members of the heavenly court (see Ps 29:1). The NRSV adopts that reading; "mighty lords" in the footnote is an uncertain meaning. See also Psalm 82, where the Lord rebukes the "gods." Then the implication of the present psalm is that they do not live up to their responsibilities for the maintenance of justice on earth. This looks like an attempt to spare the Lord, as though the heavenly court is responsible for the existence of injustice. Others would claim that human authorities are meant, on the analogy of Exod 4:16 and 7:1 (Moses is as God to Aaron and to Pharaoh); hence the psalm would refer to human beings who have judicial, God-given power, but abuse it. Structure: vv. 1–2, a calling to account of authorities who are unfair in the administration of justice; vv. 3–5, a description of the actions of the wicked; vv. 6–9, imprecation; vv. 10–11, the reaction of the just and the acknowledgement of divine justice. **3–5.** The *wicked* are corrupt since birth (Ps 51:5). There is no protection against their poisonous *venom;* they are compared to a *deaf adder* (!) that cannot be charmed by any incantation. **6–9.** The metaphors in this uncertain text abound; jaws of lions, water that seeps away, grass (see footnote), a *snail*, birth (cf. Job 3:16), and *pots* (?). The reference to the snail can perhaps be explained by its leaving a trail of empty shells; hence it melts away. The translation of v. 9 is uncertain; the comparison to the heating of pots in the NRSV refers to a very brief time (for the speedy end of the wicked). **10.** Washing one's feet in the blood of the wicked is a metaphorical gesture of revenge (Ps 68:23 and Isa 63:3–6). **11.** This is the goal of the psalm: the acknowledgment that God will judge, and in favor of the just, because the corrupt authorities will be gone.

Psalm 59. A lament of an individual. The reference in the superscription is to 1 Sam 19:11. Note the refrains: vv. 6 and 14; and the poem is divided into two parts by the hymnic refrain in vv. 9b–10, most of which also appears in v. 17. These two parts contain a quick series of pleas, complaints, and imprecations. Although an individual speaks, it is "nations" (vv. 5 and 8) who are the "enemies." Hence, some scholars think this is a prayer of a king, as representative of the community, requesting that the feared threat not come about. **1–2.** The four emphatic imperatives deal with the undefined enemies of the speaker. **3–4a.** The affirmation of innocence is common in the prayer of an individual, but it sounds strange when the enemies are identified with *nations* (v. 5). **6–7.** A vivid metaphor (cf. vv. 14–15). For the derisive laughter of God, see Pss 2:4 and 37:13. **9–10.** See vv. 16–17. **11–13.** The request in v. 11, asking for a postponement of punishment of the enemies, is strange, especially in view of the demand in v. 13 that God put an end to them. And there is little likelihood that the *people* would forget their enemies. Perhaps the text is in disorder. **14–15.** Almost identical with vv. 6–7. **16–17.** These lines are a typical anticipatory thanksgiving, but they practically repeat vv. 9–10.

Psalm 60. A lament of the nation. The superscription alludes to events of 2 Samuel 8, but the psalm speaks of defeat (v. 10), not victory. Verses 5–12 are repeated in Ps 108:6–13. Structure: vv. 1–3, accusation against the Lord for harsh treatment

of the people; vv. 4–5, request for rescue; vv. 6–8 (9?), a statement
of God's promise of victory; vv. 10–12, a complaint and request. **2–3.** The metaphors of destruction are earthquake and the
inebriating *wine* that renders the people incompetent to defend
themselves (see Jer 25:15–16). **4.** The verse is ambiguous. It
could mean that the banner is a safe place for refuge (but why?
and how?). It might also indicate that the army has been routed
and is fleeing *out of bow shot* for any flimsy refuge such as a *banner.* **6–8.** The geographical and political designations are indications of areas of the Lord's victories. Shechem and Succoth are
two cities, one east, the other west of the Jordan. The four tribes
mentioned in v. 7 are a sign of the Lord's conquest of the land
(helmet, scepter) and allotment of portions to Israel. Verse 8 mentions three prominent enemies of Israel, and the metaphors
(Moab a mere *washbasin;* Edom claimed by a toss of a *shoe)*
indicate that victory over these old enemies is easy for the
Lord. **9.** The NRSV separates this verse from v. 8, with the implication that the promise of the Lord ends with the word *triumph,*
and the quotation finishes in v. 8. But it is not clear to whom the
me refers—a king or general of the army anxious to go after
Edom? However, Edom has just been mentioned as an easy conquest. If one takes v. 9 with vv. 6–8, the speaker could be the
Lord asking for the cooperation of the people in his securing
them. **10–12.** The psalm returns to the mood of complaint, but
ends with a confident request.

Psalm 61. A mild lament of an individual. Structure: vv.
1–2a, a typical appeal for help; vv. 2b–4, a manifestation of confidence, leading to the security of the Temple; v. 5, certainty
of having been heard; vv. 6–7, a prayer for the king; v. 8, affirmation of loyal thanksgiving and fulfillment of vows. **2a.** *The
end of the earth:* this would suggest distance. But it is possible
that the meaning is from "the brink of Sheol" (so the NAB v. 3;
'erets denotes here the underworld). **2b–4.** The usual metaphors
for safety climax in the security of the Temple (the *tent*). **5.** The
certainty leads to thanksgiving and fulfillment of vows in
v. 8. **6–7.** This prayer for the king and his long reign is sudden,
even interruptive.

Psalm 62. The genre is not easy to determine, but the psalm breathes an air of trust in God. The transitions within the poem are perplexing. The word *'ak* is repeated six times (vv. 1, 2, 4, 5, 6, and 9) in the sense of "only," or "indeed," or "alone" (the NRSV prefers the latter four times). The structure is marked by sudden movements: vv. 1–2, affirmation of trust; vv. 3–4, a rhetorical address to an unidentified group (note the movement from second to third person); vv. 5–7, a kind of soliloquy or refrain, picking up vv. 1–2 and reinforcing them; vv. 8–10, now *people* are addressed, in an appeal to trust only in God, not in mortals or riches; vv. 11–12, a numerical saying **1.** *Silence:* quietly, in peace, so confident is the tone. **3–4.** Armed with such confidence the psalmist jeers at the futile efforts of those who attack people with lies and hypocrisy. **5–7.** With a slight difference (hope instead of salvation), the verses repeat vv. 1–2 along with traditional attributes (see, e.g., Ps 18:2). **8–10.** The community is exhorted to have the same kind of confidence for the following reasons: (1) mortals are a mere breath that count for even less when weighed on scales; (2) unjust pursuit of riches will get you nowhere, and even if you are becoming rich, beware! God alone merits trust. **11–12.** In the style of a numerical proverb (x, followed by x plus 1), these lines make two heavy but familiar theological points: *power* and *steadfast love* are God's; see the same combination in Exod 15:13. It is not clear how the psalmist *heard this,* especially since the message is not novel. The last line affirms the law of retribution, and is not part of the saying itself.

Psalm 63. A mild lament of an individual, dominated by joy in the Lord. Structure: v. 1, the situation of the psalmist; vv. 2–4, his yearning for the Temple and worship; vv. 5–8, the joys that come from God's presence; vv. 9–11, the fate of his enemies, and the rejoicing in God. **1.** The comparison to the waterless desert doubtless explains the superscription, although the comparison merely underlines the ardent desire of the psalmist to enjoy the presence of God in the sanctuary. **3.** An important statement. Life for the Israelites included the possession of this world's necessities, but over them all they counted the Lord's *steadfast love (hesed).* **4–8.** It is as if the psalmist cannot find words adequate to express the sense of union with God: *a rich* *feast, the watches of the night,* during which one will be alert to the presence of God and also have a sense of security and dependence upon the Lord. **9–10.** The mention of enemies is sudden and unexpected. *Depths of the earth:* where Sheol is; see the comment on Ps 61:2a. *Prey for jackals:* the point is that they are deprived of burial, a terrible fate for the ancients. *The king:* if this was originally a royal psalm, it came to be democratized for use by all. *Who swear by him:* the implication is that such persons are loyal to the God they swear by.

Psalm 64. A lament of an individual. Structure: vv. 1–6, the appeal for help quickly becomes a description of the hostility that enemies show to the psalmist; vv. 7–9, the response of the Lord; v. 10, encouragement to the righteous. **1–5.** The actions of the enemy are described in traditional terms as words that are swords/arrows (see also Pss 11:2; 37:14; cf. 10:7–11). The effect of vv. 5–6 is to emphasize how secret the designs of the wicked are. **7–8.** But God knows and will reply in kind with *his arrow.* **10.** This exhortation (as in NRSV) can be interpreted as a declarative statement, after the *upright* have witnessed what God has done for the psalmist (v. 9).

Psalm 65. A song of praise, presumably by the community. Structure: vv. 1–4, thanksgiving for forgiveness of sin is due to the Lord in the Temple; vv. 5–8, a creation hymn addressed to the savior; vv. 9–13, the Lord's grant of fertility to the soil. This simple song covers a vast area: the Temple where prayers are heard, the created world that remains in operation, and the divine provision for the earth. **2–3.** For divine forgiveness see also Ps 103:8–14. **5–8.** Both salvation and creation come together in these lines, which include both Israel and even the most distant peoples. The *gateways* are literally the "goings out," and the reference is to the distant east and west where morning and evening seem to originate. **9–13.** The *river of God* is the body of water in the heavens that descends to fructify the earth. God is a "cosmic farmer," and the *wagon tracks* are the imprint of an imaginary chariot as the Lord rides the clouds (cf. Ps 68:4) and dispenses fertility. **12–13.** This description is typically exuberant, thanks to the various personifications of nature.

Psalm 66. This psalm is a mixed type, i.e., two genres coexist: a thanksgiving song of the community, and thanksgiving by an individual. The relationship between the two parts is not clear, but it is possible that the individual in the second part speaks for the community. The prayer has strong accents of universalism (vv. 1, 4, and 7–8), and v. 1 is echoed in Pss 98:4 and 100:1. Structure: vv. 1–4, invitation to praise God; vv. 5–7, an invitation to "see" the awesome works of God, which deserve to be hailed by all; vv. 8–12, praise of the Lord who delivered the people from the test; vv. 13–15, a declaration of a thanksgiving sacrifice; vv. 16–20, an address typical of a thanksgiving psalm, giving testimony to the bystanders of the Lord's intervention. **2–4.** As often, the *name* signifies the person. The reason for the universal praise is the *power* of God; the universalism would logically mean that no *enemies* remain. **5–7.** The invitation perhaps implies that something concrete appears (cf. Ps 46:8). In contrast to Ps 65:7, the *awesome deeds* are the saving events at the Red Sea and the Jordan River (see Ps 114:3). **8–12.** The renewed call to praise is motivated by the support the Lord has given the community in their "test." Testing is a prominent biblical theme (cf. comment on Pss 17:3 and 26:2), and often for a mysterious purpose (cf. Gen 22:1 and Deut 8:2, 16). No specifics are given, only metaphors of conquest and deliverance (v. 12; cf. Isa 43:2). *Ride over our heads:* this is more than a metaphor; the winners placed their feet on the necks of the conquered, as in Josh 10:24. **13–15.** These lines begin what looks like a typical thanksgiving hymn: fulfillment of a vow to offer sacrifices because of deliverance, to which vv. 19–20 give public witness. **16.** *Come and hear:* the resemblance of this invitation to v. 5 may be a reason these two parts of the psalm are joined together. It is striking that the universalism of v. 1–12 yields to those *who fear God,* presumably believers who are present in the Temple (v. 13) and hear this testimony. The Lord certainly hears prayers (v. 20: cf. Ps 65:2). The superscription of the Latin Vulgate and LXX (numbered as 65) call this psalm "psalm of resurrection"—fittingly since the hymn describes a transition of (the people) from death to life.

Psalm 67. Identification of the genre depends on the understanding of vv. 6–7; are they a prayer for a rich harvest (so NJPS

[vv. 7–8]), or a hymn in praise and thanksgiving for the rich harvest (NRSV, NAB vv. 7–8)? Structure: There are two petitions,
vv. 1–3 and 4–5, that end in a refrain (noticeably absent after
v. 7). The conclusion follows in vv. 6–7. As in Psalm 66, the universalism is worthy of note. **1.** A restatement of the blessing of
Aaron, Num 6:24–26; see also Pss 4:6 and 31:16. **2.** *Saving power*
might normally refer to the deliverance of Israel, but here the
context is the world, which is to acknowledge the judgment of
God (v. 4) and also show reverence for the fertility of the earth
(vv. 6–7). The psalm is simple but well articulated by the repetitions: verbs, bless/praise (seven times); nouns, peoples/nations
(eight times), earth (four times).

Psalm 68. A song of praise (?). This poem is very obscure;
the text is poorly preserved in some places and many of the references are unknown. At several points translation and interpretation are quite uncertain, as the NRSV footnotes testify. It has even
been called a collection of incipits, i.e., opening lines of various
songs (a well-known view of W. F. Albright). Structure: vv. 1–3,
introduction; vv. 4–6, invitation to praise the Lord; vv. 7–10, a
description to God's saving activity (from Egypt to Canaan);
vv. 11–14, an allusion to military victories (Joshua?); vv. 15–18,
praise of the Lord's mountain (Zion); vv. 19–23, praise of the saving God, conqueror of Israel's enemies; vv. 24–27, description of
a procession; vv. 28–31, a prayer that gifts be brought by the conquered to the Lord; vv. 32–35, all kingdoms are urged to praise
God. **1–3.** Verse 1 clearly alludes to the procession of the Ark in
Num 10:35, but the following verses describe in traditional terms
the fate of the *wicked* (they perish) and the *righteous* (joy), as in Ps
1. **4.** "Cloud-rider" is a standard epithet of Baal in the Ugaritic
literature, and it is appropriated to the Lord here and in v. 33 (cf.
Deut 33:26; Isa 19:1; and Ps 18:9–10). **5–6.** These attributes of the
Lord are mentioned in view of the liberation of Israel from Egypt,
the *parched land.* **7–10.** A more detailed poetic description of the
exodus. Earthquake and rainstorm characterize a theophany, but
the gift of rain (from the Lord, not from Baal) is a blessing for
the people in the desert, on their way to the promised land.
11–14. The allusions to victory, spoil, and triumph at the heights
of Zalmon (perhaps a mountain near Bashan, but unidentified,

despite Judg 9:48), suggest the period of the Judges, but the references are obscure. The *dove* seems to be a precious item of booty. **15–16.** *Mountain of Bashan:* these heights were east of the Sea of Galilee and are personified here as reacting with envy to the choice of Mount Zion for the dwelling of the Lord. **17–18.** When one recalls what it took for David to conquer Jerusalem (see 2 Sam 5:6–10), the description of the Lord conquering and taking his *high mount* is high exaggeration! **19–23.** A song in praise of God, the savior, describing a violent victory. *Shatter the heads:* a memory of war without swords; it was literally a case of bashing heads, the vital area. Even though the enemy takes to heights or depths, Bashan or sea, they shall not escape, and Israel will witness the vengeance, described in vivid metaphor (see Ps 58:10 and 1 Kgs 21:19). **24–27.** Perhaps this sudden shift to a procession *into the sanctuary* can be linked to vv. 17–18; it is not known why these specific tribes are mentioned. **28–31.** God's power is invoked against enemies, primarily Egypt, and tribute from the nations will be exacted. **32–35.** This hymnic conclusion invites even the *kingdoms of the earth,* to hear the *voice* (i.e., thunder) of the true cloud-rider (v. 4). The emphasis on the Lord's power and might stands against the background of the political impotence of Israel; but it took them some time to realize fully that they had nowhere else to turn but to the Lord. This psalm underscores that dependence.

Psalm 69. A lament of an individual. Along with Psalm 22, this is more frequently quoted in the NT than any other psalm; it can be regarded as a description of the exemplary suffering of an innocent person who relies upon God for deliverance—and is applicable, therefore, to the Son of Man. The structure is very loose: cries for help and descriptions of misery alternate through vv. 1–29. There is no way of knowing the precise situation. The psalmist is sick (vv. 26, 29) unto death (vv. 1–2 and 14–15), and persecuted by enemies as a thief (v. 4), and as one smitten by God (vv. 10–12 and 19–20). **1–2.** The *waters* and *mire* are taken up again in vv. 14–15; they are an indication of Sheol, the nonlife that has come over him. **4–5.** The question indicates how ill-founded the accusations of the enemies are: since one has not stolen, there is nothing one can restore. At the same time, the

psalmist relies on the Lord's true evaluation of personal fail-
ings. **6–11.** The Lord should intervene for the sake of those
whom the manner in which such exemplary conduct has been rewarded will scandalize. It is a suffering *for your sake* (see also v. 9),
which the psalm does not describe in any detail. No matter what
the sufferer does (vv. 10–11), he is a subject of ridicule (v. 11);
the elders who sit at the city *gate* passing judgment are unfair
(v. 12). **13.** *At an acceptable time:* better, "for the time of your
favor" (NAB v. 4). **14–15.** Cf. v. 2. **16–18.** The appeal is couched
in traditional language; see Ps 51:1 and the comment on Ps
10:11. **21.** While food and drink may refer to the practice of giving a meal to the unfortunate, the persecutors give gall and vine-
gar instead—perhaps merely symbols here? Cf. Mark 15:23 and
parallels. **21–28.** A series of imprecations against enemies, filled
with abundant metaphors. They offered food in v. 21; now let
their food (= *table*) become a *trap* for them and their *allies* (v. 22);
this is the talion law at work. They and their children (symbolized
by *tents,* in which their families reside) are to be wiped out. There
is to be no holding back about their guilt, which their wickedness
only increases. Finally, their names are to be erased from the *book*
of life, in which the Lord who governs all has inscribed the names
of the *righteous* (see Exod 32:32 and Isa 4:3). In contrast to
them is the suffering psalmist, who relies on *salvation* from the
Lord. **30–36.** In a turnaround characteristic of most laments, the
psalmist promises a *song,* preferable to any sacrifice. Verses 32–33
express this in essence: the lesson in which the *needy* (= ʿanawim)
will rejoice. **34–36.** Although the transition from individual to
group is not unusual, these lines have the appearance of an addition that aims at including the community; it would be particularly appropriate after the destruction of Jerusalem (587 B.C.E.),
or a similar crisis.

Psalm 70. A lament of an individual, almost identical to Ps
40:13–17. There is no consensus on the relationship between the
two. The description of the psalmist's distress is vague, and has to
be inferred from vv. 2–3. Verse 4 contains the equivalent of the
Muslim cry, "Allahu akbar." Some have argued that Psalm 70 was
supposed to be read with 71, which lacks a superscription.

Psalm 71. A lament of an individual. The so-called anthological style characterizes the composition. It is made up of several expressions borrowed from other psalms (see Pss 22:10–11 and 31:1–21). This is the prayer of a sick, persecuted person, now old (vv. 9 and 18), who in the past experienced the protection of God, but now despairs at the attack of *enemies* (vv. 10–13). However, most of the prayer is permeated with hope and trust, even to proclaiming God's "mighty deeds" (vv. 15–17). The structure is loose: vv. 1–8, a plea to be delivered from the power of the wicked, accompanied by expressions of trust and praise; vv. 9–16, a complaint about the enemy, the "accusers," concluding with a vow to praise God; vv. 17–24, renewal of the plea, with affirmations of trust and praise. Throughout the psalm request, confidence and motifs of trust, and praise fairly consistently alternate. It ends with the certainty that God has heard the request. **2.** *Righteousness:* a persistent term in this prayer (vv. 15–16, 19, and 24). **7.** *Portent:* an extraordinary sign, either a kind of warning or encouragement; here perhaps a sign to the enemies that God has abandoned the psalmist. Cf. their words in v. 11, and also Deut 28:46, where *mopet* indicates punishment. **12–13.** See Ps 70:2–3. **20.** *Depths of the earth:* Sheol; see Ps 30:3. The NRSV adds "watery" because of the Hebrew *tehom* (cf. Gen 1:2).

Psalm 72. A royal psalm, perhaps composed on the occasion of the coronation of a new king in Jerusalem. The king is a descendant of David (but not the "Solomon" to whom the superscription attributes the psalm), and the dynastic oracle of 2 Samuel 7 forms the basis for the high hopes held out for his rule: justice, peace, perpetual life, and worldwide rule. The divine promise justifies Israel's adoption of the typical court style of its more powerful neighbors. The king's reign is described in "messianic" language; the currently reigning king appears in the light of the national hopes for the dynasty (see the treatment of messianism on pp. 54–58 in the Introduction). The atmosphere of the prayer is not a declaration of fact as much as a wish that the king will fulfill this tableau. In fact, the tenses of the verbs are better translated as wishes (so NRSV and many other translations). Structure: vv. 1–4, a prayer that the king will exercise (divine) justice; vv. 5–7, and also enjoy a long and beneficent reign; vv. 8–11, and that this reign be worldwide; vv. 12–14, a description of royal concern for the poor; vv. 15–17, wishes that gather up anew what the psalm has said. **1.** The parallelism (*king's son*) indicates that the new "king" is of royal lineage and not a usurper. The gift requested is the very *justice* of God. This prayer is programmatic for the entire psalm; everything depends upon the basic *righteousness* (vv. 1, 2, and 7) of the king, which vv. 4 and 12–14 pointedly specify. **3.** For this kind of hyperbole, see Isa 32:15–20. **5–7.** While long life is a typical wish for anyone, the hyperbole is justified by the hopes in the Davidic dynasty. **6–7.** See vv. 2–3. **8.** The worldwide rule seems to extend from the Mediterranean Sea to the Persian Gulf, and from the Euphrates (*the River*) to the *ends of the earth*, perhaps the Mediterranean islands. **9.** See Mic 7:17 and Isa 49:23. **10.** *Tarshish:* see the comment on Ps 48:4–8. *Sheba and Seba:* regions in Arabia. **14b.** The Lord will not allow the blood of the poor and needy to be shed; they are *precious* to God, who will not let them be oppressed (cf. Ps 116:15). **17b.** There seems to be an allusion to Gen 12:3 and other passages that describe Abraham as a source of blessing for all nations. **18–19.** The second book of Psalms ends with a doxology similar to Ps 41:13; v. 20 probably indicates the close of a collection of Davidic psalms (Pss 51–70).

Psalm 73. A thanksgiving psalm, opening the Asaph collection (Pss 73–83; plus 50); Ezra 2:41 mentions Asaph as an ancestor of Temple singers. The genre is thanksgiving, although the poem picks up on a wisdom theme, the problem of retribution (see also Pss 37 and 49). The work describes a personal crisis, but only after stating the conclusion about God's goodness (v. 1, and in greater detail, vv. 23–27, which ends in an avowal of thanksgiving, v. 28). Structure: vv. 1–3, introduction; vv. 4–12, a description of the conduct of the wicked; vv. 13–17, the doubts of the psalmist; vv. 18–20, the fate of the wicked; vv. 21–28, the fate of the psalmist. **1.** This verse is a conclusion that the psalmist reached only after much trial. Although the MT and the ancient versions read "Israel" (*lysr'l*), many scholars prefer the emendation *to the upright (lysr 'l)*, as in the NRSV. **2–3.** Envy of the wicked nearly led to a loss of faith. This was obviously a real problem in Israel; see the warnings in Ps 37:1, 7; and also Prov 23:17, and Ps 49. **4–12.** Although the text is unsteady, especially vv. 7, 10, the description of the wicked focuses upon their wickedness and their self-satisfaction, which apparently prompt them to *oppression* of others. Verse 9 pictures them with mouths huge enough to consume heaven and earth. **10–11.** According to the NRSV they gain the favor of the people, even though they blaspheme. For similar quotations of the wicked, see Ps 10:4, 6, 11, and 13. **13b.** A reference to the liturgical act of purification (Ps 26:6). But it is in vain since hardly a day goes by without what is considered a punishment from God (v. 14). **15–20.** Realizing the implications of these thoughts, the psalmist goes to the sanctuary to ponder their *end* (lit., their "after"). But the description of their fate in vv. 18–20 contains nothing new; it is the traditional destiny of the wicked. Perhaps there is a true conviction that the wicked will be somehow punished. **21–22.** These words are best taken as indicating the stupidity of not recognizing the truth of claims that the following verses, 23–28, enunciate. The comparison to a *beast* is reminiscent of Ps 49:12, 20 (see the comment on that psalm). **23–28.** One of the most remarkable passages in the Bible. The author has an insight into the lot of the just: companionship with God. Verse 23 indicates a lively sense of the presence of God in life. What is the result of reliance on divine guidance (v. 24b)? Lit., "after, glory, you take me." The "with honor" of NRSV is vague, even ambiguous; *kabod* can also mean "glory." Does the Hebrew text intend a deliberate ambiguity? Many interpreters understand this verse to mean that the psalmist is referring to the Lord's deliverance of him from the quandary (vv. 1–2) or the "punishment" (v. 14). Others think that the insight is a breakthrough, that the poet somehow sees a continuing union (beyond death) with God in this and in the following verses. See also the discussion in the comment on Ps 49. If this psalm does show a breakthrough on the idea of life with God after death, it was not picked up in the biblical tradition until late. And even if there is no breakthrough on this score, the intensity of the description of union with God remains noteworthy. The question is not settled by adverbs like *continually* or *forever* (vv. 23, 26); these merely indicate indefinite duration. **25.** *In heaven:* not in a "theological" sense; it means what is above, physical space, in contrast to *earth*. For the writer, in all God's creation, only God is at the center. **26.** This repeats the previous verse from another point of view; the meaning is: "alive or dead," one must rely on God. This attitude is not far from Rom 14:7–8. **27–28.** Everything comes down to nearness to God, that is, living with a sense of the Lord's presence (whether in this life or the next is not the issue, for all is gift, not reward).

Psalm 74. A lament of the community, on the occasion of a destruction of the Temple (perhaps in 587 B.C.E.?). Structure: vv. 1–11, a complaint and description of the dire situation; vv. 12–17, a hymn praising God's creative power; vv. 18–23, a second appeal to God. After the initial "why?" (repeated also in v. 11), are two lengthy appeals to "remember" (vv. 2, 18). They are separated by the creation hymn, which itself serves to remind the Lord of the divine power that should work in Israel's favor. **1–3.** Highly evocative language reminds the Lord of past involvement with this people and with Zion, the divine dwelling place—all with an aim of inducing God to intervene. **4–11.** The fiery tone is matched by the vivid description of the desecration of the Temple. How can the Lord tolerate such actions? **9.** *Emblems:* a play on the mention of the banners of the enemies in v. 4. The verse means that there are neither "signs" from God, nor any kind of message, for the prophets are mute. **12–17.** How does this creation hymn fit into the sad lament? Implicitly, it asks for a display of the awesome power of the Lord in creation, which is also described as *salvation* (v. 12). The presentation is in terms of the mythical primordial battle between the Lord and chaos (represented by *Yam,* or *sea,* and the *dragons,* and the *heads of Leviathan;* cf. Isa 27:1; Ps 104:26). See the treatment of creation in the Introduction (pp. 40–44). There can be no question about the divine power, but will God put it to work? **18–23.** The Lord is called upon to *remember* (as in v. 2). This is far from being a mental exercise, despite the *do not forget* repeated twice (vv. 19 and 23). Saving action is necessary. The treatment of Israel is portrayed as an insult to the divine *name* and a bad reflection on the *covenant.* Even the plight of the *poor and needy* receives attention. There is no gentle ending to this psalm, as v. 23 testifies.

Psalm 75. The classification is uncertain; the opening suggests thanksgiving. Both the community and an individual speak praise, and a solo voice delivers an oracle of judgment. Structure: v. 1, introductory thanksgiving; vv. 2–5, an oracle of judgment; vv. 6–8, a warning that judgment is coming for the wicked; v. 9, a solo voice praising God; v. 10, an oracle against the wicked. **1.** The community speaks. *Your name is near* is peculiar; some ancient versions speak of invoking the name. The *wondrous deeds* usually refer to the marvels of the exodus story (e.g., Exod 3:20), or less often to a personal deliverance, as in Ps 26:7; at issue here are just judgments upon proud malefactors. **2–5.** The *I* who speaks is certainly the Lord. At a chosen *time* God will proclaim judgment, an action that relates to dominion over the world (see Ps 46:2, 6, 10). The addressees are unspecified except for their proud, boastful attitude. *Horn:* a common symbol for strength (Ps 18:2). **6–9.** NRSV understands this as a warning uttered by the speaker of v. 9. The geographical references in v. 6 indicate where the true source of *lifting up* exists (vv. 4–5). And God is the one *putting down* as well, for in the divine hand is the devastating *cup* of wine that ultimately destroys anyone who drinks of it. This is a frequent metaphor for the wrath of God (e.g., Isa 51:17–23). It is *well mixed,* i.e., heavily spiced and potent. **9.** The reaction of praise is obviously uttered by a (representative?) member of the community, but the speaker of the final verse must be God, since it echoes vv. 4–5.

Psalm 76. A hymn of praise, or song of Zion (cf. Pss 46 and 48). Structure: vv. 1–3, an acknowledgement of the Lord's protective dwelling in Zion; vv. 4–10, an address to God, in praise of the victory achieved and the judgment rendered; vv. 11–12, encouragement to fulfill vows to this fearsome Lord. It is not possible to associate the song with a particular incident. The atmosphere of fear and awe dominates in vv. 7–8 and 11–12. **2.** *Salem:* an older name of Jerusalem (Gen 14:18). **3.** See Ps 46:9 for the motif of the divine breaking of weapons; this suggests that the victory is the Lord's alone. This and the following verses are more a generalization about the inviolability of Zion than a reference to a particular battle. **4–6.** Addressing the *God of Jacob* directly, the verse implies that the army opposing Zion is rendered impotent by the all-powerful *rebuke,* the same rebuke administered to the waters of the deep (Ps 104:7) or the waters of *sea* (Isa 50:2). Their *sleep* is not the sleep of death, but torpor and daze; they are silent before the awesome (vv. 7 and 11). **7–9.** The emphasis shifts from war to *judgment,* and across the entire world, as the Lord intends the salvation of the *'anawim,* or the poor. **10.** Any translation/interpretation of this verse is very doubtful. **11–12.** An order is given to fulfill vows of thanksgiving to this *awesome* God.

Psalm 77. A lament of an individual, followed by praise of God. There is a rather vague and unusual topic for a lament: the change of the *right hand of the Most High.* Structure: vv. 1–10, the lament; vv. 11–12, transition to the song of praise; vv. 13–20, a hymn recalling ancient memories. **1–9.** An elaborate description of anguish, night and day. Just the thought of God keeps the psalmist awake, but the mood is tantalizing. Although the psalmist begins with an outcry (v. 1), no request to be delivered follows. The consideration of *days of old* (v. 5) touches off a series of tormenting questions (vv. 7–9). This questioning remains in the realm of theory: what has happened to the love and mercy of God? Does the old confession of Exod 34:6 hold true any more? But the reader still does not know the actual cause of the great sorrow. **10.** Finally the reason for the depression is revealed, but then only in an oblique way, because one has to catch the nuance of the *right hand,* which hearkens back to the exodus memories in the Song of Moses (Exod 15:6, 12). Apparently the grief has been caused by a current disaster, although this is never spelled out. **11–12.** In response to this crisis, the psalmist recalls the past with all its *wonders* and *mighty deeds* of God. It is almost as if he wills a return of the "right hand" by reciting the hymn that follows. **13.** The holiness of God's *way* is not meant in an ethical sense; God is different, mysterious, and hence incomparable (v. 13b; cf. Exod 15:11). **15.** The metaphor of the right hand has been changed to the *arm* (NRSV adds "strong") of Exod 15:16. **16–20.** The text describes the passage through the Red Sea in terms of a victory over the primordial waters by the God of thunder and lightning, who comes *through the sea* (cf. Hab 3:15) without even leaving a trace. The ending is abrupt; no effort is made to connect it with the initial depression. It is as though a master poet caught the depressed mood of the people and sought to change it with this poem.

Psalm 78. A historical psalm (Pss 105 and 106) in hymn style, that suggests wisdom influence (vv. 1–4; 5–8). This is history, not in the sense of a relating of dry facts, but a rehearsal for a didactic purpose, reminding the people of how their past impinges on the present, if they will but listen. In a broad sense, the structure consists of an introduction, vv. 1–8, and the historical summary from the Exodus to the time of David (vv. 9–72). The historical summary breaks down further: vv. 12–31, guidance on the journey from Egypt through the wilderness; vv. 32–58, the story of rebellion, despite the memory of the plagues; vv. 59–72, disaster in the promised land, along with the Lord's response with the choice of Zion and David. There is a delicate mix of pedagogy and history as the writer chronicles the continual infidelity and disobedience of Israel, which is matched by the continual forgiving response of the Lord who punishes but also saves. This yields a certain pattern to the historical events: the divine intervention, then the rebellion of the people, followed by punishment. A refrainlike quality appears in the observations of Israel's failures introduced at vv. 17, 32, 40, and 56. **1–2.** The opening is in typical wisdom style (cf. Ps 49:1–4; Prov 3:1; 5:1). **5.** For reference to the continuous tradition, see Exod 10:2; Deut 4:9 and 32:7. The emphasis on handing the tradition on to future generations is exemplified by the existence of such a psalm as this. **7.** Remembering and forgetting are woven into the presentation (see vv. 11, 35, and 39). **9.** The reference to Ephraim is sudden and puzzling. It was the most important tribe in the north, and it is singled out in v. 67 as the tribe that the Lord did *not* choose. It is not clear why it merits first mention (vv. 9–11) in the history that really begins at v. 12. *The day of battle:* the reference is not known. These verses reflect the prejudice of the Judeans against the Northern Kingdom. **12.** *Zoan:* identified with Tanis, the Hyksos capital in the Nile delta, which is not mentioned in the Exodus narrative. **13–16.** A litany of the familiar wonders associated with the crossing of the Red Sea and the traversing of the desert: waters, cloud/light, and drinking water. **17–20.** A dramatic presentation of one of several instances of rebellion in the desert

(Exod 16:1–3; Num 11:4–6). **21–31.** See Num 11:4–13, 31–34. The overgenerous supply of quail and manna is presented as a punishment from an angry Lord. **23.** *Yet:* read "so." **24–25.** The familiar expression, *bread of angels,* appears again in Wis 16:20. The MT reads literally "bread of mighty ones" (cf. Ps 103:20). Note the contrast between mortals and "angels." **26–29.** The dramatic presentation continues in the Lord's disposition of nature to ensure the food. **30–31.** Then, very dramatically, with the *food still in their mouths,* death strikes, even the *strongest of them,* the *flower of Israel.* **32–33.** In response to Israel's obstinacy, the Lord has them die in futility and suddenly (such is the meaning of v. 32, *pace* NRSV*).* **35–39.** The "remembering" on Israel's part was insincere. Nonetheless the Lord was merciful and *remembered* (v. 39) that they were only *flesh,* another symbol of human transience (cf. Ps 103:14–16). **40–41.** An impatient exclamation over Israel's "testing," a frequent theme (see also vv. 18, 56). **42–51.** Again, remembrance (v. 42). The psalmist jogs Israel's memory by recalling the plagues *(signs, miracles)* in the following order, which differs from that in Exodus (in parentheses): water into blood (1), *flies* (4), *frogs* (2), *locusts* (8), *hail* (7), *cattle* disease (5). Verses 49–50 personify the plagues *(destroying angels)* to express the divine *anger.* **51.** The climax is the tenth plague of the book of Exodus, but it is only the last of seven in the psalm. *Ham,* as the parallelism indicates, is another designation of Egypt (cf. Gen 5:32; 10:6). Obviously, there is no concern to be exact in the various versions of the plagues, as Ps 105:28–36 also shows. **52–55.** A description of the Lord's solicitous guidance in a brief summary, ending with Zion *(holy hill),* as also in Exod 15:17. **56–72.** The final perspective extends from Shiloh (v. 60) to David, and it is prepared for by Israel's infidelities. **57.** A *treacherous bow* is one that is literally slack, and hence ineffectual. **58.** *High places:* originally traditional sites of worship, which came to receive condemnation especially in Deuteronomistic theology and in the prophets (the Deuteronomistic history is the name scholars give to the fairly unified material from Deuteronomy through 2 Kings). 60–61. The reference is to the Philistine conquest of the Ark, and the end of the *tent* (a building of some kind) at Shiloh. **63–64.** Once again, hyperbolic expressions of extreme grief over the events described in 1 Samuel 4.

65. These are bold metaphors to express the Lord's decision, especially the shaking off of the effects of *wine.* **66.** Most versions agree with the polite and correct translation of the NRSV, but the Vulgate expresses more colorfully the reference to hemorrhoids *(in posteriora)* mentioned in 1 Sam 5:6, 12. **67–68.** The Lord chooses Zion/Judah for a dwelling place, over against Ephraim (see v. 9). **69.** The comparison of the Temple is unique; the metaphors indicate height and solidity. **70–72.** The Lord chooses a shepherd to shepherd his heritage (not *inheritance;* cf. v. 62). This "historical" psalm illustrates not only sad pages in Israel's history but also the perpetual struggle between divine mercy and wrath. This "inner" life of God is similarly portrayed in the famous lines of Hos 11:1–9.

Psalm 79. A lament of the community (cf. Ps 74) over some unnamed disaster. The description of the defilement of the Temple indicated in v. 1 suggests the year 587 B.C.E., if it is not an exaggeration. It is hardly as late as the Maccabean period, for which it nevertheless remained relevant; 1 Macc 7:17 takes up the highly charged language of vv. 2–3. Characteristic of this psalm is the emphasis on the Lord's involvement. The divine honor is at stake (cf. vv. 9, 10, and 12). It is almost as if Jerusalem's tragedy is the concern of God, and not of the people. While one can readily sympathize and even identify with the author, caution is necessary today. The "kingdoms that do not call on your name" (v. 6) cannot be dismissed so easily. Structure: vv. 1–4, the complaint; vv. 5–10, several pleas with reasons the Lord should intervene; vv. 11–13, final plea and vow to give thanks. **3.** Lack of burial was felt to be a terrible plight (cf. Deut 28:26). **4.** *Taunt:* this motif crops up again in vv. 10 and 12. **5.** The question echoes Ps 13:1. **6.** The *nations* are not specified, but clearly they, not Israel, should be the object of divine wrath. **8–10.** While it is not denied that the tragedy is due to *sins,* more is at stake: the glory of the divine *name* (Ps 74:18). God must act. *Where is their God?:* a stereotypical taunt, to move the Lord to intervene (Pss 42:3, 10 and 115:2). *Outpoured blood:* the choice of language is again deliberate and provocative. **11.** *Prisoners:* this is another motif. The iconography of the ancient Near East often depicts captives being led off by victors. They are indeed *doomed,* literally "sons of death" (also in Ps 102:20). **12.** *Bosom:* the expression derives from the ample folds of the outer garment that served as a receptacle, and hence an appropriate metaphor for full punishment.

Psalm 80. A lament of the community. The occasion and date cannot be determined, despite the references to Ephraim and Manasseh (the Northern Kingdom?) in v. 2. Note the refrains in vv. 3, 7, and 19, which echo the Aaronic blessing in Num 6:25. Structure: vv. 1–3, a cry for help; vv. 4–6, description of the present dire situation; vv. 8–13, a question asking why God has abandoned the care for the vineyard; vv. 14–18, a renewed appeal for concern for the vineyard. **1.** *Shepherd:* see Gen 48:15; 49:24; and Ps 77:20. The Lord was conceived of as invisibly *enthroned upon the cherubim,* the mythical winged figures, half-human and half-animal, associated with the Ark as protective genii. **5.** *Bread of tears:* a pregnant phrase; weeping is as frequent as eating (cf. Ps 102:9 and also Job 3:24, where Job's "sighing" is his "bread"). **8.** *Vine:* a frequent figure for Israel (cf. Hos 10:1; Isa 5:1–7; 27:2–6; and Ezek 17). **10.** *Mighty cedars:* lit., "cedars of God," giant trees that, like "mountains of God" (Ps 36:6) are exclusively the work of God, so superlative are they. **11.** A hyperbolic description of the extent of the vine; see the comment on Ps 72:8. **15–16.** Uncertain translation; see NRSV footnote. **17b.** *The one whom:* lit., the "son of man whom," can refer to Israel, or to the reigning king who sits at the "right hand" (Ps 110:1). The phrase "son of man" itself means a human being ("mortal"), and is frequent in Ezekiel.

Psalm 81. The genre is not clear. The poem calls for and describes a liturgical celebration in which the word of God is proclaimed. Structure: vv. 1–5b, a hymnic introduction; vv. 5c–16, an oracle delivered in the name of the Lord, perhaps by a prophet. For other examples of oracles, see Pss 12:5; 32:8–9; and 50:7–15, 16–23. **2–3.** Musical accompaniment is customary (Ps 150:3–5). **5c.** Literally this reads: "I heard a tongue [language] that I did not know." It emphasizes that what follows is not the word of the speaker, but an introduction to what is clearly a divine statement. **6–8.** There are references to a series of events: freedom from slavery (the *basket* is for carrying the clay bricks in

Egypt), and the *secret place of thunder* (perhaps Sinai; cf. Exod 19:16–19). For Meribah, see Num 20:2–13, and for testing, Exod 17:7. The recollection of these saving actions of God prepares for the command that follows. **9–10.** The basic commandment (Exod 20:2–3) is repeated and justified on the basis of God's generosity. **11–15.** Because Israel would not *listen,* God left them on their own. But would that they might *listen,* and thus find their enemies defeated. **16.** Israel's reward for fidelity is symbolized by the choice *wheat* (Ps 147:14) and the hyperbolic honey from the rock, as in Deut 32:13.

Psalm 82. The genre is again not clear; the poem presents a judgment scene in the heavenly court, where God arraigns *'elohim,* gods or *elohim*-beings, and condemns them to death because of their injustice and abuse of power. See the discussion of monotheism in the Introduction (pp. 32–33), as well as the parallel situation in Psalm 58, which also blames injustice in this world on the members of the heavenly court. Structure: v. 1, here comes the judge; vv. 2–4, God accuses the "gods" of unjust activities; v. 5, a reflection about the effects of injustice on earth; vv. 6–7, the sentence to death; v. 8, plea of the psalmist that the Lord rise to judgment on the earth. **1–4.** The implication is that the "gods" have failed to live up to their task of exercising judgment. Specifically, they are guilty of *partiality,* abusing their power and oppressing those classes most in need of just treatment. Lit., they "lift up the face" of (v. 2b, *show partiality to*) the wicked **5.** This can be attributed to God or the psalmist. The connection between injustice and the physical world also appears in Pss 75:3–4; 96:10; Isa 24:1–6; and Amos 1:2. **6.** They are gods, sons of Elyon *(the Most High);* they are the heavenly beings whom God assigned to the nations, according to Deut 32:8–9. **7.** The sentence is death— to die like any mortal—a terrible judgment since immortality belonged to the divine sphere. The motif of the fall of the gods (cf. also Ezek 28:17 and Isa 14:15) derives from ancient mythology. The use of this text in John 10:34 is conditioned by the contemporary understanding of Jesus' audience. It is possible that another level of meaning was reached, namely that the "gods" are really human judges. Judgment is God's prerogative (Deut 1:17; cf. Exod 21:6). **8.** The appeal is for the Lord to take charge of things, since everything *(all the nations)* comes under divine control. This unusual psalm opens up a new vista on reality, and on the modern world. It seems to presuppose that a profound unity exists between justice and the world as we know it, between the exercise of (judicial) power and the justice of God.

Psalm 83. A lament of the community. Despite the mention of the nations in vv. 6–8, the specific setting of the psalm escapes us. Indeed, the union of all these peoples on one occasion is hardly possible. They may represent a programmatic statement of general conspiracy. The mention of Assyria could point to the ninth–seventh centuries, and the absence of Babylon could suggest a date before 612 B.C.E. (the fall of Nineveh, capital of Assyria). Structure: vv. 2–8, a cry for help against the machinations of hostile nations; vv. 9–18, a request for God to destroy them, as he did Israel's enemies in the past. **1–5.** As in Psalm 79, the stakes are high and the Lord must intervene *(your people; against you)*. The quotations in vv. 4 and 12 make the appeal all the more dramatic, comparable to Ps 79:10, "Where is their God?" **6–8.** These ten peoples were neighbors, and most of them often hostile to Israel, but as a unit they never attacked Israel. The *children of Lot* has a pejorative nuance (cf. Gen 19:36–38 and Deut 2:8–22); as Moab and Edom, they have already been mentioned in v. 6. **9–12.** These early victories, detailed in Judges 4–8, were high points to which Israel looked back, e.g., "the day of Midian" in Isa 9:4. Only Endor is unusual, but its site near Taanach according to Josh 17:11 would indicate some connection with the battle against the Canaanite kings of Judg 5:19. **12.** *Our own possession:* the nuance to the phrase is that they aim to undo Israel's initial "possession" of Canaan; see the use of "occupy" in Deut 12:1 to indicate the possession of the land. **13–18.** The imprecations are couched in traditional metaphors of destruction, *chaff, fire, tempest.* **16.** This verse does not imply any letup in the treatment of the enemies. Verse 16b is to be understood, not as a statement of purpose (so NRSV), but as a result clause; the enemies will finally be forced to acknowledge the Lord as Elyon, the *Most High* (v. 18). The result will be an admission (there is no god like *YHWH*), not conversion or assimilation. **17.** *Forever:* as so often, this does not designate infinite time, but indefinite duration; in context, it is one element

in the hyperbolic description of the punishing blows to be visited
upon the enemy.

Psalm 84. A hymn in praise of the Temple, a song of Zion.
It is most likely a song of pilgrims approaching and entering Zion
and/or the Temple—in the style of the *Songs of Ascents,* Psalms
120–34. Structure: vv. 2–4, an ardent desire for presence in the
Temple; vv. 5–7, the joys of those who make the pilgrimage;
vv. 8–9, a prayer for the king; vv. 10–12, the joy and blessings
coming from the Lord and the Temple. **2–4.** The intensity expressed in these lines matches that of other psalms: Ps 27:4–5
(beauty); 42:1–2 (the thirst of a deer); 63:1–3 (thirst, love better
than life). **3.** Birds nesting, perhaps in the Temple area, become a
symbol of the security enjoyed by those who are also around the
altars. **4.** The poet expresses a gentle envy of the priests and Levites
who have special rooms and functions in the Temple. **5–7.** The
text has some obscurities. The *valley of Baca* remains unidentified. Perhaps this is a description of a pilgrimage, where the arid
valley becomes a spring, thanks to the poet's imagination and to
the *early rain.* For the theme of water in the desert during the new
exodus envisioned by Deutero-Isaiah, see Isa 35:1–10; 41:18–20.
7. The NRSV provides the traditional translation in 7a, with the
meaning, "increasing in strength." The Hebrew is ambiguous and
modern translations differ. In 7b NRSV adopts the reading of the
MT, which softens the verb, *will be seen;* actually the text indicates
that the pilgrims *see* God. **8–9.** The prayer for the king *(your
anointed)* is unexpected, suggesting a preexilic date. He is called a
shield (cf. Pss 47:9 and 89:18) as the protector of the people and
the channel of divine power and blessings. **10.** *Elsewhere* is added
for the sense; see the "one thing" asked for in Ps 27:4. The rest of
the comparison contrasts outside (at the threshold like a *door-
keeper)* with inside *(tents).* The mention of *wickedness* (or, the
wicked) is surprising, but it can underline the fact that only the
faithful will enjoy such intimacy with God, as vv. 11–12 indicate. **11.** Nowhere else does the OT explicitly call God *sun,* but
there is an association with the sun in Isa 60:19–20. This psalm
testifies to the lively sense of proximity to the Lord that the
Temple represented for the Israelites. The comment on vv. 2–4
indicates both the frequency and power of this theme. The final

verse addresses God, proclaiming the happiness of everyone *who trusts in you,* namely these pilgrims. The appreciation of the religious meaning of pilgrimage is familiar to early and medieval Christianity, but less so in the modern era. One should recall that three important pilgrimage feasts emerged in Israel: Unleavened Bread/Passover, the harvest feast or Feast of Weeks *(Shabu'ot),* and Tabernacles/Tents *(Sukkot).*

Psalm 85. A lament of the community, to which a divine oracle is given as an answer. The situation and date cannot be determined absolutely, but it is clear that the people are suffering grievously. Structure: vv. 1–3, see the comment below; vv. 4–7, a prayer for restoration, for salvation; vv. 8–13, an oracle of salvation. **2–4.** These lines have been interpreted as a reference to a past event (more probable), such as the restoration from exile, or to a future deliverance (verbs in the prophetic perfect), or against the background of a liturgical re-presentation (verbs representing confidence). **7.** Several key terms begin to appear: salvation and steadfast love, along with faithfulness and righteousness (vv. 10–11). **8–9.** The psalmist awaits a prophetic oracle (cf. Ps 81:6), which v. 8 confidently summarizes as "shalom," or *peace.* **10–11.** These verses have an oracular air. Prime qualities of the Lord are boldly personified (cf. the personifications in Isa 58:8 and 59:14–15). The image of the *kiss* continues somewhat in the meeting of *ground* and *sky* (see Ps 36:5–6 for the reach of righteousness and fidelity). **12.** The ground mentioned in the previous verse is now pictured as producing the fruits of the earth. **13.** The personification is striking because it has the divine *righteousness* in front of the Lord creating a path, almost like a light; contrast Ps 43:3, where the psalmist asks for the divine light and faithfulness as a personal guide.

Psalm 86. A lament of an individual. It provides very few specific indications of distress. Indeed, the poem resembles a collage in that it alludes to many other psalms, as will be indicated. Because of this, the structure is loose: vv. 1–7, renewed appeals to the Lord for help; vv. 8–10, a short hymn in praise of the incomparable Lord; vv. 11–13, a request and thanksgiving; vv. 14–17, confident prayers for help, not unlike the spirit of vv. 1–7. **1.** A plea to God is repeated almost endlessly in this psalm. The phrase, *poor and needy ('ani we'ebyon)* is frequent (e.g., Ps 35:10), and it is intended to strike a chord with a *good and forgiving* (v. 5) God. **2.** *Preserve my life:* a repetition of Ps 25:20a. *You are my God:* the statement is not as flat as it sounds; the cry, "my God," has the nuance of intimacy and appeal in the Psalter. *O Lord:* this is not the sacred name, but the substitute, Adonai, which unaccountably occurs in vv. 4, 5, 8, 9, 12, and 15. Hence the NRSV and other versions properly do not print it in small caps, which is reserved for *YHWH.* **4b.** Repeated also in Pss 25:1; 143:8. **5.** The verse recalls traditional attributes (cf. also v. 15). **6.** Compare Ps 5:1–2. **7.** Cf. Ps 17:6. **8–10.** The divine incomparability is a familiar theme (e.g., Exod 15:11), and v. 10b is an indication of the way in which it came to be understood. With the uniqueness of God comes the submission of *all the nations.* **11.** The request to be taught the Lord's *way* echoes Ps 25:4, 8, and 12. *In your truth:* not abstract truth, but obedience in fidelity to the covenant, an *undivided heart.* **12–14.** Verse 12 looks like a vow of thanksgiving, in view of the deliverance that is affirmed in v. 13. But the transition from v. 13 to v. 14 is difficult unless the verbs are understood as timeless perfects (confidence). **15.** An old credal formula is expressed here and in many other places (see Exod 34:6 and Ps 103:8). **16.** The request repeats v. 3 in part. The child of a *serving girl* is one who is born in the master's house and belongs to the master (Exod 21:2–4). Hence the term connotes total devotion. **17.** The request for a *sign* is in harmony with v. 16, but the reason given in the last line is again a rough transition; has help already been given? The frequency of the repetitions from other biblical verses may be an indication that one should not expect an ordered sequence of ideas. The peculiar attraction of this psalm is the obvious prayerlike quality of almost every verse, which makes the psalm a veritable collage of short conversations with God.

Psalm 87. A hymn, or song of Zion. The text is difficult in places, and many changes have been suggested. However, the NRSV captures the main ideas: (1) the Lord has chosen Zion; and (2) the city of God is the honorific "birthplace" of all Jews in the Diaspora. Structure: vv. 1–3, the preeminence of Zion because of the Lord's love; vv. 4–6, a list of those who can claim citizenship

or even birth in Jerusalem; v. 7, conclusion. **1.** The choice of
Zion is central to OT belief, and celebrated frequently (e.g., Ps
132:13–17). *Glorious things* are exemplified by Psalms 46 and
48. **4–5.** These lines seem to be spoken by God (or the personified Zion?). It is significant that the nations are those who were
typically the enemies of Israel, especially Egypt, Babylon, and
Philistia. *Rahab:* not the monster of Job 26:12, but another name
for Egypt (Isa 30:7). The entire Fertile Crescent is targeted in v. 4.
While it certainly refers to Diaspora Jews, the text is also open-
ended so as to embrace the entire world. The Lord is consistently
mentioned as the Lord of all, and the one true God who controls
the nations. But we have no real grasp of this universality. Does it
mean that the nations are, or will be, subject to the Lord—that
they in some way acknowledge God, either in the present or in
the future? Even the so-called "God-fearers" (proselytes) in the
Diaspora observed only certain features of Jewish life; they were
not truly "converts." The great vision of Isa 2:2–4 envisions the
nations streaming to Jerusalem to learn the Lord's ways. But is
this the same as the birthright envisioned in this psalm? See also
Ps 86:9, and the comment on 83:16. Note the threefold repetition
"was born there" (vv. 4, 5, and 6). **6.** The Lord is represented as a
heavenly census taker (cf. also Ps 139:16). **7.** Presumably this is a
description of a celebration in Jerusalem, where singers are at
work (there is no verb in the MT). Literally, "all my water
sources" (roots? home?) are in *you* (= Zion). The modern taste
for discovering one's roots finds an analogy in the vivid poetry
here; there is also a recognition of a bond of unity greater than
mere physical accident: where is one's true home?

Psalm 88. A lament of an individual in the greatest distress,
perhaps mortally sick, although the formulaic language would be
suitable for any affliction. It is a stark picture of abandonment by
friends, and, apparently, by God. Structure: vv. 1–2, an appeal to
the "God of my salvation"; vv. 3–12, a description of suffering,
with reference to the motif of Sheol; vv. 13–18, renewal of
plea and complaint. **1–2.** *God of my salvation:* in view of the despairing mood of the psalm, this phrase should be kept in
mind. **3–7.** Sheol and Pit are equivalent notions, and they are
conceived as dynamic powers that pursue and ultimately conquer

mere mortals (cf. Ps. 30:3). They represent nonlife, the distress that afflicts the psalmist. The description remains general, and the reader cannot specify the trouble; for the divine *waves* see vv. 16–17 and Ps 42:7. **10–12.** The *shades* (whoever is in Sheol) are no longer in loving contact with the Lord and so cannot praise him. This motif frequently serves to move God to pity (see the discussion of Sheol on pp. 34–36 in the Introduction). **14.** "Hiding the face" is another frequent idiom expressing divine unconcern or even wrath (see the comment on Ps 10:11). **17.** The watery images of the Pit and the waves of v. 7 are picked up in the *flood.* **18.** It is remarkable that the prayer ends on this foreboding note of *darkness* (cf. also vv. 6 and 12). This psalm is generally regarded as the most "pessimistic," perhaps unfairly. It is grim, but not despairing, as v. 1 indicates, and twice more the psalmist cries out to God (vv. 9 and 13). That very fact is significant; even in the direst straits one may appeal to Lord.

Psalm 89. This is a lament (vv. 38–52), and a very artfully constructed one. It has hymnic qualities from the very outset, praising the creator (vv. 5–18) and rehearsing the oracle concerning the Davidic dynasty (vv. 19–37). The author, doubtless speaking for the community, dwells on the steadfast love and faithfulness in the very first verse, and repeats one or both terms in vv. 5, 8, 14, 24, 28, and 33, so that the final agonizing appearance in v. 49 appears climactic. Structure: vv. 1–4, introduction, praising God, especially for the Davidic covenant; vv. 5–18, a hymn to the power of God, manifested in the work of creation; vv. 19–37, a rehearsal of the oracle concerning David and his dynasty; vv. 38–51, a complaint accusing God of failing in the covenant promise. The occasion of this moving psalm cannot be determined exactly; it could fit into several historical periods (e.g., the death of Josiah in 609 B.C.E. or the fall of Jerusalem in 587); v. 52, final blessing. **1–4.** The introduction sets the tone and states the topic: God's (acts of) love *(hesed)* and fidelity *('emunah)* as reflected in the Davidic covenant. **5–8.** These lines lead into the creation hymn by celebrating the incomparability of the Lord (Ps 86:8) and the reverence that the holy ones, members of the heavenly court (cf. Ps 82), show him. **9–10.** For the mythological allusions, see the discussion of creation in the Introduction (pp. 40–44) and the comment on Ps 74:12–17. Like Leviathan (Ps 104:26), *Rahab* is a monster personifying the powers of chaos (in contrast to Ps 87:4). **11–13.** In view of the final complaint, the poet takes pains to exalt the divine power, which even mountains like Tabor and the fabled Hermon acknowledge. **14.** Line *a* is found again in Ps 97:2. The attributes in line *b* are personifications (Ps 85:13). **15.** *Festal shout:* the Hebrew term is associated with acclamation and procession (of the Ark; 2 Sam 6:15). **17–18.** The power (= *horn*) of the people is rooted in the Lord (vv. 11–13), and shown in the *king* (= *shield,* as in Ps 84:9). **19–37.** Following the hymn is an expanded version of 2 Samuel 7. **19.** The promise to Nathan is described as spoken in a *vision to your faithful one* (Nathan), and the psalm develops this theme all the way down to v. 37. It highlights royal prerogatives that are assured by the Lord: anointing (v. 20), protection (v. 21), victory over his foes (vv. 22–25), adoptive sonship (vv. 26–27), personal and dynastic security (vv. 28–37). Verses 28–37 present the covenant with David (like the covenant with Abraham) as unconditional. Individual kings may be punished, but the dynasty will go on (cf. 2 Sam 7:14–16). However, this covenant is conditional in the understanding of 1 Kgs 6:12 and Ps 132:12, which demand observance of the divine covenant by the kings if their sons are to sit on the throne. Differing views appear to have existed concerning the interpretation of the oracle of Nathan. **39–45.** The complaint begins with a strong "and [= but] you." The Lord is accused of having renounced the *covenant* with David; the proof is a disastrous war, as all the metaphors in vv. 40–43 indicate. The most dramatic touch is the ending, the hurling of the *throne,* and cutting short *the days of his youth* (death?). As with much of the language in complaint, it is not legitimate to take these outrages as specific historical data. That is why one cannot specify the setting of this psalm. **46–51.** The personal agony of the poet finds expression in traditional motifs (*how long. . . ?* as in Ps 13:1–2). However, the mention of a short life and the threat of Sheol seem out of tune with the general tone of the complaint. Verses 49–51 are more in character, especially the mention of the commitment to *steadfast love* and *faithfulness,* on which the Lord has reneged. **52.** A doxology completes the third book of Psalms (cf. 41:13; 72:18–19). This psalm is rich in creation theology and messianic imagery, but it is particularly intriguing in the way in which it confronts the Lord with a *fait accompli* and introduces the issue of divine responsibility.

Psalm 90. While the genre of the poem seems to be a community lament, only v. 13 explicitly sounds that note. The entire poem has more of a meditative, tentative character, which is unusual in the Psalter. Although a community speaks, it seems clear that the composition is the careful work of a single poet who is sharing ideas with all. In the past the work has been considered as a composite of two separate psalms; that explanation is simply unnecessary. It is the only psalm attributed to Moses, "the man of God," as Deut 33:1 also describes him. Structure: vv. 1–12, the lament, contrasting God's eternity with the fleeting and troubled life of humans; vv. 13–17, a request for the Lord to turn, and show favor. **2.** This verse, like Prov 8:22–31, invites the reader to go backward from the creation of the world to consider what we call the "eternity" of God. **3.** The *turn back* is the same "turn" that appears in v. 13 (cf. Gen 3:19). **4.** The brevity of time for God is exemplified by the sensation of *yesterday* and the night *watch*. Second Peter 3:8 uses the idea in the context of the "delay" in the second coming of the Lord. **5–6.** Although the Hebrew of v. 5a is obscure, the general theme is the brevity of human life, in contrast to v. 2. The theme is a common one (e.g., Isa 40:6–8; Ps 102:11; Sir 18:9–10). **7–8.** These verses reflect on the human condition rather than offer a specific complaint. It is a confession of the sinfulness that has merited the wrath of God. This is the first mention of *anger* (see v. 11), and the identity of the poet is subsumed in an undefined "we." **9–10.** Under the shadow of divine *wrath,* the brevity of human life is all the more lamentable (cf. Job 4:19–21). Somewhat optimistically, the "biblical" age is pitched at three score and ten or, at the outside, eighty years, but humans have little to show for their efforts. **12.** There is considerable depth to the teaching requested by the psalmist. *So* in NRSV should be translated as "rightly," modifying *count,* with NJPS, NAB, NIV. What does the context suggest? A sober and serious consideration of time spent with both God and world, which leads one to wisdom, *a wise heart.* The transitory character of human life is transcended by a time that is counted correctly, in the light of God and the biblical "fear of the Lord," which is the beginning of wisdom (Prov 1:7). **13.** The poet calls out to the Lord to take a different *turn* than in v. 3. *Have compassion:* lit., "repent concerning," "change your mind about." Moses uses this language when pleading with God in Exod 32:12, a text exhibiting the same movement: turn . . . repent (also Jonah 3:9). **15.** The prayer is that the time of affliction be at least equaled by the time of joy. **16.** A spirit of confidence exudes from the request that future generations see the divine *glorious power* (better, "splendor," "majesty," "glory"). **17.** The unconquerable optimism closes fittingly with a repetition that God will *prosper* (lit., "establish") what the community is trying to achieve (which is not apart from God). The psalm gives the reader much to think about: the eternity of God, the moment of humans, time, wisdom, and the future.

Psalm 91. A psalm of trust, probably describing a liturgical action. Structure: vv. 1–2, an address to one who finds refuge in the Temple; vv. 3–13, a description of the protection that the Lord provides; vv. 14–16, a divine oracle, assuring salvation. **1–6.** *You who live:* literally, "the one who lives." The Hebrew is singular, but the translators have rendered the plural for the sake of gender inclusivity (cf. comment on Ps 1). The "you" is inserted, and with good reason, since the rest of the poem refers to "you" (in the singular). *Will say:* a mere revocalization of the MT would make this an imperative, and thus the rest of v. 2 forms the prayer recommended to the one who looks to the Temple for security. One of the personnel of the sanctuary advises the psalmist to pray trustfully for protection, and then develops the reasons in the following verses. The hostile powers are described in traditional metaphors: snares, plague, night terrors (demons), arrows, sun rays (v. 6), lions, and serpents. *Wings:* see also Pss 36:7; 57:1. In this Temple context one can easily imagine the wings of the cherubim over the Ark. *Faithfulness:* personified again, and here as protective gear; the *buckler* is a small round shield. **7.** See also Ps 3:6 for *ten thousand* as a preferred exaggeration. **8.** No action is necessary, except to watch as the Lord eliminates the *wicked.* **9.** *Refuge:* occurs for the third time (vv. 2 and 4). *Most High:* as in v. 1. **11–13.** See the reply of Jesus to Satan in Luke

4:10–12. The work of God's angels is illustrated in Gen 24:7, and in the books of Tobit and Daniel. The metaphor in v. 12b derives from the rocky roads in Palestine. **14–16.** Without any introduction, a divine oracle is given. Those who *know* the name of the Lord (so also Ps 9:10; cf. 5:11) are those who believe and call on divine aid, which will be forthcoming (v. 15), culminating in a typical OT blessing, *long life* and *salvation*.

Psalm 92. The genre of the poem is thanksgiving, and its prime concern is retribution upon the wicked. However, in contrast to Psalm 73, it has no problem believing that the virtuous will prevail and the wicked will be punished (cf. Ps 37, and the friends of Job, who also share this belief). Structure: vv. 1–4, introductory thanksgiving for God's (unspecified) deeds; vv. 5–9, praise of the divine plans, which the wicked fail to understand; vv. 10–15, affirmation of the Lord's care of the psalmist and the righteous. **2.** See the comment on Psalm 89 for a different celebration of *steadfast love* and *faithfulness*. **4.** The *works,* which normally refer to the Lord's interventions in Israel's history, denote in vv. 5–9 the upholding of proper justice among human beings. **6b.** *Stupid:* the Hebrew word *(ba'ar)* connotes the animal level of understanding and is used pointedly in this sense in the key texts of Pss 49:12; and especially in 73:22, where the poet has nearly given up in the struggle to understand the Lord's works. **7–8.** Although *grass* usually symbolizes evanescence, here it describes the flourishing of the wicked. However, they will be destroyed *forever,* i.e., an indefinite period. Oddly, the length of time for the fate of the wicked corresponds to that of the Lord's exaltation, although the Hebrew expressions are different. **9.** The verse sounds like an adaptation of the praise of Baal current centuries earlier in Ugarit: "Now thine enemy, O Baal, Now thine enemy wilt thou smite, Now wilt thou cut off thine adversary" (*ANET,* p. 131). **10.** The metaphors of *horn* (= strength) and *fresh oil* indicate power and renewal. **11.** The wicked of v. 7 are now characterized as *my enemies;* for witnessing their *downfall,* see Ps 91:8. **12–15.** The metaphor of a *tree* for the righteous is frequent (cf. Ps 1:3). The conclusion reaches beyond injustice in human affairs: in the Godhead no iniquity exists.

Psalm 93. A hymn of praise, commemorating the Lord as king. See the discussion of Mowinckel's theory of "enthronement" psalms in the Introduction (p. 10), and also the comment on Psalm 47. Structure: vv. 1–2, acclamation of the Lord as "eternal" king and creator; v. 4, divine dominion over the waters of chaos; v. 5, conclusion. **1–2.** The cry of enthronement ("the Lord is king") does not preclude kingship from the very beginning; the divine rule is manifested in establishing the *world*. Royal garments are not those of an earthling, but *majesty* and *strength*, personified. The poet struggles to express the notion that there was never a time when the Lord was not, even before creation. Note the change from the third person to the second; this is frequent in Hebrew poetry, and does not signify a real change, or justify inferences about a change of speaker or subject matter. **3–4.** The waters of chaos, which might just possibly destroy creation, (cf. Ps 46:2–3) are held in check by divine power; similarly, in Ps 29:9–10 God sits enthroned above the waters, while all proclaim: "Glory." **5.** Royalty involves laws *(decrees),* and the transcendent holy one sanctifies the Temple by residing there.

Psalm 94. This is a lament of an individual and also a community. Violence and injustice threaten the community (vv. 1–7; cf. Pss 14 and 53), and an individual complains about the situation, ending by expressing confidence that the Lord will establish justice. There is no need to distinguish two separate psalms. Structure: vv. 1–3, the introductory appeal; vv. 4–7, the complaint about oppression within Israel; vv. 8–15, a wisdom lesson both for fools (vv. 8–11) and for the righteous (vv. 12–15); v. 16, a complaint that is smothered by confidence that the Lord will correct the situation. The issue is an old one; retribution upon the wicked is treated especially in Psalms 37, 73, and 92 among others, and here the author presents an argument in favor of divine discipline (cf. Prov 3:11–12). **1–3.** The appeal is a very strong request for the Lord to *shine forth* (Ps 50:2) as an avenger. This is not a hate-filled cry, but an appeal to the Lord for justice. Neither is it new, because "vengeance is mine" (Deut 32:35). God must defend the oppressed and administer justice, in the situation described in the following verses. **4–7.** Without identifying the wicked, the psalm portrays their evildoing in typical language of oppression in vv. 5–6, with the characteristic dismissal of *the God of Jacob* as one who does not know and will not act (see Ps 73:11). **8–11.** To the jeer of the wicked in v. 7, the poet gives a rhetorical response in the wisdom style (cf. Ps 33:13–15 and Prov 20:12). **12–15.** The positive aspect of the wisdom lesson is to recognize the value of the Lord's discipline (Prov 3:11–12) and teaching. Verse 13 recalls the proverbial wish about the wicked falling into the pit they have dug for others to fall into (Ps 7:15; Prov 26:27; and Eccl 10:8). **16–18.** These verses (esp. v. 18) are reminiscent of the experience of the author of Ps 73:2. The *silence* of Sheol (Ps 115:17b) would have been his but for the Lord. Somehow he saw divine justice at work, punishing the wicked. **20–23.** NRSV understands them to be *rulers* (v. 20), an inference from the Hebrew which reads "the seat of injustice." The implication is that they have manipulated the law. But the condemnation of the wicked is clear from the repetition of *wipe them out* in the final verse.

Psalm 95. A hymn of praise, commemorating the Lord as king; see comment on Psalms 47 and 93 about enthronement psalms. There is a marked liturgical character here, resembling that of Psalm 81. Structure: vv. 1–5, introductory and cohortative invitation to a group to unite in praise of the Lord as king and creator; vv. 6–7a, an exhortation to worship Israel's shepherd; vv. 7b–11, a proclamation of the Lord's warning against obstinacy, based on the people's history. **3.** The exaltation of the Lord beyond all gods is a familiar theme (Exod 15:11 and see the comment on Ps 82). **4–5.** Note the extremes: height and depth, water and earth, in an inclusio, marked by the *hand* of God. **6–7a.** The opening invitation is renewed, to worship the Lord who has also created Israel as the chosen flock. These lines are a kind of repetition; note the occurrence of *hand.* **7b.** As in Deut 30:11–20 and often elsewhere, *today* indicates that the ancient covenant is being renewed in a liturgical re-presentation. **8–11.** Someone speaks in the name of the Lord, recalling examples of rebellion in the desert: at *Meribah* (= strife), where they quarreled with God and at *Massah* (= testing), where they put God to the test. See Exod 17:1–7; Num 20:1–13; and Heb 3:7–11. *Rest:* originally (Deut 12:10 and 25:19) referred to the possession of the promised land, which is really the Lord's "rest," the heritage given to Israel. In the context of the psalm it has the overtones of peace with God; the people now know where their true rest is. In contrast to the reassuring ending of Psalm 81, this poem ends on a very stern note, recalling the Lord's anger (cf. Heb 4:11).

Psalm 96. An enthronement psalm; see comment on the preceding psalm. First Chronicles 16:23–33 inserts this song in the context of David's bringing the Ark to Jerusalem. There is a noticeable similarity to Psalm 98, and many phrases occur elsewhere in the Bible (Isa 42:10–11). Notice also the threefold repetition: "sing to the LORD" (vv. 1–2); "ascribe to the LORD" (vv. 7–8); and the repetition of "he is coming" in v. 13. Structure: vv. 1–3, introductory invitation to sing praise; vv. 4–6, the reasons for the praise; vv. 7–10, the invitation to praise extends to the nations; vv. 11–13, all creation is invited to join in praise of the Lord who is coming to judge. **1.** Perhaps this song is *new* because the liturgical occasion is a new one, or the words "renew" divine praise (cf. Pss 33:3 and 40:3). Line *a* is repeated in Ps 98:1 and Isa 42:10. **4–5.** See comment on Ps 95:3; other gods are "zeroes" (better than NRSV, "idols") in comparison to the creator. **6.** These divine attributes become personified as attendants upon the Lord (Ps 89:14). **7–9.** The style is reminiscent of Ps 29:1–2, but the audience is now the *families of the peoples.* **10a.** The vivid cry of enthronement (Ps 93:1) addresses the *nations.* Some Old Latin and Greek manuscripts added here "from the tree," in reference to the crucifixion of Christ; this is reflected in the famous *Vexilla Regis* hymn. **11–12.** Note the strong personifications in these verses. The coming of the Lord stirs nature, and it may have been re-presented in the cult by a procession of the Ark (see the comment on Ps 47:5).

Psalm 97. This is an enthronement psalm with obvious hymnic quality, but only the first and last verses mention addressees. Verses 8–9 seem to address the Lord directly, but the transition from third person to second is not unusual; see the comment on Ps 93:2. The body of the psalm is taken up with declarations about the Lord. Structure: v. 1, the cry of enthronement and address to the world; vv. 2–5, description of the theophany;

vv. 6–9, universal recognition of the Lord's supremacy and rule; vv. 10–11, assurance of the Lord's care for the faithful; v. 12, an address to the righteous. **1.** Even the *coastlands* (Mediterranean islands) take part in the enthronement cry. **2–5.** Typical theophanic traits, indicating divine presence, are repeated here (see Deut 33:1–5; Judg 5:4–5; and Ps 18:7–13). Verse 2b is practically a repetition of Ps 89:14. The description is vivid; the Lord is wrapped in clouds, darkness, and fire, while he shoots out lightning causing the earth to tremble (Ps 96:9) and *mountains melt like wax.* **6–7.** So universal is this that there seems to be no room for worship of anyone else (read "zeroes" for *worthless idols*). **8–9.** *Zion* is mentioned because of its unique relationship to the Lord, who is the "most high" (*'elyon*; see the comment on Ps 46:4), beyond all *elohim*-beings (= *gods* in v. 7, translated as "angels" in the LXX: cf. Heb 1:6). **10–12.** The poem takes a sudden turn to the topic of retribution, and it follows traditional doctrine, calling the *righteous* to *rejoice in the LORD* (cf. Ps 32:11). The reader is invited to ponder these so-called "enthronement" psalms. What were the expectations of the people, especially in view of the dire political situation during most of their national existence? One can well imagine that they fed into contemporary eschatological expectations. Certainly later, in NT times, readers understood them as describing the approach of the kingdom of God.

Psalm 98. An enthronement psalm, similar to Ps 96; note the opening cry (v. 1), and also the endings (vv. 7–9 with Ps 96:11–13). Structure: vv. 1–3, an invitation to praise the Lord because of the victory that has taken place; vv. 4–9, the initial appeal is widened to invite all nations and all creation to join in the rejoicing at the Lord's coming. There is no obvious historical reference for the "victory." The delirious tone of the poem approximates the mood so prominent in Deutero-Isaiah (the name scholars give to the anonymous author of Isa 40–55), as well as in the other enthronement psalms. **1.** See the comment on Ps 96:1. The *marvelous things* is a term that often refers to the saving deeds of the Exodus story, and the term *victory* occurs three times in vv. 1–3. However, there is a certain timeless quality to these lines; the marvels cannot be specified. The language is characteristic of

Deutero-Isaiah (e.g., the hand/arm as the means of salvation/victory). Note also the parallelism between salvation and justice. **2.** *Vindication;* lit., righteousness (cf. v. 9); the psalm does not explain exactly to what event this refers or how God has revealed it before *the nations.* **3.** Vindication is described as a manifestation of the traditional attributes (*hesed* and *'emunah;* Ps 89 and Exod 34:6) *to the house of Israel.* Cf. Isa 52:7–10, where similar hyperbolic language refers to the return from Babylon. **4.** *All the earth:* probably its inhabitants, although inanimate things are referred to explicitly in vv. 7–9. **8–9.** A joyous welcome is given by nature to the coming of the Lord as judge, contrary to the many times judgment is seen as threatening. Again, the unusual vision shown in the enthronement psalms challenges the reader. How is the *righteousness* of the the Lord manifested in victory? The open-endedness of these verses indicates that it would be a mistake to limit them by tying them in with one historical period.

Psalm 99. Another enthronement psalm, as the opening affirmation indicates. In contrast to the previous psalm, Psalm 99 has no similarities with Deutero-Isaiah, and it places more emphasis upon data in Israel's history. The refrain of "holy" (vv. 3, 5, and 9) divides the poem; in addition, the command to "worship" appears twice. Structure: vv. 1–3, an acclamation of the Lord's kingship, universally acknowledged; vv. 4–5, reasons for worshiping God; vv. 6–8, a description of the Lord's dealings with priest and prophet; v. 9, a command to worship the Lord. **1–3.** The enthronement is described in terms of the majestic presence on the Ark between the *cherubim,* where God is lifted high (*exalted,* v. 2; and extol in vv. 5 and 9, means to "lift high"). Note the theophanic effects in v. 1; the mood of these verses could be cohortative, as in NRSV, or simply declarative. **4.** *In Jacob:* these attributes of the Lord are performed and activated in Israel, whereas Ps 9:7–8 reports these same virtues displayed over the world. **5.** *Footstool:* the Ark of the Covenant. *Holy:* the cry recalls the threefold "holy" of the Seraphim in Isa 6:3. **6–7.** Three heroes of Israel serve to illustrate calling on the *name,* or interceding (cf. Exod 32:31–32; Num 17:10–13; and 1 Sam 7:8–9). *The pillar of cloud:* refers to Exod 33:9, where the cloud hovered over the Tent of Meeting whenever Moses entered it to commune with the Lord. **8.** In contrast to the obedience noted in v. 7 stand the *wrongdoings,* punished, but also forgiven by God—a tension typical of the OT and of human existence. **9.** The cry of vv. 3 and 5 is rephrased as the reason for worshiping the Lord on the *holy mountain,* the Temple. This suggests that the psalm is emphasizing the aspect of holiness that marks the transcendent presence of the Lord in Zion. Verses 1–3, which also mention Zion, elaborate on the fear of God and awe. This same Lord who appeared in a frightening theophany is the one who "answered them" (v. 6).

Psalm 100. A hymn of praise best explained as an exhortation to people celebrating (in procession?) in the Temple. The tone of joy is characteristic of a text from such an occasion, as the psalm's emphatic quality also shows, for there are seven imperative verbs in vv. 1–4. Structure: vv. 1–2, a call to worship; v. 3, the reason for worshiping; v. 4, another call to worship; v. 5, the reason for worshiping. **1.** *All the earth:* as in Ps 98:4. The universality is surprising, if considered from the point of view of Israel's worldly importance. But from the point of view of a God whom Israel celebrates as creator, king, and ruler of all, this viewpoint has its own logic. **3.** The reason concentrates on Israel's privileged relationship to the Lord, who is truly God, in covenant with *his people,* and is the shepherd of *his pasture.* **4–5.** The call to worship is motivated by the twin benefits God constantly shows, which the psalms so often record (e.g., Ps 98:3). Although the text contains no mention of enthronement, the spirit and vision of this call to worship are akin to the enthronement psalms that precede it.

Psalm 101. A royal psalm, spoken by a king, concerning the norms he follows in his administration; for another detailed description of an ideal king by a court poet, see Psalm 72. Structure: vv. 1–2a, introductory proclamation concerning regal justice; vv. 2b–8, a personal statement of royal standards. **1–2a.** The ideal is obviously the concern, but the question in the NRSV is tantalizing, as though he is singing of an ideal that may be beyond reach. Another translation of the MT is possible: "When will you come to me?" This makes it an invocation of divine aid. **2b.** *Within my house:* refers to the royal administration, the honesty and goodness of his officials; vv. 6–8 also lay out such a goal. The king's personal *integrity* (= blameless, v. 2a) is reflected in the structures of his realm. **3–4.** *Anything . . . base:* lit., "a thing of Belial"; this has a different meaning in Ps 41:8. The king may be speaking of his personal ideals, but he would presumably enforce these among his courtiers and subjects. **5–6.** The standards for his ministers are clear, negatively in v. 5, positively in v. 6, where *the faithful in the land* will receive royal *favor.* **7.** The bane of those in power are yes-men, sycophants who practice *deceit;* they will be banned. **8.** A daily supervision will ensure the expulsion of the wicked *in the land* (cf. the phrase in v. 7); they will be cut off from Jerusalem, *the city of the* LORD. One may interpret the program announced in this psalm as a royal promise, or simply a statement of the ideals that inspires the monarch.

Psalm 102. A lament of an individual, the fifth of the seven "penitential" psalms (cf. comment on Ps 6). The superscription is admirable for its succinct description of the setting. Structure: vv. 1–2, an appeal to God to hear the prayer; vv. 3–11, description of personal distress; vv. 12–22, a confident appeal to the Lord as the restorer of Zion; vv. 23–24, the resumption of the personal lament; vv. 25–28, conclusion, on the theme of the Lord's permanence. The transition from personal complaint to expressions of hope for the restoration of Zion has led to various interpretations. Is it a natural development, or the result of incorporating another poem? If the entire psalm is taken as a unit, the poet is complaining about personal suffering, yet vv. 12–22 show more concern with the fate of the people than with personal destiny. **1–2.** These lines echo many other psalms (e.g., Pss 27:9 and 39:12–13 on hiding the face; see also the comment on Ps 10:11). **3–5.** Metaphors of evanescence (*withered like grass,* taken up again in v. 11) and physical sickness (fever and emaciation) make it difficult to specify the reason for the complaint. *Smoke* is a symbol of the ephemerality of life (Ps 37:20; cf. Ps 68:2). **6–7.** The vivid comparisons underscore loneliness and desolation. **8.** *Use my name:* the psalmist has become the parade example of an accursed person; his very name is used in a curse: "may you be cursed as N. is." **9.** More expressive metaphors; mourning and sadness (signified by the *ashes*) are as much a part of daily existence as consuming food and drink. **11.** *Evening shadow:* the reference is to the lengthening of the shadow, portending the end of life, although v. 23 refers to *midcourse.* **12–17.** In contrast to the brief lifetime of mortals stands the Lord's permanence, a theme that will appear at the end in vv. 25–27 (cf. Ps 90:2, 4). The turn to the fate of Zion is sudden; but the claim that this is an insertion is unnecessary. The passage clearly presupposes the destruction of Jerusalem and the period of exile. **14.** Note the tender feelings of the populace for Zion's *dust.* **15–16.** Ezekiel similarly described the return of the *glory* of the Lord (Ezek 43:2–4); now *all the kings of the earth* will see it. Again, the easy transition to a universal perspective is striking. **18–22.** Zion remains the subject, but the passage calls for a written record that a future generation may contemplate, that they may praise God for freeing the prisoners (those in exile). Again, a universalist perspective appears in v. 22. **23–27.** A switch back to the lament; see the comment on vv. 3–5. Again the psalm highlights the permanence of God (cf. v. 12). In a colorful metaphor, the psalmist compares all creation to a mere garment that wears out (Isa 51:6). In contrast, *you are the same* (lit., "and you, he/it"), living without *end.* The letter to the Hebrews applies vv. 25–27 to Christ to indicate his superiority over the angels (Heb 1:10–12). **28.** The poet returns to the topic of future generations (cf. v. 15); something of the permanence of God is attached to Israel. One should grant the author freedom to make the sudden transitions found in the poem. Moreover, the themes of the various parts of the psalm interrelate: the ephemeral existence of humans as against God's eternity, and the poet's plight as against the fate of the community, present and future.

Psalm 103. A song of praise of deep religious sensitivity. It is a simple and beautiful reaction to the goodness of God. Structure: vv. 1–5, a colloquy urging praise for personal benefits; vv. 6–18, an acknowledgement of the Lord's kindness to the people; vv. 19–22, conclusion. **1–2.** *Bless:* is equivalent to "praise" and designates the Lord as the supreme one. *Soul:* the term inadequately expresses Hebrew *nephesh,* which means something like life-force, or the person *(all that is within me).* The address is to the self. The opening line forms an inclusio with v. 22; the twenty-two lines of the poem correspond to the number of letters in the Hebrew alphabet. The poem begins and ends forcefully on a note of blessing (vv. 1–2 and 20–22). As so often, *name* is a parallel to *the* LORD. **3–5.** A thanksgiving for the personal benefits that are mentioned; the parallelism in v. 3 reflects the association of sin and sickness (e.g., Ps 32:1–5; 107:17; Job, *passim*). *Steadfast love:* repeated in vv. 8, 11, 17; *mercy* occurs in v. 8. The *eagle* was a symbol of vigor and strength. **6–18.** This confession begins with the acts of God in Israel's history, and dwells on the divine mercy, especially toward those in the covenant (v. 18). **6.** *Vindication:* lit., "righteousness," forming an inclusio with v. 17. **7.** *Ways:* this is exactly what Moses prays to know in Exod 33:13. **8.** The classical formula of Exod 34:6 is repeated here and often (e.g., Num 14:18; Ps 86:15; and Jonah 4:2). **9.** See the affirmation in Isa 57:16. **10.** See Hos 11:8–9 for the struggle between mercy and justice. **11–13.** The poet, searching for comparisons that would be adequate to convey the *compassion* of God, seizes upon space and family (*as a father;* cf. Prov 3:12). **14–16.** Although the perspective is Israelite, the reasons are pertinent to all humanity, which is made from *dust, like grass* (Pss 37:2; 90:5; Isa 40:7). **17–18.** The compassion focuses on those who are loyal and *fear* God. **19.** The verse serves as a theological reason behind the following conclusion. **20–22.** All quarters of the globe are called upon to *bless the* LORD, who rules over all. The reader will surely notice the emphasis on blessing in this and the following psalms. Like Psalm 103, Psalm 104 begins and ends with "bless the LORD, O my soul!" (vv. 1, 35), an inclusio. The final Hebrew tag in Ps 103:22, "hallelujah," (lit., "praise Yah[weh]"), may actually function as the beginning of the next psalm and form an inclusio with 104:35. Notice also that Ps 106 begins and ends with a hallelujah (vv. 1, 48). These seem to be signs of editing.

Psalm 104. A hymn of praise of God as creator; one of the most remarkable songs in the Psalter. The similarity to the "Hymn to the Sun" of Pharaoh Akhenaton (cf. *ANET,* p. 370) has often been noted, especially for vv. 19–23. Any dependence is largely indirect; the main source of the creation traditions in Ps 104 seems to be Genesis. Structure: vv. 1–4, invitation to praise the divine glory in the heavens; vv. 5–13, God's taming the waters of chaos and making water available to creation; vv. 14–23, God's providence, culminating in the function of night and day; vv. 24–26, admiration for God's wisdom, especially regarding the sea; vv. 27–30, the dependence of living things upon the divine breath; vv. 31–35, conclusion. **1.** See the comment on Ps 103:1. **2–5.** The comparison of *light* to a cloak makes sense when one views light as a "thing" (Job 38:19). God was thought to dwell above the firmament (the *tent,* Gen 1:6–8) and to ride on the *clouds* (Ps 68:4). Lightning *(flame)* and *winds* are merely God's servants. The firmness of earth results from *foundations* (Job 38:4–6). **6–9.** Creation is described in mythological terms: the waters of chaos cover the earth, but the Lord brings order out of this with *thunder* (the divine voice), and waters find their proper place, never to rebel again. **10–18.** The formerly unruly chaotic waters now have the mission of giving drink to creation and making the earth produce good things for all creatures. The mention of beasts, birds, bread, wine, oil, goats (even the "unessential" *coneys* or rock-badgers, v. 18), and humans evokes a touching scene. **19–23.** A quaint picture is drawn: night is for the beasts, and day is for humans to work. The same sequence appears in the Egyptian hymn indicated above, in which the Egyptian sun-god, Aton, retires at night when evil power takes over. However, in v. 21 the Lord hears the beasts; the roaring of *lions* is their prayer for food. **24–26.** The author pauses to admire the wisdom displayed in creation and especially in the abundant life of the sea. As for *Leviathan,* the monster of chaos (Ps 74:14; Isa 27:1; and Job 41:1–34), the writer imagines it as merely a plaything. **27–30.** Besides feeding all creatures, God keeps them alive by the creative *spirit* or *ruah.* This term can also mean "wind," and on this level it could refer to the winds that provide the rainy season for creatures. But against the background of Gen 2:7, it refers to the divine breath that makes creatures live. On a third level, the Christian liturgy has appropriated v. 30 to refer to the action of the Holy Spirit and the feast of Pentecost. From the point of view of the "breath of life," existence depends upon God's breathing. When the breath of God stops, creatures die (cf. Eccl 12:7). This lively creation poem emphasizes the concept of the world as a continuing event, a continuous creation. **29.** The hiding of the face has occurred often already in the psalms (see comment on Ps 10:11). *Dismayed:* better, "terrified." **31–32.** Although according to Genesis 1, God saw that what was created in the six days was "good," it is naive or even extraordinary to invite the creator to take a simple joy in it. This is all the more striking in view of the affirmation of the ferocity of Leviathan's power. **33–35.** The author returns to the personal note that marked v. 1: he commits himself to a lifetime of praise of the Lord, hoping that the psalm itself is pleasing to God! The imprecation against *sinners* does not lessen the power of the poem. From the point of view of a "perfect" world, they constitute a blemish in the divine creation; so let them be eliminated. The LXX connects the final hallelujah with the next psalm.

Psalm 105. A "historical" psalm (cf. Pss 78, 106, and 136), or better, a song of praise that rehearses the divine actions in Israel's history. It ranges from the patriarchs to the settlement in the land (v. 44), but commemorates Abraham in a special way (vv. 6, 9, and 42); it may be characterized as the story of God's fidelity to the promises made to Abraham. Structure: vv. 1–6, an invitation to Abraham's children to praise the Lord for the marvels in their history; vv. 7–15, the covenant with Abraham and descendants; vv. 16–22, the story of Joseph; vv. 23–43, the Exodus from Egypt through the desert; vv. 44–45, Israel in the land. Verses 1–15 appear in a cultic setting in 1 Chr 16:8–22. **1–6.** The invitation singles out the reason for praise, the *wonderful works* (vv. 2, 5). **4.** *Strength:* the word refers to the Ark of the Covenant in Ps 78:61 (NRSV, "power"; cf. Ps 132:8), and is thus parallel to *his presence* in line *b.* **7–15.** The covenant with the patriarchs is seen primarily from the point of view of the gift of the *land of Canaan.* God protected their lives, for at first they were only temporary residents (v. 12, NRSV, *strangers*) and subjected to various difficulties narrated in the book of Genesis. The quotation in v. 15 is an idealization of the patriarchs, naming them *anointed ones* and *prophets.* **16–22.** See Genesis 37–50. The psalmist introduces the note of providence at the beginning: God *sent a man ahead* (v. 17). **23–36.** Cf. Exodus 1–12. The experience of Abraham's descendants in Egypt (*Ham;* vv. 23, 27) is introduced on a sobering note: Jacob was a (resident) *alien,* away from the land that God had promised him. But divine providence comes into view in vv. 24–25, and especially in v. 26: God *sent his servant Moses.* The sequence of the ten plagues differs from the Exodus account: the Exodus plagues appear in the order 9, 1, 2, 4, 3, 7, 8, 10, with no mention of the fifth or sixth plagues. See the comment on Ps 78:42–51. **37–43.** The departure and journey through the desert is surprisingly brief, lacking any mention of the Red Sea. The theme of providence continues and culminates in the Lord's fidelity to the *promise* to Abraham (v. 42). **44–45.** The conclusion ties in Sinai *(statutes, laws)* with salvation history; obedience to the laws equals gratitude for gift of the land of Canaan. In contrast to Ps 78, this poem handles only the beginnings of Israelite history, and emphasizes especially the Abrahamic covenant. Could this be explained by the historical situation, after the exile, when there was less reason to speak of the covenant with David? It was then that the Abrahamic covenant would be a consoling memory.

Psalm 106. The genre remains uncertain; it is a "historical" psalm, conceived in terms of a national lament and confession of sin. It is similar to, but also very different from, Psalm 105. The latter praises God for the saving deeds of past history; here the recital of the sacred history is a way of expressing sorrow for the people's constant rebellion. This is preeminently a confession of sin, while at the same time it glorifies the Lord because of the mercy shown to Israel, and it also pleads for a restoration "from among the nations" (v. 47). There are traits of an individual song (vv. 4–5), but the psalm remains a lament over the community's failure to respond to the continuous mercy of God. Structure: vv. 1–5, introduction; vv. 6–46, several episodes are described, from the Red Sea to Canaan and the scattering among the nations; v. 47, an appeal for deliverance in the present situation. **1–5.** In a sense v. 1 says it all: praise the Lord because of the *steadfast love* (vv. 1, 7, and 45) that has been continually shown to the people. The first-person singular subject in vv. 4–5 speaks for the community and is clearly looking forward to future deliverance. **6.** The present generation is linked to the rebellious *ancestors.* **7.** The rebellion refers to Exod 14:10–12 (see also Exod 15:24 and 16:2), when Israel recoiled at the sight of the pursuit of the Egyptian army. NRSV calls attention in a footnote to the literal translation of the Hebrew phrase that the LXX rendered "Red Sea"; it was a marshy body of water east of the Nile. **13–15.** The grumbling in the desert is described several times (cf. Exod 15:24; 16:2; and Num 11:1–23). **16–18.** The reference is to the rebellion against Moses in Numbers 16. **19–23.** The golden calf episode is described in Exod 32:1–14 and Deut 9:7–21. **23.** *Breach:* Moses is pictured standing at a hole in the wall to protect the people from the Lord's *wrath* (Exod 32:11; Deut 9:25). **24–27.** Cf. Num 14:1–25, describing the refusal to enter Canaan. The punishment is the famous forty years *in the wilderness.* Verse 27 seems to reflect the tradition found in Ezek 20:34, perhaps in view of the setting of the psalm (v. 47). **28–31.** The events of Baal-Peor and the role of Phinehas appear in Numbers 25. **32–33.** *Rash:* another interpretation of why Moses never entered the promised land (cf. Exod 17:1–7 and Num 20:2–13). **34–39.** Israel's "mingling" *with the nations* (v. 35) refers to their being seduced by *the idols of Canaan,* while it also reflects the current situation of v. 47. **37.** *Demons:* the precise nuance of the Hebrew term remains unclear. Verses 40–46 summarize later history (Judges to Kings; cf. v. 43) in a general Deuteronomistic style; the *compassion* of the Lord was ever at work. **47.** This verse reflects vv. 1–2 and epitomizes the entire psalm, pointing to the situation of the community at a time after the exile. **48.** The doxology is not part of the psalm; it signals the end of Book IV of the Psalter (cf. comment on Pss 41:13; 72:18–19; and 89:52).

Psalm 107. A hymn of praise or thanksgiving, as vv. 1–3, 22, and 32 indicate. *Steadfast love* is an inclusio (vv. 1, 43; and cf. 8, 15, 21, and 31). The arrangement is striking: four groups of people are presented; four refrains center on their crying (vv. 6, 13, 19, and 28), and four refrains summon them to thank/praise God (vv. 8, 15, 21, and 31). Structure: vv. 1–3, an invitation to the *redeemed* to thank God; vv. 4–9, the first group, who were delivered from distress in the desert; vv. 10–16, the second group, freed prisoners; vv. 17–22, third group, the sick who have been cured; vv. 23–32, sea voyagers who have been rescued; vv. 33–42, a hymn praising God's power manifested in favor of the upright; v. 43, a conclusion in the wisdom style (cf. v. 1). These four groups can be understood literally or metaphorically, i.e., as referring to the concrete experiences of disparate groups, or as typifying the various trials from which God has delivered the community. Both levels of meaning are possible, but the metaphorical approach is more likely. Then the prayer can be seen as a postexilic communal thanksgiving, and the four groups have symbolic intent; the redeemed are those liberated from exile. **1–3.** *Redeemed:* the term refers to deliverance from Egypt and then from Babylon. The reference to the four corners of the earth introduces a community restored from the exile. Then the introduction would indicate the way vv. 4–32 should be understood. **4–9.** *Some:* this word is not explicit in the Hebrew of vv. 4, 10, 17, and 23, but it is needed to indicate the four groups. Note how a conclusion follows the refrain of v. 8. The distress of none of these groups can be pinpointed to a particular event; but the experience of exile would fit. **10–18.** The rebellion of the *prisoners* may suggest Israel's infidelity; the exiles are referred to as prisoners in Isa 42:7, 22. Note again the nature of the conclusion following the refrain (vv. 15–16). **17–22.** Sin and suffering are associated in v. 17, and the description resembles the typical psalmic depiction of distress, followed by the exhortation to liturgical sacrifice (v. 22). **23–32.** The seafarers experience God's *wondrous works* in the unruly sea which the Lord has hushed. Like v. 22, v. 32 exhorts praise of God, a communal dimension of the psalm. **33–42.** The psalm departs from the pattern and exalts the power of God in destruction and in blessing. **43.** The appeal calls attention to the entire psalm as a subject of meditation on God's *steadfast love* (v. 1).

Psalm 108. A composite psalm, made up of Ps 57:7–11, the lament of an individual, and Ps 60:5–12, a communal lament. The result is a new psalm, in the sense that it begins with the praise of God and only a hint of trouble (v. 6, but cf. v. 11), and it adds a promise of salvation (vv. 7–9) with assurance of victory (vv. 12–13). Psalms that rearrange previous (liturgical?) texts can reflect a new situation as this psalm seems to do. The poet resides *among the nations* (v. 3) and calls upon the Lord for deliverance. This appeal is met by an old promise that lays claim to territory, maintaining Israel's rights against three traditional enemies. The psalm makes sense in the situation of the exile or some perilous period during the diaspora. See comment on Psalms 57 and 60.

Psalm 109. A lament of an individual. Structure: vv. 1–5, a complaint against the calumny of enemies; vv. 6–19, a series of curses; vv. 20–31, a request that God punish the enemies but bless the speaker, concluding with a vow of thanksgiving (vv. 30–31). The imprecations in vv. 6–19 have often been interpreted as the words of the psalmist against enemies. But they can be better understood as the charges and curses directed against the speaker by the enemies, because the subject is singular, while the enemies are always described in the plural (vv. 1–5 and 20–31). In v. 20 the psalmist wishes that the preceding curses recoil upon the enemies who uttered them. This is an example of the talion law in action, and an effort to offset the calumny and curses that have been directed against the speaker, perhaps in a legal proceeding. **1–5.** The silence of God is held up in vivid contrast to the words from the *deceitful mouths.* **4b.** The Hebrew is obscure: "I am prayer"; if "prayer" denotes judgment (cf. v. 7 where the same word is parallel to *tried*), the sense would be that the speaker is being judged. Unfortunately, the NRSV rendering seems to suggest that the "prayer" is vv. 6–19. **6.** *They say:* NRSV inserts these words, because it interprets vv. 6–19 as the words of the accusers; note the quotation marks. **6b.** *Accuser:* Hebrew *satan* means adversary, and in this case a kind of prosecuting attorney who stands *on his* (the defendant's) *right* in what seems to be a court trial; in contrast, God will be at the right hand of the poor in v. 31. The term also appears in vv. 4a, 20, and 29. The *satan* of the OT is not the devil of the NT. In Job 1–2 he is not a human being, but a member of the heavenly court, suspicious of mortals, but not opposed to the Lord although he puts his own judgment against that of God (cf. also Zech 3:1–2). The evils envisioned in this list of imprecations are death and loss of everything, with consequent hardships on the family; even the descendants are to be wiped out, as the curse envelops the whole group (vv. 13–15). Verses 18–19 vividly describe the power of a curse; let his curses clothe and permeate him. **20–21.** The speaker returns the imprecations of vv. 6–19 upon the accusers and appeals to the *steadfast love* (vv. 21, 26). **22.** Instead of persecuting the *poor and needy* (see v. 16, which perhaps contains the specific charge leveled against the author), he is one of that group, experiencing the piteous situation in vv. 22–25. **23.** The slight effort it takes to shake off a *locust* is an image for frailty. **26–29.** The author renews the appeal, and prays that the Lord's blessing will offset the curses of enemies, who will also come to realize that the *hand* of the Lord was with him in the whole process. The comparison of the *mantle* in v. 29 recalls the "garment" of v. 19. Clothing was not an insignificant matter. **31.** *Right hand:* recall the position of the accuser in v. 6. The above interpretation is not an effort to absolve the psalmist of uttering a string of curses. Rather, it stems from a concern to understand what is happening within the poem. In fact, there is no "absolution"; the psalmist hurls back at the accusers all the curses they wished upon him. There is no room here for "Love your enemies . . . " (Matt 5:44). Neither is there justification for anyone to dismiss this psalm. As indicated in the Introduction above (pp. 48–50), the reader can allow the violence and vengeance of such prayers (e.g., Jer 17:14–18) to be a mirror of the vengeance that lurks in their own hearts, and so a challenge to their readiness to forgive their enemies.

Psalm 110. A royal psalm, difficult to understand because of its obscurity (vv. 6–7) and textual uncertainty (v. 3). It figures in the NT more than any other psalm. Early Christian writers quote or allude to it in a messianic sense. Structure: vv. 1–3, an oracle of assurance for the king, followed by comment; vv. 4–7, another oracle (v. 4b) concerning royal priesthood, followed by a comment on victory. **1.** Someone proclaims an oracle of the Lord to the *lord* king. The *right hand* is the favored position, and one of power. *Footstool:* ancient Near Eastern iconography sometimes shows victors with their feet on the prostrate bodies of captives. **2–3.** The point of these verses is to assure the king of victory. NRSV pictures the *forces* of the king and a renewal of the king's youth comparable to the freshness created by the dew. A well-known reading follows the LXX and Vulgate (but not Jerome's translation from the Hebrew) in interpreting *youth* as "I have begotten you" (cf. Ps 2:7). There is simply no certainty about the meaning of v. 3. **4.** The second oracle is firm and unchanging: the priestly character of the king is asserted by associating him with Melchizedek, i.e., apparently with the dignity of the priest-kings of Jerusalem (= Salem in Gen 14:18). The priesthood is on the model of that famous king. **5–7.** It is not clear if these words are part of the oracle. They seem to deal with the military exploits of the king. Verse 7 is totally obscure. Despite this exaltation of the Jerusalemite king, the prophets (e.g., Isaiah, Jeremiah) did not fail to deal with them as mere mortals capable of mistakes. The astonishing thing is that such a psalm as this was transmitted through the postexilic period when there was no longer any mon-archy. Perhaps a messianic interpretation was operative early on, as the application in the NT implies (e.g., Matt 22:41–46).

Psalm 111. A song of praise in acrostic style; the half-lines begin with successive letters of the Hebrew alphabet. Some clas-sify this as a wisdom psalm; although vv. 5 and 10 provide a basis (*"fear"*), the *works* that are celebrated are on the historical level (*wonderful deeds* in v. 4; *covenant* in vv. 5 and 9). The similarities between Psalms 111 and 112 have often been noted; they are "hallelujah" psalms, an acrostic pair, intended to match. If Psalm 112 reflects wisdom traditions, then Psalm 111 exemplifies the sage's style of praise—teaching by example. Structure: v. 1, hym-nic introduction; vv. 2–9, reasons for the praise: the greatness of the works/deeds of the Lord (the root *'asah* appears six times); v. 10, a wisdom ending. **1.** Hallelujah is literally, "praise Yah(weh)." The worshiping community intones the hymn, prob-ably through a single representative, stressing inner appreciation (*with my whole heart;* cf. Deut 6:5). **2–4.** The events of salvation history, normally not part of wisdom lore, are in view. The *re-nown* of the Lord is indicated in Exod 34:10; see also 34:6. **5.** The *food* may be an allusion to the timeless divine generosity, but also a reference to the manna in the desert. **6–8.** The grant of Pales-tine *(the heritage)* and the Law are commemorated. **9.** Note the parallelism between *redemption* and *covenant.* **10.** A wisdom tag line (Prov 1:7 and 9:10). Praise of the Lord continues indefinitely (*forever;* cf. vv. 3, 8, and 9). This poem inculcates salvation history as wisdom teaching.

Psalm 112. See the comment on Psalm 111. The ideal wise person is portrayed here, just as in Psalm 1. The NRSV adopts the plural form for the sake of gender inclusivity. The psalm has no particular structure; rather, there is a sequence of sayings that characterize the one who fears the Lord (cf. Ps 37). The wisdom mood is typically upbeat, and is so here, indicating the blessings of the righteous and wise: children, wealth, sharing with others, especially the poor. They are *secure in the LORD* (v. 7). **1.** Cf. Ps 1:2. **3.** *Righteousness:* see v. 9b and also Ps 111:3. The wisdom literature binds together wisdom and virtue. *Forever:* as in Ps 111, the term occurs often (vv. 6 and 9), and in the sense of indefinite duration. **4.** *Light:* in what sense? God is a light for others (cf. Pss 27:1; 36:9), and the character traits in v. 4b reflect those of God. Perhaps they provide inspiration and hope. Light stands in contrast with *darkness,* which could be a symbol for those in the dark who need help. **8–10.** There is a kind of dialectic between the righteous and the wicked; the former will eventually witness the downfall of enemies (Pss 54:7 and 118:7). Similarly the wicked will witness the exaltation of the just (*horn* is a symbol of strength).

Psalm 113. A song of praise. Structure: vv. 1–3, summons to praise the name of the Lord; vv. 4–9, exaltation of the Lord who cares for the poor. **1.** Hallelujah continues as a superscription; cf. Psalms 111–112. *Servants of the LORD:* perhaps priests and Levites, but possibly all the faithful. **2–3.** Note the emphasis on the *name;* neither *time* nor space can limit praise of the Lord. **4–9.** The exaltation *on high* is deliberate here, because God can look *down* and see everything, thus delivering the *poor* and *needy* (cf. Ps 35:10). The *barren woman* recalls the story of Hannah and her song in 1 Sam 2:1–10. The hallelujah that ends the psalm may actually belong to the next one, as in Psalms 111–112. In Jewish tradition Psalms 113–118 are known as the "Hallel," and they are recited at the Passover Seder service. They are sometimes referred to as the Egyptian Hallel on account of Ps 114:1 and the Passover connection. Psalm 136, incidentally, is called the "Great Hallel."

Psalm 114. A song of praise; LXX and the Vulgate combine it with Psalm 115. The usual hymnic introduction is lacking, but this only underscores the lively description of the salvation history. The association of the two crossings, of the Red Sea and the Jordan River, appears already in Josh 4:23–24. **1–2.** The poem moves rapidly from the Exodus to the period of the monarchy, indicated by the separate mention of *Judah* and *Israel.* **1.** *Of strange language:* the phrase conveys the sense of alienation that the Hebrews experienced in Egypt, especially after the rise of a Pharaoh who "did not know Joseph" (Exod 1:8). **3.** *Sea:* the Red Sea, personified here as fleeing without fighting; it gives up the battle that the mythological Sea engages in with the Lord (cf. Ps 77:16–20). The *Jordan* river could do no less! **4.** *Mountains:* also personified, probably those of Sinai, trembling at the theophany (v. 7). This playful exercise of poetic imagination is not lacking in other poetic descriptions (cf. Pss 96:11–12 and 98:7–8). **5–6.** The dramatic repetition of the frolicsome questions prepares for the climactic ending in the following verses. **7–8.** If nature reacted so picturesquely in the previous lines, what can *earth* (Sinai, Canaan, or perhaps the entire world) do, but tremble? Tempering the fearsome theophany of the Lord is the reference to Kadesh, where God wondrously provided water for the people (Num 20:1–11 and Ps 105:41).

Psalm 115. There is no easy classification of the psalm's genre; it combines lament, confidence, petition, and praise in what seems to be a choir song of Temple liturgy. It is certainly distinct from Psalm 114, with which it has been connected in some Hebrew mss. and ancient versions. Structure: vv. 1–3, a motif from a lament; vv. 4–8, a hymnic satire about idols; vv. 9–18, a liturgical dialogue. **1–3.** A request for aid is implicit, and to be realized, not by Israel but by the Lord alone, who acts for the sake of the *name* (cf. Ps 113:1–2). The stereotypical question dramatizes the ridicule of the *nations* (Ps 79:10). It is answered by the confident statement about *our God* in v. 3, and in the ensuing description of the ineffectiveness of the nations' idols. **4–8.** Partially repeated in Ps 135:15–18. This is a satire against dead idols in the style of Isa 40:18–20; 44:9–20; Jer 10:3–16; and Wis 13:10–15:17. As Israel deepened its idea of monotheism, any divine image came to represent a zero; hence, the image has *eyes,* but no vision, etc. Notice the imprecation in v. 8. **9–11.** This appeal to *trust* appears to be directed to all *Israel,* to the priests *of Aaron,* and to the "proselytes" *(you who fear the LORD,* v. 11). The same series of worshipers also appears in Pss 118:2–4 and 135:19–20. *Help and shield:* for this repetition see Ps 33:20. **12–13.** The three classes just mentioned seem to unite in hymnic antiphonal response *(us).* **14–15.** Perhaps a solo voice replies in a blessing addressing the speakers of vv. 12–13 *(you).* **16–18.** *We* suggests that the entire community speaks these lines in a final cadenza. The mention of the plight of the *dead* in Sheol is not as strange as it may appear at first sight. The blessings have to do with life—the very opposite for those who are in *silence.* The issue is praise of God, which the shades cannot perform. Only *we* on the *earth* given to us by God can do that; to live is to praise God.

Psalm 116. A song of thanksgiving, divided in the LXX and Vulgate into two psalms (vv. 1–9; 10–19). Verses 17–19 suggest a setting in the Temple where the psalmist fulfills vows and offers a thanksgiving sacrifice. Structure: vv. 1–2, acknowledgement of the Lord's response to supplication; vv. 3–4, description of past distress; vv. 5–6, a lesson from the way the Lord delivered the psalmist; vv. 7–9, an acknowledgement of new life; vv. 10–11, a flashback; vv. 12–19, acknowledgment of the Lord as rescuer. **1.** Literally the MT reads, "I love because the LORD has heard. . . ." **3.** See the comment on Ps 18:5 for the imagery. *Death* appears also in vv. 8 and 15. This kind of language is typical of the psalms' efforts to express distress of any nature. **4.** To call *on the name of the LORD* means here to ask for help, but in vv. 13 and 17 it means to proclaim the sacred name in thanksgiving. **5–6.** The didactic tendency of the thanksgiving psalm is exemplified in a lesson preached to those who are present in the Temple. **9.** *In the land of the living:* the phrase seems obviously to refer to being alive again, restored from the death that threatened (cf. Pss 27:13; 52:5; Isa 38:11). Others take it to refer to the psalmist's presence in the Temple. **10–11.** See the comment on Ps 30:6–10. **11.** *Liar:* i.e., not dependable or trustworthy. **13.** The *cup of salvation* seems to be part of a libation rite that pours out the contents of the cup. **15.** The death of the *faithful* is *precious,* i.e., the faithful are are too dear to the Lord to be allowed to die. For blood (= death) being precious, see Ps 72:14. **16.** *Serving girl:* see the comment on Ps 86:16.

Psalm 117. A song of praise, the shortest psalm in the Psalter. The structure is a model of hymn style: a summons to praise, then the reason for it. The Gentiles are invited to praise the Lord because of the saving acts that God performed on behalf of Israel—*hesed* and *'emet,* the love and fidelity that are the enduring qualities of God's relationship to Israel. Many other psalms have displayed universalism (e.g., Ps 96), but this short summons is very direct, even imperious. Paul picks it up in Rom 15:11.

Psalm 118. A song of thanksgiving. It has received many varying interpretations, but as a whole it fits the description of a thanksgiving liturgy. Structure: vv. 1–4, a summons to praise the Lord; vv. 5–18, a typical thanksgiving song of an individual; vv. 19–28, a proclamation and indication of a liturgical procession and dialogue; v. 29, an inclusio with v. 1. If the *I* is not the king, it is still an important leader who heads a public thanksgiving and procession to the Temple. Jewish tradition associated the poem with the joyous feast of Tabernacles. **1.** See v. 29. This proclamation addresses the entire community. Then it is partially taken up in the litany that follows (vv. 2–4), uttered by the three classes indicated in Ps 115:9–11. **5–9.** An acknowledgement of rescue, typical of thanksgiving psalms. It expresses supreme confidence in the Lord (vv. 6–7) and offers two "better"-sayings in the wisdom style. **10–13.** The song returns to the distress, portrayed with exaggeration and emphasis (*cut them off,* three times). The *nations* are never identified. **15–16.** The speaker makes the victory songs come alive with a quotation about the *right hand of the* LORD, which is so prominent in Israel's history (Exod 15:6, 12). **17–18.** Physical death is meant, and a full life on earth is implied. The treatment *(punished)* from the Lord is measured, perhaps comparable to the discipline of a father (Prov 3:11–12). **19.** This cry initiates a dialogue between the speaker and Temple personnel. **20.** The reply to the appeal to open the gates in v. 19. The gates are presumably gates of the Temple, where the "righteousness" of the one who enters is emphasized (cf. Pss 15 and 24); only the just *(tsaddiqim),* or victors, can enter. **21.** The prayer of thanksgiving is taken up again (cf. vv. 5, 14). **22.** The symbol of the cornerstone derives from the practice of stonemasons of choosing only the best quality to be in a key position of the building. The NT interpretation makes copious use of this verse in reference to Christ (cf. Matt 21:42; Acts 4:11, etc.). **24.** The *day* is the time in which the Lord acted and delivered (vv. 5, 14, and 16). **25.** *Save us:* the abbreviated form of the Hebrew appears in English as "hosanna." **26.** We do not know who *comes in the name of the LORD,* but the person who is hailed thus is obviously important, and is to be identified with the speaker in this psalm, perhaps a king. He receives a blessing from an unidentified group *(we bless you),* who are doubtless Temple personnel. **27.** The proclamation, whether by the speaker or the group, reflects the light that comes from God, as in Num 6:25 (also Ps 36:9). Verse 27b is obscure; the text envisions some kind of liturgical action at the *horns of the altar.* **28.** The speaker of this praise of God seems to be the main actor of the psalm. **29.** See v. 1.

Psalm 119. An acrostic poem of 176 verses. Each of the eight verses of the first stanza begins with the first letter of the Hebrew alphabet *(alef);* each verse of the second stanza begins with the second letter *(bet);* and so on for all twenty-two letters of the Hebrew alphabet. In contrast to the NIV, NAB, and other translations, the NRSV does not print the Hebrew letters designating the stanzas. There are eight verses to a stanza, and in practically every verse a synonym for the Torah (= teaching) occurs: the list includes, law (or teaching, *torah,* twenty-five times), decrees, statutes, commandments, ordinance(s), word, precepts, and promise. There are only a few instances in which one of these terms does not appear: vv. 3, 37, 90, and 122. There is little profit in trying to determine the exact nuance of each Hebrew word; the general term, *torah,* serves as the umbrella under which the others fit. Torah does not mean the Pentateuch, nor merely "law" in a narrow legal sense. The devotion to law in this psalm is not to be confused with legalism; it is rather devotion to the divine will, the divine word, which for Israel was being continually actualized in its experience.

Despite what has just been said, the skeleton structure of the psalm and its repetitions strike many as flat and boring. That judgment is not fair. There is a certain mantralike style of repetition that is at work here; one can be mesmerized by the various aspects of the divine word in a manner that is conducive to devotion. There is considerable movement within the psalm: motifs of complaint, request, praise, admiration, praise, contrition, trust, love, salvation, and life. There is also a certain charm in the lack of logical progression and in the sudden leaps from faith to grief, from admiration to puzzlement.

1. This is a programmatic statement; *torah* is not an abstraction, but is the law *of the* LORD, the revelation of God's will for Israel. As in Ps 1:1, the plural is used for the sake of gender inclusivity. *Way:* another of the frequent synonyms; cf. vv. 3, 5, 14, 15, etc. **2.** For wholehearted devotion, inspired by Deut 6:5, see vv. 10, 34, 58, 69, and 145. **14.** The note of joy in the observance of Law is sounded very often: vv. 16, 24, 35, 47, 50, 77, 92, 111, 143, and 174. The comparison of wisdom with *riches* (see also vv. 72 and 127) is characteristic of the doctrine of the sages (e.g., Prov 3:13–16). Curiously enough, the psalm does not highlight wisdom, although later, by the time of Ben Sira (about 200 B.C.E.), Jews identified wisdom and law (Sir 24:23). **19.** *Alien:* the Hebrew *ger,* sojourner or wayfarer, is one who has no claim to possession of territory. The meaning is spiritualized here to indicate one for whom the Lord is the only claim; the pilgrim seeks not land, but to know the divine will. **22–23.** Motifs from the lament genre occur often, as here, and in vv. 28, 49–54, 61, 81–88, 132–36, and 153–58. However, the extravagant language of the lament appears only rarely (e.g., *wineskin* in v. 83). **25b.** Note the connection between *word* and life, vv. 28 and 107. **32b.** The literal Hebrew is better: "you make wide my heart." **34.** *Understanding:* meant in a religious sense, like "fear of the Lord" (cf. vv. 73 and 144). **41.** Note the parallelism between *steadfast love* and *salvation.* **49.** *Remember:* usually this call to God in the psalms occurs in desperate straits; here it is a mild reminder of the *hope* that the writer places in the *word* (cf. vv. 81–82). **83.** Containers for wine or water were often made of leather, which would become brittle in the warmth of a home. **89.** *Forever:* is matched by the same word in v. 93, and it means indefinite duration. For other instances of the idea, see Isa 40:8 and Ps 89:1–2. **96.** The thought is obscure. *Perfection* is a hapax legomenon. Perhaps the NRSV means that the human fulfillment of God's *commandment*, which is *exceedingly broad*, falls short of what it should be. **98–102.** A certain wisdom flavor appears in these verses that deal with teachings of the sages (vv. 99–100), and the Lord has been the teacher of the psalmist (cf. also vv. 124–125). **105.** A famous quotation concerning Scripture. See also v. 130. **120.** Strong language for fear or awe before the Lord; this is not servile fear, but a fear that lives also with love. **127.** See vv. 14 and 72, and also Ps 19:10. **145–160.** The stanzas marked by *Qof* and *Resh* contain more intense pleas for deliverance and life. **150–151.** Note the contrast between who is *far* and who is *near*. **159.** See v. 40. **161.** As in v. 23, *princes* is practically a metaphor for people of influence. **162.** The metaphor of rich *spoil* suggests only the rejoicing of the psalmist. **164.** *Seven times:* the number may denote an indefinite series of repetitions, but for later readers, it also sets the tone for the monastic recitation of the Office of the church. **169–176.** The *Tav* stanza reflects many emotions scattered through the poem: pleas, praise, joy, salvation, and life. The final verse, v. 176, is in curious contradiction to v. 110; this forthright admission at the end serves as a motive for the Lord to continue to aid a weak human being.

One can only admire the dexterity of the author in working within the narrow framework of an acrostic, and yet capturing so many various dimensions of human existence before God. The poem is an example of the "anthological composition" that became common toward the end of the OT period, i.e., a borrowing of phraseology from earlier (biblical) works. Yet, this is no mean art. It presupposes on the part of both author and reader a fundamental and complete knowledge of "the law, the prophets, and the later authors," as the translator wrote in the preface to his Greek presentation of Ben Sira, who himself epitomized this style of writing. The so-called *Hodayot* (= praises) from Qumran offer another example, replete with phrases from previous books of the Bible.

Psalm 120. "A Song of Ascents" is the NRSV translation of the superscription at the beginning of each of the psalms numbered 120–134. The phrase has been variously interpreted, as referring to the fifteen steps leading from one court to another in the Temple (hence they have also been known from the Latin Vulgate version as "gradual" or "step" psalms), or as songs of the exiles "going up" to Jerusalem. Today there is a consensus that they are pilgrimage songs which the faithful would have used in going up to the Jerusalem Temple to celebrate. As a group, they are shorter than most; many of them have collective applications (e.g., Ps 130:8). Note also a striking repetitive style, e.g., "keep" in Psalm 121, "peace" in Ps 122:6–8; "unless" in Psalm 127; "often" in Psalm 129.

Structure of Psalm 120: vv. 1–2, an appeal to the Lord; vv. 3–4, an imprecation; vv. 5–7, a complaint about the present situation. **1–2.** NRSV translates v. 1 as though it were a lament, and v. 2, the appeal. But it is possible, with the NAB, NJPS, and other translations, to render the verbs as past tense, indicating thanksgiving; then v. 2 is the prayer that the poet uttered in distress. **3–4.** The imprecation is directed against the personified *deceitful tongue* (perhaps slander). The question derives from the self-imprecation formula, "Thus may the Lord do, and more," which appears elsewhere in the Bible (2 Sam 3:9). The reply is colorful, an arrow for the tongue, and also the intense heat given off by the *broom tree*. **5.** Geography makes this impossible; Meshech is the name of an ancient people of northeast Asia Minor; Kedar is the name of a desert tribe from north Arabia. They are so far apart that they have to be taken metaphorically, perhaps as an expression of the alienation the poet feels. **6–7.** Wherever the psalmist may be, he resides *among those who hate peace*—at cross-purposes with his peaceful intent.

Psalm 121. A psalm of trust, characterized by the sixfold repetition of the term *keep* or "guard." Structure: vv. 1–2, question and answer; vv. 3–8, an address to the speaker. **1–2.** *Hills:* a reference to the safe haven of the Temple mount in Jerusalem, or to the dangers in the hills of Judah? Perhaps the question is deliberately ambiguous, but it seems to be solved in v. 2; the poet knows where *help comes* from. The verses mark a dramatic beginning for the rest of the psalm, which is best understood as a further assurance, from one of the Temple personnel, of divine help (cf. Ps 91:3–13). **3–6.** The reply is dominated by the word *keep,* and the various characterizations of the Lord, who never sleeps, and protects from moon stroke (a reference to lunatics? cf. Ps 91:5–6) and from sunstroke (Isa 49:10). **7–8.** Not only safety from dangers, but the personal attention of the Lord is promised "forever" in all activities, *going* and *coming* (cf. Ps 139:1–3).

Psalm 122. A song of Zion, on the occasion of a pilgrimage to Jerusalem. Structure: vv. 1–2, arrival at Jerusalem, the cause of joy; vv. 3–5, praise of Zion; vv. 6–9, prayers for Jerusalem. **1.** Presumably on arrival at Jerusalem, the pilgrim recalls the joy with which he or she received the invitation to make the pilgrimage. **3–5.** The admiration for the holy city echoes the awe of Ps 48:12–13. God *decreed* (Exod 23:14–17) three annual pilgrimages to Jerusalem, which became the place of worship after David transferred the Ark there (Ps 132). Here also *judgment* by royal officials was pronounced (cf. 1 Kgs 7:7). **6–9.** The opening line of v. 6 has a particularly beautiful sound. Roughly it goes this way: "*Sha'alu shalom Yerushalayim.*" The third mention of Jerusalem in the poem is a play on the name. The prayers for the city center upon *peace,* or "shalom," which is reflected in the name, Jerusalem; *nomen est omen.* The centerpiece of it all is of course *the house of the LORD* (an inclusio with v. 1). There are few cities that can equal the symbolic power of Jerusalem (cf. also Rev 21) in the history of the human race.

Psalm 123. A soft lament that is filled with confidence, probably reflecting an exilic or postexilic attitude. Structure: v. 1, a gesture of expectancy; v. 2, a comparison; vv. 3–4, an appeal for mercy. **1.** A representative of the community speaks, as seems clear from the plural in vv. 3–4. The *eyes* lifted heavenward become the key symbol in the threefold repetition to follow. **2.** The brevity of the comparisons conjures up a vivid picture, most of it left unsaid, but very suggestive. The *eyes* on the *hand* suggest alertness, readiness, expectancy, and obedience, which derive from the final gaze—*to the LORD.* As one looks to the largesse (as well as the command) that comes from the hands of master/mistress, so one looks expectantly to God. **3–4.** The repetition in this short prayer is particularly striking: *eyes,* and *have mercy upon us,* and *more than enough/fill.* The repetitive style is characteristic of the Songs of Ascent. The *contempt* mentioned in the final verse cannot be further specified.

Psalm 124. A thanksgiving song of the community. Again, the repetitive style is conspicuous: *If . . .* (repeated in v. 2); *then* (three times); *escaped* (twice). Structure: vv. 1–5, a description of a failed threat from unnamed enemies; vv. 6–7, thanksgiving for deliverance; v. 8, a proclamation of trust. **1–5.** This vivid repetitious outcry expresses what would have been, but for the Lord's help. It is a rhetorical invitation for the community to join with the psalmist *now;* as v. 1a makes clear, the danger is over. Verses 4–5 compare hostile powers in a perennial metaphor to the unruly *waters* (Isa 51:10) that the Lord consistently rebukes (Ps 104:6–7). **6–7.** The metaphors change to those of teeth of a wild animal, and also the trap of *fowlers.* The latter was a wooden instrument, with nets triggered to capture the prey. **8.** For this avowal, see Pss 121:2 and 146:5–6. In one form or another, this is a frequent theme in Christian liturgy.

Psalm 125. A national psalm of trust in God in the face of difficulties. Structure: vv. 1–2, a description of those who trust in the Lord; vv. 3–5, a prayer for the upright. **1–2.** The reasons for trusting are two: (1) the inviolability of *Zion* (cf. Ps 48:8), which shares in the very permanence of God; (2) the protection of the Lord, comparable to the *mountains* that *surround* Zion. **3.** The Bible rarely expresses the reason for this as concretely as this psalm does here: for the sake of the upright, wickedness must disappear from the land. This is in order to keep Israelites from temptation to do *wrong.* Their historical records and the prophets show that they did fail. The metaphor of the *scepter* refers to either internal or external oppression, or perhaps both. *The land allotted to the righteous:* the phrase hearkens back to the division of the promised land (Josh 15:1 and 17:1). **4–5.** An appeal for the Lord to intervene with appropriate judgment for the *upright* and the *evildoers.* The poem concludes with a prayer for the *peace* of Israel, just as in Ps 128:6 (cf. Ps 122:8).

Psalm 126. More important than genre classification (lament of the community) is the capture of the mood of the psalm, which has been neatly expressed as "joy remembered and joy anticipated" (J. L. Mays, *Psalms*, 399). Structure: vv. 1–3, a historical survey; vv. 4–6, a plea for restoration. **1–3.** The speakers, whether or not they were participants, refer to the joyous end of the exile. Those who returned could hardly believe that they had. Their experience was like a *dream*. The deliverance was such that even the *nations* acknowledged it—an exaggeration typical of the Psalter. Note the characteristic repetition in vv. 2–3. The emphasis on joy is clear from the terms for rejoicing (five times) **4.** The implication is that the postexilic period has not been all that it was envisioned to be (cf. also Isa 40–66). In the poet's own time, the Lord's continuing intervention remains necessary. The comparison to the wadis *in the Negeb* bears on the transformation undergone by the dry and caked valleys, once water courses through them. **5.** This has the air of a proverb that v. 6 explains more fully. The toil and labor involved in planting will be followed by the joy of the harvest.

Psalm 127. A slice of wisdom (note the ascription to Solomon who was famous for his wisdom and building exploits). In a sense, this is hardly a "psalm"; it looks more like proverbial exhortations. The structure pivots on the theme of building: vv. 1–2, a house; vv. 3–5, a family. **1.** The comparisons are to a material building and to the guarding of a city (cf. Ps 121). **2.** The Lord is the giver of every gift, no matter the human effort in earning a living by *anxious toil*—a teaching also found in Prov 10:22. This idea underlies much of the OT understanding of life. Even so, laziness is roundly condemned in the wisdom literature (e.g., Prov 10:4–5). But here lies a paradox as well: the Lord gives to a favored one *during sleep* (reading the NRSV footnote). God gives as God pleases. **3–5.** This understanding of a role of *sons* in a family typifies OT life. The comparison to *arrows* (see also *quiver* in v. 5) lies in the protection that males provide for a family, as v. 5 specifies. In the judicial processes that take place at the *gate* of the city (cf. Prov 31:23), their large number will be a support to the father.

Psalm 128. A psalm of "blessings," showing wisdom influence. Verses 3–4 reflect the outlook indicated above in Ps

127:3–5; the common theme is children. Structure: vv. 1–4, a beatitude that spells out prosperity for the family; note the inclusio in vv. 1 and 4; vv. 5–6, another blessing, on the individual and on Zion. **1.** Note how *fear of the LORD* is interpreted in v. 1b. The emphasis on the *ways* is characteristic of Psalm 1 and also Prov 4:10–27. **2–4.** The reward for such fear of God is prosperity and a large progeny. The comparisons, *vine* and *olive,* derive from staples of Israelite life, and here symbolize a fruitful wife. **5–6.** The blessing on the God-fearer continues, as a blessing from the Lord in Zion, which will be extended also to future progeny and will involve the prosperity of Jerusalem itself. It may be presumed that this blessing would be given by one of the Temple personnel. The last line is repeated in Ps 125:5.

Psalm 129. Like Psalm 126, this psalm looks both backward and forward; in view of the past difficult experiences, let the Lord hear the appeal to punish Zion's enemies. Structure: vv. 1–4, a summary of Israel's sad history of oppression and deliverance; vv. 5–8, a prayer for punishment of Zion's enemies. The problem lies in the mood: are vv. 1–4 a thanksgiving song of relief that the difficult period is over, as in Psalm 124? More likely it is a recalling of past oppression that seeks to move the Lord to grant the present appeal (vv. 5–8). **1–3.** *Let Israel now say:* see Ps 124:1b. The past history of oppression is over, according to v. 1b, but it was severe. Israel has barely survived. Israel did not merely serve as a beast of burden, but it was itself thoroughly *plowed.* Note the characteristic repetition; *from my youth* suggests that the period envisioned is from exodus to exile. **4.** *Cords of the wicked:* this continues the plowing metaphor; the Lord cuts the ropes that would have yoked the animal. **5–8.** The focus is on *Zion,* the center of the postexilic community. **6.** *Grass on the housetops:* such grass that happens to grow on the roofs of beaten earth has no root and cannot last. Of course, there will be no harvest cry since there is nothing to reap. **8.** *Blessing,* such as that of the harvesters (cf. Ruth 2:4), will not be heard by the enemies, whom vv. 6–7 have already compared to unharvested crops. It is not clear if the last line is a separate blessing, but the whole is idealistic; those *who hate Zion* (v. 5) would never hear such soothing words.

Psalm 130. A lament of an individual, popularly known by its Latin incipit, "De profundis." It is the sixth of the seven "penitential" psalms; see the comment on Psalm 6. Structure: vv. 1–2, an ardent appeal for God to listen; vv. 3–6, reason to trust in the Lord's forgiveness; vv. 7–8, an address to the community. **1–2.** The opening cry is typical of the lament (e.g., Ps 5:1–3). *Out of the depths:* from the watery deep, chaos, the sphere of death and Sheol, far from God. Sheol occurs frequently as a symbol of distress in this life. *Depths* can refer broadly to all troubles, psychological or otherwise. Interestingly, it is the only reference in the poem to trouble, since the next verse goes on to appeal to God's mercy in a subtle way. **3–4.** The question in v. 3 has no rival. Were the Lord to keep score, there would be no hope for anyone. But immediately the text recalls the forgiving nature of God (cf. Exod 34:6–7). This poignant question underlines divine generosity. The experience of God's mercy leads into fear; *revered* suggests too superficial a meaning. Fear of God is many things, from trembling to simple obedience; all this is involved in v. 4. **5–6.** The *word* so ardently awaited may be an oracle of salvation from a priest, indicating divine forgiveness. Note the repetition in v. 6, so characteristic of the Songs of Ascent. **7–8.** Again (cf. Ps 123), there is a movement from the individual to the community; v. 7a is repeated in Psalm 131:3a. Israel is urged to adopt the same hope that has just been expressed, for the Lord is one who redeems Israel not only from Egypt, but *from all its iniquities,* just as the psalmist believes.

Psalm 131. A psalm of trust. The speaker implicitly offers loyalty and modest achievement to the Lord in a spirit of serene confidence. Structure: v. 1, a statement of personal humility and limited goals. v. 2, an affirmation of childlike trust; v. 3, a recommendation to Israel. **1.** The things *too marvelous* are not specified, but they would indicate various issues confronting a person. Job uses the same phrase in Job 42:3b to indicate what he had been struggling with. This is a counsel not to give up, but to recognize one's limitations, and implicitly to control a competitive spirit. **2.** The comparison to a *weaned child* in a mother's lap evokes all the safety and quiet imaginable, and it is intensified by the repetition characteristic of this group of psalms. *With me:* the

Hebrew is ambiguous; the reading in the footnote is preferable; NRSV implies that a mother is speaking. **3.** The appeal to the people repeats Ps 130:7a, and follows the pattern of proceeding from the individual to the community.

Psalm 132. A royal psalm that does not identify the speaker(s). It rehearses two oaths, those of David (vv. 1–10) and of the Lord (vv. 11–18). David swore to provide a house for the Lord; the Lord swore to provide a house for David by the choice of Zion and the dynasty (or "house") of David. The poem is an imaginative and probably liturgical version of 2 Samuel 6–7. Structure: vv. 1–5, a prayer for David for his concern about the Lord's dwelling; vv. 6–10, a description of a procession of the Ark that was found; vv. 11–12, the Lord's oath to assure David of a dynasty; vv. 13–18, the Lord's eternal choice of Zion. **1.** *Hardships:* perhaps referring to David's struggle with Saul? The speaker of this prayer might be, in view of v. 17, the king or one of the Temple personnel. **2.** The oath appears to be a creation of poetic license; the tradition in 2 Sam 7:1–3 is different. *The Mighty One of Jacob:* not a common title (cf. Gen 49:24), but appearing also in v. 5. **6–7.** The sudden transition is difficult. Who is the *we*? What does *it* refer to? This seems to be a recreation of the finding of the Ark of the covenant (hence the *it*) at Kiriath-jearim (here, *the fields of Jaar*). *Ephrathah* is an area associated with Bethlehem. Whatever the geographical and historical details may be, the cry in v. 7 *(let us)* represents dramatically the joy at the finding of the Ark (the *footstool;* Ps 99:5 and 1 Chr 28:2), and bringing it to Jerusalem (1 Sam 7:2 and 2 Sam 6:1–19). This suggests, along with the following verses, a liturgical scene in which the Ark was carried in procession. **8–10.** The Chronicler inserts these words in his version of Solomon's prayer at the dedication of the Temple (2 Chr 6:41–42). *Rise up:* so begins the cry of Moses when the Israelites carried the Ark in the desert. **9.** *Clothed with righteousness:* there is a kind of identity between clothing and being (cf. Pss 30:11–12 and 109:29). Note the repetition in v. 16. **10.** *Anointed one:* the currently reigning king. **11.** The oracle to Nathan (2 Sam 7:1–17) was not technically an oath, but Ps 89:3 so describes the Davidic covenant. The promise secures the permanence of the dynasty, provided the descendants are faithful; this proviso does not appear in Ps 89:20–37, where this covenant with David is unconditional, as is the case with 2 Sam 7:14–15. **13–18.** The choice of *Zion* underscores the *resting place* (v. 8) of the Lord. The quotation marks in the NRSV indicates that these lines are the Lord's blessing. Note the triad: bread for the *poor, salvation,* and *joy.* **17.** *Horn to sprout:* the mixed metaphor involves the *horn* of an animal as a symbol of strength, and a plant *sprout* to designate a descendant *(tsemah)* of David as in Jer 23:5; Zech 3:7, etc. The metaphor of the *lamp* derives from the Temple lamp that burned perpetually (Lev 24:2). **18.** See the comment on v. 9. This psalm bears witness to a lively messianic hope that perdured during the postexilic period and found expression in the New Testament (e.g., Luke 1:69).

Psalm 133. The genre of the poem is unusual; it praises the unity of a group of Israelites, culminating with those in Zion, where the Lord's blessing occurs. **1.** *Kindred:* lit., "brothers"; this should be understood in the broad sense of an extended family, or even the entire people. What is praiseworthy is their *unity.* **2.** The vision of unity and peace resembles the holy *oil* running copiously on the beard of Aaron, the high priest (cf. the anointing in Exod 30:30). **3.** The second comparison is to the *dew of Hermon,* the mountain range north of Palestine, which would have provided water runoff from its snowy heights. It is an imaginative leap to think it irrigates the *mountains* (in the plural!) *of Zion.* But Jerusalem is the poet's goal, for the divine *blessing* rests *there. Life forevermore:* not eternal life, but continuing prosperity and *shalom.*

Psalm 134. A liturgical blessing, the last of the Songs of Ascent; the psalm is dominated by the word, *bless;* cf. the preceding psalm. **1.** *Servants of the LORD:* priests, Levites, even a choir, are summoned to praise the Lord (see Pss 113:1 and 135:1–2). **3.** This blessing is addressed to a single individual, but perhaps *you* is a collective. As it stands, it may be a blessing of the Lord, which the *servants* pronounce over a pilgrim.

Looking back on the Songs of Ascent (Pss 120–134) as a whole, we become aware of the rich liturgical life that they suggest. They also provide a selective compendium of Israelite beliefs. No doubt, too, the deep expressions of spiritual life arise from their association with pilgrimages, a use that seems probable. Zion/Jerusalem, and all that God's choice of this place as his dwelling involves, lie at the heart of these prayers, and that may explain the absence of references to Sinai and the Exodus.

Psalm 135. A hymn of praise that echoes phraseology from other psalms in the style of the so-called anthological composition. Structure: vv. 1–4, introductory summons to praise; vv. 5–14, reasons for the praise; vv. 15–18, the futility of idols; vv. 19–21, a concluding exhortation to praise the Lord. **1–4.** Note the repetition of *praise* and LORD. *Servants:* see the comment on Ps 134:1. **4.** The choice of Israel as treasured *possession,* a favorite term in Deuteronomy (see also Exod 19:5), is paradoxical. On the one hand, Israel is really not a great nation, and Deut 7:7 makes that clear. On the other hand, all creation and peoples belong to the Lord, yet Israel has unique status, for they received the *heritage* of the land (v. 12). **5–14.** The *I* seems to be a representative of the community who rehearses in conventional terminology the power of the Lord as creator and as conqueror of Egypt (note the bravado style in the address of v. 9) and also of the Canaanites (cf. Num 21:21–35). **13–14.** This closes the rehearsal of the praises. **15–18.** Virtually identical with Ps 115:4–8; see comment there. **19–21.** The mood of the ending reflects the opening verses, vv. 1–3. The invocation proceeds from the nation to those who fear the Lord, groups that Pss 115:9–11 and 118:2–4 already also distinguish.

Psalm 136. A song of praise in the form of a litany, in Jewish tradition called the "Great Hallel" and recited at the Passover Seder service. Structure: vv. 1–3, introduction; vv. 4–22, praise because of the Lord's creative power and saving actions on behalf of Israel; vv. 23–26, conclusion. The song seems to be designed for antiphonal rendering: the first line by a soloist and the refrain by the congregation. The importance of the refrain drives away the monotony that repetition can create. The *steadfast love* (Hebrew: *hesed*) of the Lord has appeared all though the Psalter and indeed the OT as a key theological term, and it is now dramatically celebrated in liturgy. In view of Israel's checkered history and often puzzling relationship to the Lord, the confession is all the more moving. **1–3.** The opening invitation recalls the first lines of Psalms 106 and 107. The Hebrew idiom for the superlative is apparent in *the God of gods.* **4–9.** The cosmological picture is much the same as that of Genesis 1; as in the Pentateuch creation serves as a prelude to the salvation history. **13–15.** In contrast to Ps 135:8–10, these verses commemorate the crossing of the Red Sea. **17–22.** Cf. Ps 135:10–12. **23–25.** *Us:* the present community is also the recipient of the Lord's gracious intervention, but the date of the psalm cannot be determined. It may be postexilic. If so, the prayer is a lively witness to the belief in divine deliverance. Now the text returns to a universal note of God's providing *food.* **26.** An inclusio with v. 1, but *the God of heaven* is a unique title in the OT (cf. Jonah 1:9).

Psalm 137. A lament of the community, dating from the exile or the postexilic period. Structure: vv. 1–3, a flashback to the experiences in Babylon; vv. 4–6, an imprecation on the poet should he forget Jerusalem; vv. 7–9, an imprecation on those who destroyed Jerusalem in 587 B.C.E. **1.** *Rivers:* the reference is to settlement of the exiles in Babylon, where countless irrigation canals from the Tigris and Euphrates watered the plain. **2–3.** The situation is dramatized: there is no joy in Babylon. The request of the captors is analogous to the motif of the frequent question appearing in the lament, "where is your God?" (e.g., Pss 42:10 and 79:10). The "songs of Zion" has been adopted as a convenient classification of certain hymns (Pss 46, 48, 76, 84, 87, and 122). **4–6.** The poet introduces himself with a question that is an answer to the taunting demand of v. 3. It implies that "foreign" land is unclean and unfit for worship, as well as hostile. Cf. the request of Naaman for Israelite soil on which he might be able to stand when worshiping the Lord in Damascus (2 Kgs 5:17). While delivering this self-imprecation, the psalmist is at the same time singing a song of Zion! The reference to *hand* and *tongue* refers the reader back to harp and song. It is not clear what happens to the right hand; *wither* of NRSV is justifiable; others understand the verb as "forget" (its skill). These lines betray an intense loyalty to Zion and the Lord. **7–9.** *Edom* ravaged Judah during the fall of Jerusalem (Lam 4:21 and Obad 8–15). **9.** All warfare is barbaric, and no one practice is more brutal than another. Both ancient and modern warfare involve atrocities (cf. Hos 10:14; 13:16; and Nah 3:10). The mention of children here is a kind of cliché that sums up the usual horrors of war inflicted upon all, young as well as old. The writer is asking for the implementation of the talion law: let Babylon be punished in payment for what it did to the Israelites. The talion law (Exod 21:23–25 and Lev 24:17–22) was designed to produce equity in retribution. See the discussion of "enemies" in the Introduction above (pp. 46–52).

Psalm 138. A thanksgiving psalm. Structure: vv. 1–3, a thanksgiving for deliverance; vv. 4–6, a hymnlike proclamation of the universal recognition of God; vv. 7–8, an expression of trust and acknowledgment of the Lord's work. **1–3.** Hebrew *'elohim* can stand for God, or *gods*, and angels, the members of the heavenly court. Verse 2a suggests that this prayer is uttered in the court of the Temple. **4–5.** This idealistic and enthusiastic universalism has been met before in the Psalter (cf. the enthronement psalms, such as Pss 96 and 98). **6.** The very height of the Lord provides a view of everything (cf. Ps 113:5–6). **8.** The poet returns to the theme of the Lord's *hesed*, or *steadfast love* (cf. v. 2). That is the reason for the confidence expressed in v. 7. The final plea is not only for the psalmist (*the work of your hands*, as in Job 14:15; cf. Job 10:8), but for all.

Psalm 139. The classification of this famous psalm is uncertain: is it a hymn, a meditation on God's active presence, or the prayer of an accused person? It is possible that it is an affirmation of innocence—that would be the import of vv. 19–24—that follows considerations concerning God's loving presence. The "I-Thou" character of the poem makes it one of the most personal expressions in the Bible; abstract notions of divine omniscience and omnipresence take concrete form. Structure: vv. 1–6, an address to God concerning his intimate knowledge of the speaker; vv. 7–12, the impossibility of escaping the divine presence; vv. 13–19, admiration of the divine involvement in the very birth and predestination of the psalmist; vv. 19–24, a plea to see divine justice at work, and to remain faithful. **1–3.** Merism is common in Hebrew poetry; one is either sitting or standing, walking or not; this figure of speech stands for completeness, "at all times." Note the inclusio in v. 23, *search.* **6.** The manifestations of divine *knowledge* elicit admiration. **7.** In an imaginative flight the poet describes how one cannot elude the divine *spirit.* Were one to be taken up like Elijah (2 Kgs 2:9–11), or to sink to the depths of Sheol like Korah and Dothan (Num 16:29–33), there is no escape from God. Although there is no loving contact with God in Sheol, this does not mean that even it is beyond divine reach (cf. Amos 9:2!). **9–10.** The speed with which the dawn comes will not suffice to evade the *hand* of God, no matter where one flees. **11–12.** In the *darkness* of Sheol, "night shines as the day," as v. 11b literally expresses it; v. 12 reaffirms that there is no darkness for God (only the "dark night of the soul" for humans?). **13–15.** The mystery of gestation is open to God—another sign of intimate presence (cf. Job 10:8–11). The *depths of the earth* means the womb, but the phrase may originally have reflected the story of the creation of humans from "mother" earth (cf. Gen 2:7, where *adam* was made from the *adamah*). **16.** The text is difficult, but it reflects the belief that God was thought to have the names of all human beings inscribed in a *book* (Pss 56:8 and 69:28). **17–18.** Another expression of admiration at the divine transcendence (cf. v. 6). On the divine *thoughts*, see Isa 55:8. **19–20.** The transition to this personal problem is very abrupt; the psalmist considers his opponents, the *wicked*, his personal foes. **21–22.** Personal *enemies* are identified as the enemies of God as well; as such they are seen as hateful. The emotional connotation of hatred is not present; this amounts to a declaration of loyalty, as if to say "your enemies are my enemies." Of course anyone may say this too glibly. As sinners, the enemies of God are worthy of rejection, but it should be added that it is for God to determine who these are, not the psalmist. See the discussion of "enemies" in the Introduction (pp. 46–52). **23–24.** These verses soften considerably the apparently self-righteous tone of the preceding lines. There is no complacency here, for the psalmist intones *search me!* The writer is aware of personal weakness, that the *way* is crooked. Should there be any wavering in personal loyalty, that same God, who is all-knowing (vv. 1–18), is also able and willing to bring about a change and lead into the paths of old. *Way everlasting:* a unique phrase, probably referring to tried and true fidelity to the

Lord. This psalm is castrated in some prayer books that eliminate vv. 19–22 as disturbing to "prayer." This seems wrongheaded. Should not prayer be realistic and confront human reality?

Psalm 140. A lament of an individual. The poet is beset by calumnies of wicked people, but the description is too general to permit specific conclusions (cf. Ps 64). Structure: vv. 1–3, a plea for protection against enemies; vv. 4–5, the same plea, renewed; vv. 6–7, a confident prayer; vv. 8–11, an imprecation (?); vv. 12–13, a confident conclusion. **3.** The metaphors resemble Pss 52:2–3; 58:3–4; and 64:3. **5.** For the metaphor of the *trap*, see Ps 64:5 and comment on Ps 124:7. **9–11.** Although the text is uncertain, the poet invokes the talion law (see comment on Ps 137:9) and wishes to see the enemies defeated by their own devices (cf. comment on Ps 7:15). **12–13.** This affirmation is supremely confident, as the speaker implicitly associates himself with the *upright*.

Psalm 141. A lament of an individual. Structure: vv. 1–2, a cry for God to hear; vv. 3–7, a prayer not to be led astray; vv. 8–10, a confident plea. **2.** In the liturgy God accepts sacrifice—so also may this prayer be received, *as incense*, literally "smoke." This would be the smoke rising from incense burned with sacrifice (Lev 16:13). Uplifted *hands* are the typical gesture of prayer (Pss 28:2 and 134:2). **3–4.** The fear is that of being seduced by the wicked (cf. Ps 125:3 and the warning in Prov 1:10–19). **5–7.** Hence any discipline from the *faithful* can only be beneficial. NRSV footnotes indicate how uncertain the text is; the translation seems to affirm the eventual punishment of the wicked. **8–10.** The psalmist prays that the *wicked* fall into the very traps they have prepared for the *defenseless*.

Psalm 142. A lament of an individual, marked by simplicity, humility, and trust. Structure: vv. 1–2, description of an appeal to God; vv. 3–4, the direct appeal; vv. 5–7, a renewed appeal with confidence of being heard. **1–2.** Despite the emphatic beginning, the psalm does not specify the *complaint*. **3–4.** The direct appeal *(you)* rests on the fact that God knows the *way/path* of the psalmist, and that a *trap* (the same word as in Ps 140:5) has been set, and no one cares. God must verify it. **5–7.** The appeal is renewed as the psalmist introduces the metaphor of *portion* (*heleq,* as in Ps 16:5) to describe the relationship to God. It is like the "portion" allotted to Aaron, namely the Lord (Num 18:20). *Prison:* probably another metaphor for the forlorn condition. But the outlook is positive, as the poet looks forward to a thanksgiving sacrifice, surrounded by the *righteous* (bystanders; cf. Ps 30:4).

Psalm 143. A lament of the individual, the seventh and final "penitential" psalm. It echoes the phraseology of other psalms in the style of anthological composition (cf. Ps 135). Structure: vv. 1–2, appeal to be heard; vv. 3–6, complaint; vv. 7–12, series of petitions. **1–2.** The appeal is rather puzzling. It is made to divine *faithfulness* and *righteousness,* and this motivation appears as an inclusio in v. 11. Like Psalm 26, this text makes an implicit claim that one has been loyal to God, who should respond in kind. At the same time, however, there is to be no strict *judgment!* The reason given is fairly common in the OT: no one is *righteous* before God (e.g., Job 4:17; 9:2; 25:4, etc.). In the earnestness of this appeal the psalmist wants to have it both ways (cf. Ps 130:3). **3–6.** *Darkness* is associated with the abode of the dead, as in Job 10:21–22. The memory of *days of old* is all the more tantalizing since those days seem unrepeatable; no wonder there is a *thirst.* **7.** For the hiding of the *face,* see the comment on Ps 10:11. **8–10.** As often, dawn is the time when God answers (cf. Ps 5:3). *Teach me the way:* this is practically the same as the request in v. 10a; the *way* is the *will* of God. The way out of the difficulty is to follow leadership of the *good spirit* (an uncommon phrase; cf. Neh 9:20) of God. For the Lord as teacher, see Ps 32:8–9. **11–12.** A certain directness and sincerity characterize the prayer: you are my God (v. 10); *I am your servant* (v. 12). At the same time, the psalmist makes a claim upon the Lord, *for your name's sake.* The attitude toward enemies (v. 12, *destroy all my adversaries*) reflects a steady fear in the Psalter. This category "enemies" is broader than what the modern reader imagines—they include not just personal enemies but the invisible world of unknown powers that affect the human condition. But the OT expresses more than one point of view. In 1 Kgs 3:10–12 the Lord

tells Solomon that because he did not ask for the life of his enemies, he would receive the "listening heart" that he requested. See
the discussion of "enemies" in the Introduction (pp. 46–52).

Psalm 144. The classification is difficult, due to shifts in
the poem. It finds echoes elsewhere (anthological composition;
cf. Ps 143), especially in Psalm 18, and it has elements of both lament and thanksgiving. It may even be called a royal psalm, as
v. 10 would indicate. Structure: vv. 1–2, a thanksgiving for divine
aid; vv. 3–4, a rhetorical question relative to human frailty;
vv. 5–8, a plea for deliverance; vv. 9–11, a vow of thanksgiving;
vv. 12–15, a communal prayer for prosperity. **1–2.** See Ps 18:2,
35, and 47. **3.** Although this verse recalls Ps 8:4, its tone differs
from the amazement expressed there. Now the question merely
underlines the fleeting existence of the mortals God has created,
as in Pss 39:5, 11 and 109:23. **5–8.** Cf. Ps 18:7–14; but here
the mood is that of pleading. Note the typically wide expanse
of the description of the dangers: *mighty waters, aliens,* and *lies.*
9–10. The vow of thanksgiving is phrased like Ps 33:2–3. **11.** In
an odd move, this verse practically repeats the plea of vv. 7–8.
12–15. The text is obscure, and its connection with the previous
lines is difficult to ascertain. NRSV interprets it as a wish, climax-
ing in the beatitude of v. 15. The picture is one of prosperity, with
references to the blessings of children (v. 12, sturdy indeed), produce of food and animals, and the safety of the city. It is no surprise, then, to see a double beatitude for that community (v. 15).

Psalm 145. This unusual psalm is the only one to be called
"praise" in the superscription, and praise it is. Moreover it is or-
chestrated in an acrostic pattern (cf. Pss 9–10 and 119). Each
verse begins with successive letters of the alphabet, *alef, bet,* etc.
The *nun* letter and verse is missing from the MT but found in the
ancient versions and is supplied here in v. 13b. Within the constraints of an acrostic pattern, the poem ranges widely, as the alternation between second and third person indicates. Structure:
vv. 1–3, direct address to the Lord with a shift to the third person
in v. 3; vv. 4–9, direct address, with a shift in vv. 8–9; vv. 10–14,
direct address, with a shift in vv. 13b–14; vv. 15–20, statement of
praise in the third person, with a shift in v. 20; v. 21, an inclusio

with v. 1. **1–2.** Note the repetition of bless/praise. Literally, the Lord is invoked as "my God the King," and kingship is taken up in vv. 12–13. **3.** Mortals can be "searched," as in Ps 139:1, 23, but not the Lord, who is simply unfathomable. **4–9.** Yet the poet proclaims the deeds/works of the Lord (cf. Ps 111:2–4), commemorated in the praise that has passed down through generations. The praise is, as it were, concentrated in v. 7, which recalls the credal formula of Exod 34:6–7, a confession that Israel often makes (Ps 103:8). **10–13a.** The poet weaves in the works/deeds of vv. 4–6, and the "king" of v. 1 in acclaiming the *kingdom* of God (note the repetition). **13b–14.** Supplying the missing *nun* verse allows for a kind of lead into the direct address that follows. **15–16.** The beneficent providence of God reflected in these lines has made them a popular prayer, especially at mealtime, in the Christian tradition (see also Ps 104:27–28). **17–20.** The beneficence of the Lord appears particularly to the worshipers, those who invoke, *fear*, and *love* God, in contrast to the *wicked*. **21.** *All flesh:* the nineteenth occurrence of *all* in a poem that looks at praise from many angles. Perhaps the most adequate commentary on this psalm is the witness of both Christian and Jewish tradition. St. Augustine opens his famous *Confessions* with a quotation of v. 3, and goes on to say: "Thou dost so excite him [referring to mortals] that to praise Thee is his joy. For Thou hast made us for Thyself and our hearts are restless till they rest in Thee" (*The Confessions of St. Augustine* [trans. F. J. Sheed; New York: Sheed & Ward, 1943], 3). In the Talmud we read: "Everyone who repeats the *Tehillah* of David thrice a day may be sure that he is a child of the world to come" (*Berakot*, 4*b*). The Hebrew word *tehillah* means "praise," and it is used here, the only time that it occurs in a superscription, to refer to Psalm 145.

Psalm 146. A song of praise. The Psalter comes to an end with five "hallelujah" psalms (Pss 146–150), i.e., they begin and end with the exclamation "praise Yah" (see the comment on Ps 113). Structure: vv. 1–2, hymnic introduction; vv. 3–4, admonition about trust; vv. 5–10, a beatitude, followed by a description of the Lord. **1–2.** See Ps 104:1, 33. **3–4.** The frequent motif of human mortality (Ps 90:3–6) serves here to point out the contrast to the following verses, which praises the Lord as one to be trusted in every crisis. *Princes:* symbols of powerful and rich leaders. **5–10.** This catalogue of divine attributes and performances emphasizes concrete actions (as is typical of the traditional conception of the Lord). Even the resident aliens (NRSV *strangers*), all those in need (cf. Exod 22:21–24), come under divine providence. **10.** An appeal to Zion, as the heart of the people.

Psalm 147. A song of praise. The structure revolves around three invitations to praise: vv. 1–6, the Lord as restorer of Israel and creator; vv. 7–11, the providential direction of nature; vv. 12–20, God's care of the people, regulating natural phenomena. The poem reflects other psalms and also Isaiah 40–66. **2.** The reference is to the end of the exile. **3.** See Isa 61:1. **4.** Cf. Isa 40:26–28. **5.** Surprisingly, references to the Lord's wisdom are relatively late in the OT. **6.** Cf. Pss 145:14 and 146:8. **8–9.** A description of continuous creation (cf. Ps 104:13–23). **10–11.** The metaphors are familiar (Pss 20:7; 33:16–17; and Prov 21:31). Material advantages count for little; one must *fear* the Lord. **13–14.** These are the primary blessings Israel hoped for (cf. Pss 127–128). **15–18.** The *word* of God is responsible for the cycle of the seasons so vividly described. **19–20.** A special divine *word* is reserved for Israel (see Deut 4:8 and 32:8–9).

Psalm 148. A summons to praise. Structure: vv. 1–6, to all in the heavens; vv. 7–12, to all on earth. It is reminiscent of the "Benedicite" canticle, or Song of the Three Young Men, in the additions to the Greek text of Daniel (Dan 3:52–90, Greek text; cf. NRSV, Apocrypha). **4.** *Highest heavens:* lit., "the heavens of the heavens"; this would be the area over the firmament where "the waters above the dome" (Gen 1:6–7) were located, as indicated in v. 4b. **5.** The verse states the reason for the praise (cf. Ps 33:6–7). **7–14.** *From the earth:* corresponding to the "heights" are the various earthly entities, animate and inanimate. The last two verses resume the invitation and provide a very traditional reason *(name)* for the praise. For the symbol of the horn (= strength), see Pss 112:9; 132:17; but here it is applied to *the people of Israel.* The poem stands behind the famous "Canticle to the Sun" of St. Francis of Assisi.

Psalm 149. A song of praise. Structure: vv. 1–4, invitation to the community to praise God for victory; vv. 5–9, another invitation to praise God and carry out divine judgment. It is not possible to associate this with a particular historical event, although some have suggested that the first part refers to the exodus and the second to the taking of Canaan. **1–4.** Israel is to praise the Lord because the victory of *the humble* has been achieved by the *Maker* (cf. Prov 21:31). **5.** *On their couches:* the meaning remains unclear; couches served as places to recline while eating at a banquet, but such a reference seems strained here and not in harmony with the activity in the succeeding verses. **6–9.** The Israelites are urged to exercise *vengeance on the nations.* This is interpreted as *the judgment decreed,* presumably by the Lord, e.g., the "oracles against the nations" in many of the prophetical books (Isa 13–23; Jer 46–51). Nothing can be gained by attempting to be more specific about the warlike intent of these lines. Indeed, the import of the psalm remains difficult. To define it as an eschatological vision seems merely to postpone the discovery of its meaning by hiding it in a mist of allegory. For the treatment of violence and vengeance, see the discussion of "enemies" in the Introduction (pp. 46–52).

Psalm 150. Book Five of the Psalter closes with this doxology (cf. comment on Ps 106:48). It is a song of praise that is almost entirely a hymnic introduction; "praise" occurs eleven times (and note the imperative mood), in addition to the opening and closing hallelujah. As a whole, the poem answers the questions, "where" (v. 1), "why" (v. 2), and "how" (vv. 3–5). It illustrates the various types of musical instruments that Israel used in liturgical celebration. **1.** If the two cola in v. 1 are strictly parallel, the reference is to a liturgy among the heavenly court (cf. Ps 29), rather than in Jerusalem. But both realms may be in view. **6.** The breath of life recalls Gen 2:7 and 7:22, and the "spirit" of Ps 104:30.

Select Bibliography

Out of the myriad of books dealing with the psalms, the following list includes those the author found most useful for his own study and for the audience this work envisions.

Balentine, S. E., *Prayer in the Hebrew Bible* (Overtures to Biblical Theology; Minneapolis: Fortress, 1993). This supplements the brief treatment of prayer in the psalms.

Brueggemann, W., *The Message of the Psalms* (Minneapolis: Augsburg, 1984). A compact, insightful commentary.

Davidson, R., *The Vitality of Worship* (Grand Rapids, Mich.: Eerdmans, 1998). A lengthier commentary that is helpful.

Gerstenberger, E., *Psalms: Part I, with an Introduction to Cultic Poetry* (The Forms of Old Testament Literature 14; Grand Rapids, Mich.: Eerdmans, 1988). A thoughtful treatment of the genres and especially the setting of Psalms 1–41.

Gunkel, H., *Introduction to the Psalms* (Macon, Ga.: Mercer University Press, 1998). Along with his untranslated commentary, this is arguably the most important book on the psalms in the last century.

Holladay, W. L., *The Psalms through Three Thousand Years* (Minneapolis: Fortress, 1996). A fresh look at the Psalter as it has traveled through the years.

McCann, J. C., *The Book of Psalms* (NIB 3:641–1280; Nashville: Abingdon, 1996). A commentary on both the NIV and the NRSV, oriented toward explaining the context of each psalm within the Psalter (understood as a relatively unified entity).

Mays, J. L., *Psalms* (Interpretation; Louisville: Westminster John Knox, 1994). A succinct, insightful treatment of the psalms.

Miller, P. D., *They Cried to the Lord* (Minneapolis: Fortress, 1994). Like Balentine's book, a broad treatment of prayer and an analysis of genres.

Mowinckel, S., *The Psalms in Israel's Worship* (Nashville: Abingdon, 1962). The title indicates a greater attention to liturgical possibilities, for example, enthronement psalms.

Westermann, C., *Praise and Lament in the Psalms* (Atlanta: John Knox, 1981). A careful analysis of literary genres, in some respects going beyond Gunkel.

General Index to Part One

The page references can be supplemented by consulting the appropriate psalms in the commentary of Part Two.